# JOURNAL OF LEGAL PLURALISM
## and Unofficial Law

NUMBER 64 / 2011.

AF742485

**Bibliographic information published by the Deutsche Nationalbibliothek**
The Deutsche Nationalbibliothek lists this publication in the Deutsche Nationalbibliografie; detailed bibliographic data are available in the Internet at http://dnb.d-nb.de.

ISSN 0732-9113
ISBN 978-3-643-99869-9

**A catalogue record for this book is available from the British Library**

©LIT VERLAG GmbH & Co. KG Wien,
Zweigniederlassung Zürich 2012
Klosbachstr. 107
CH-8032 Zürich
Tel. +41 (0) 44-251 75 05
Fax +41 (0) 44-251 75 06
e-Mail: zuerich@lit-verlag.ch
http://www.lit-verlag.ch

LIT VERLAG Dr. W. Hopf
Berlin 2012
Fresnostr. 2
D-48159 Münster
Tel. +49 (0) 2 51-620 320
Fax +49 (0) 2 51-23 19 72
e-Mail: lit@lit-verlag.de
http://www.lit-verlag.de

**Distribution:**

In Germany: LIT Verlag Fresnostr. 2, D-48159 Münster
Tel. +49 (0) 2 51-620 32 22, Fax +49 (0) 2 51-922 60 99, e-mail: vertrieb@lit-verlag.de

In Austria: Medienlogistik Pichler-ÖBZ, e-mail: mlo@medien-logistik.at

In Switzerland: B + M Buch- und Medienvertrieb, e-mail: order@buch-medien.ch

In the UK: Global Book Marketing, e-mail: mo@centralbooks.com

# JOURNAL OF LEGAL PLURALISM
## and Unofficial Law

POLICY

The Journal of Legal Pluralism and Unofficial Law (JLP) is a refereed, independent, inter-disciplinary, international journal devoted to scholarly writing, documentation, information on current developments, and communications about all aspects of legal pluralism and unofficial law anywhere in the world and at any time. Issues 1-18 bear the name *African Law Studies*.

MANUSCRIPTS

Manuscripts for the Journal of Legal Pluralism should be submitted to the editor-in-chief:

Melanie G. Wiber
Department of Anthropology, University of New Brunswick
P.O. Box 4400, Fredericton, N.B.
Canada E3B 5A3
Fax: (+ 01) (506) 453-5071
Email: wiber@unb.ca

or to one of the associate editors. Unless the editors are otherwise informed, submission of a manuscript implies the undertaking that it is not currently being considered by another journal and that if accepted it will be available for publication.

Manuscripts must conform to the style and other instructions contained in the JLP 'style sheet' (to be found on the JLP web site under the title 'Author guidelines'), and should generally be submitted in electronic form.

SUBSCRIPTIONS

From nr. 49 (2004) the Journal of Legal Pluralism has been published by LIT Verlag, Münster-Hamburg-Berlin-Vienna-London, whose address for inquiries about subscriptions and for orders is Grevener St./Fresnostr.2, D-48159 Münster, Germany, Fax (+49) (0)251 23 19 72, vertrieb@lit-verlag.de.
Back numbers of African Law Studies and the Journal of Legal Pluralism to nr. 48 are available from William S. Hein & Co., Inc., 1285 Main Street, Buffalo, New York 14209-1987, USA..

INDEXES AND DATABASES

Articles appearing in the Journal of Legal Pluralism are indexed in the principal legal and social science indexes and online data-bases. It is planned to make available the full text of all articles published more than two years previously on the website of the Journal of Legal Pluralism at www.jlp.bham.ac.uk . Currently the site contains the full text of all articles in nrs. 15 to 57, and abstracts of articles in nrs. 43 to the current number.

CITATION

The Journal of Legal Pluralism and Unofficial Law should be cited as: *Journal of Legal Pluralism*.

**EDITOR-IN-CHIEF**

MELANIE G. WIBER, Anthropology, University of New Brunswick

**ASSOCIATE EDITORS**

FRANZ VON BENDA-BECKMANN, Max Planck Institute for Social Anthropology, Halle/Saale
KEEBET VON BENDA-BECKMANN, Max Planck Institute for Social Anthropology, Halle/Saale
JENNIFER CORRIN, Law, University of Queensland
ANNE GRIFFITHS, Anthropology of Law, University of Edinburgh
CHRISTIAN LUND, International Development Studies, Roskilde University
YÜKSEL SEZGIN, Harvard Divinity School
FAUZIA SHARIFF, Law and Anthropology, London School of Economics
GORDON WOODMAN, Law, University of Birmingham

**EDITORIAL ADVISORY BOARD**

ELS BAERENDS
Sociology of Law, University of Groningen
DONALD BLACK
Sociology, University of Virginia
MARTIN CHANOCK
Legal Studies, LaTrobe University
MARIE-CLAIRE FOBLETS
Social and Cultural Anthropology, Catholic University of Leuven
DAVID M. ENGEL
Law and Social Policy, State University of New York
MARC GALANTER
Law and South Asian Studies, University of Wisconsin
CAROL GREENHOUSE
Anthropology, Indiana University Bloomington
PHILLIP H. GULLIVER
Anthropology, York University
ROBERT KIDDER
Sociology, Temple University
ETIENNE LE ROY
CNRS, Paris
SALLY ENGLE MERRY
Anthropology, Wellesley College
SALLY F. MOORE
Anthropology, Harvard University
LAURA NADER
Anthropology, University of California, Berkeley
FILIP REYNTJENS
African Law and Politics, University of Antwerp
SIMON ROBERTS
Law, London School of Economics
ADRIAN VAN ROUVEROY VAN NIEUWAAL
African Studies Centre, Leiden
BART RWEZAURA
Law, Open University Tanzania
BOAVENTURA DE SOUSA SANTOS
Economics, University of Coimbra
RÜDIGER SCHOTT
Ethnography, University of Münster
ROGER SOUTHALL
Political Studies, Rhodes University
FONS STRIJBOSCH
Catholic University of Nijmegen
JACQUES VANDERLINDEN
Law, Free University Brussels
RICHARD WERBNER
Anthropology, University of Manchester

# CONTENTS

## FROM THE EDITOR

In September 2011, the Commission on Legal Pluralism celebrated a Jubilee Congress in Cape Town, South Africa. The Congress was hosted by the Center for Legal and Applied Research (CLEAR) from the Faculty of Law at the University of Cape Town, and the local organizer was Professor Hanri Mostert. The Congress theme was "Living Realities of Legal Pluralism", which brought together many international scholars and practitioners from around the world, particularly from various African states. The presentations highlighted theoretical and methodological approaches to the study of legal pluralism; case studies of legal pluralism generated by the activities undertaken by government, civil society, and market entities; the pluralist discourses of rights over land and natural resources; the increasing intertwining of human rights and development discourses; and the relationship between law, custom and religion. Many of these themes are represented in the articles published in this issue of the Journal of Legal Pluralism. Given that there were over 160 speakers at the Congress, this volume represents only a very small sample of the scholarship represented there. Several themes that remain perennial interests in legal anthropology are found in this volume, including the effects of legal pluralism on gender issues, on the management of natural resources, on attempts to reform legal systems, on the relationship between minority religions and the modern state, and on the application and outcomes of science and technology. This volume also benefits from two thoughtful plenary presentations, one on the relationship between legal pluralism and governability, and one on the paradigms employed in legal pluralism research. Further publications from the Congress are expected in the form of several edited volumes to be produced in South Africa.

The next international meeting of the Commission on Legal Pluralism will be held in conjunction with the congress of the International Union of Anthropological and Ethnological Sciences. The IUAES congress theme is "Evolving Humanity, Emerging Worlds" (for more information see http://www.iuaes2013.org/index.html). It will take place in Manchester, UK from 5-10 August. See the Commission website (at www.commission-on-legal-pluralism.com) for information on panel organizers in legal pluralism and for the recent call for papers.

# ABSTRACTS OF ARTICLES

**JLP 64: 1-31**

## ACCESS TO JUSTICE IN PEMBA CITY: HOW EXPLORING WOMEN'S LIVED REALITIES WITH PLURAL LAW UNCOVERS PROGRAMMATIC GAPS

Giselle Corradi

This contribution explores the links between women's lived realities with plural law and development interventions that aim at improving women's access to justice. Based on a case study in Pemba city, northern Mozambique, the paper illustrates the relevance of incorporating 'actor oriented' perspectives on gender and legal change within justice sector aid. First, it describes the justice landscape of Pemba city in terms of the legal actors to whom women resort, their procedures, the types of case that they deal with and how they relate to each other. Secondly, it depicts the kinds of strategy that have been supported at the national level and in Pemba city in order to improve women's access to justice, and analyses how these relate to the justice landscape of Pemba. Third, it examines the testimonies provided by different women in Pemba city regarding their perspectives on justice processes and their experiences with the law while exploring how the latter are related to programmatic efforts. This exercise reveals that the enforcement of justice forum decisions is a crucial area for women's access to justice that remains out of sight. The conclusion argues that understanding women's lived realities with the law is essential in two ways. On the one hand, it is necessary for assessing the kinds of process that interventions set in motion and the extent to which the latter contribute to the realisation of women's rights. On the other hand, it uncovers areas of intervention that remain unaddressed despite their potential to generate positive changes.

**JLP 64: 33-63**

# LEGAL AND JUDICIAL PLURALISM IN NAMIBIA AND BEYOND: A MODERN APPROACH TO AFRICAN LEGAL ARCHITECTURE?

Oliver C. Ruppel and Katharina Ruppel-Schlichting

The focus of this article is twofold: Firstly to shed light on the concept of legal pluralism from a Namibian perspective. Namibia is a vital example for an African country in which legal pluralism is not only anchored in the Constitution, but also a living reality in legal practice. The article sketches some historical developments in Namibia relevant for the understanding of the coexistence of different legal systems in the country, before discussing the existing and emerging legal setting in the context of national law applicable in Namibia and its international obligations. A focus is placed on the interplay between Roman-Dutch Law, the Common Law and Namibian Customary Law. In order to demonstrate how such pluralism plays a role in the complex national judicial framework, the Namibian court system is briefly introduced and challenges are highlighted by way of examples.

Secondly, Namibia is a member of various political and economic formations on the African continent such as the Southern African Development Community (SADC) and the African Union (AU) and also faces international obligations resulting from these memberships. The article also aims to reflect on this African legal architecture, i.e. not only addressing legal pluralism on the national but also on the regional and continental level. After all, the majority of people in southern Africa is not only faced by legal pluralism at the national level, but is increasingly governed by multilayered political or economic regimes which have manifold legal implications. This complex system of multi-level governance depends on the strength of interdependence between the regional, national and local levels. With a view towards a more transnational legal pluralism the article intends to offer an appropriate account of contemporary African legal reality and to reflect legal pluralistic insights beyond territorially-based application in a modern African legal environment.

JLP 64: 65-90

# NAVIGATING BETWEEN TRADITIONAL LAND TENURE AND INTRODUCED LAND LAWS IN PACIFIC ISLAND STATES

Sue Farran

As in other parts of the world, islands in the south Pacific region experienced British colonial administration accompanied by the introduction of non-customary land laws and policies. In some cases colonial administrators took land which they deemed to be uncultivated or lying 'waste and idle' and claimed it for the Crown or later, the state. In other cases they reshaped customary institutions and structures in efforts to acknowledge local indigenous polities but at the same time understand them on their own terms. On independence, and in the years just prior to and after independence in many countries, land that had been alienated to foreigners was restored to indigenous people, but the slate could not be wiped entirely clean of the colonial legacy. Indeed few countries rejected the colonial systems of laws and courts, so that even today, introduced laws and dispute resolution forums remain relevant and influential.

Alongside shifts from rural residency to urbanisation, from subsistence agriculture to cash-cropping and waged labour, there are other pressures both internal and external, to commercialise and capitalize land and its resources. There are demands for registration and demarcation of customary land interests, for the simplification of complex kinship rules which determine land rights, for greater individualization of land rather than communal access and multiple rights, and for the establishment of certainty through final court decisions rather than negotiated settlements which may be revisited and renegotiated. For some, both from within and without Pacific island countries, customary land tenure is seen as an obstacle to economic development, for others it is seen as essential for maintaining social stability and security and for ensuring the equitable distribution of resources in states where governance is weak and public provision virtually non-existent.

Drawing on legal and anthropological research, and focussing on the island countries of Melanesia, this paper looks at contemporary examples of how governments and individuals are negotiating the space between the two systems of customary land tenure and introduced land law highlighting how plural systems offer scope for developing coping strategies and the development of hybrid legal approaches.

**JLP 64: 91-120**

# CAUGHT BETWEEN DIFFERENT LEGAL PLURALISMS: WOMEN WHO WEAR ISLAMIC DRESS AS THE RELIGIOUS 'OTHER' IN EUROPEAN RIGHTS DISCOURSES

Amy R. Jackson and Dorota A. Gozdecka

Legal pluralism is a phenomenon defined differently by scholars researching European law and scholars researching issues concerning cultural and religious accommodation. Whereas European law scholars focus on possible theoretical tools for conflict resolution between intersecting European legal systems, scholars focusing on multiculturalism argue that cultural and religious legal pluralism conveys a dynamic relationship between official and unofficial law drawn out by migration and issues of accommodating a primarily Muslim *diaspora* in Europe. Yet, seemingly differently defined, these pluralisms have an equally important impact on the understanding of fundamental human rights in Europe. They both influence national law and shape the boundaries of rights, such as freedom of religion.

Building upon established notions of legal pluralism, the paper provides a critical analysis of the application of human rights standards in European normative orders and argues that the rights of the religious 'other' are caught in an interplay of various types and forms of legal pluralism(s) in which issues of inclusion often remain secondary. It focuses upon the key example of women who wear a *hijab* (headscarf) or a *jilbab* (a long coat like garment which covers the body except the hands and face) and who were the central focus of European Court of Human Rights cases such as *Dahab v Switzerland* and *Sąhin v Turkey*, and of domestic cases, for example, *R (on the application of Begum) v Headteacher and Governors of Denbigh High School*. The paper re-orders and re-constructs certain forms of legal pluralism and also focuses on the relationships between them.

JLP 64: 121-148

## WHO IS GOVERNING FOOD SYSTEMS? POWER AND LEGAL PLURALISM IN LOBSTER TRACEABILITY

Courtenay E. Parlee and Melanie G. Wiber

This paper uses a recent lobster traceability project in the Canadian Maritimes to examine the emerging governance institutions in our global food systems. Given the central importance of lobster to family-based, independent fishing enterprises, this lobster traceability project was a unique opportunity to investigate the people, organizations and governance institutions that are impacting lobster fisheries enterprises and management. This case study illustrates the many "jurisgenerative institutions" (Anderson 1998) at various scales that are currently involved in governing lobster as it enters our food systems, and also traces some of the impacts of those multiple institutions on each other, and on the fishing enterprise. We conclude that legal pluralism is an important constituent in global food security and food governance, and that this characteristic of our emerging food governance institutions requires more careful study.

JLP 64: 149-172

## LEGAL PLURALISM AND THE GOVERNABILITY OF FISHERIES AND COASTAL SYSTEMS

Svein Jentoft

Conditions for, and limits of, governability of fisheries and coastal systems cannot be properly understood without an examination of legal pluralism. Governing systems that do not take legal pluralism into account are likely to fail. This article discusses how interactive governance theory and legal pluralism may benefit from each other and how legal pluralism can be assessed from a governability perspective. Interactive governance theory offers a conceptual framework for investigating legal pluralism and how it contributes to governability, whereas the legal pluralism literature provides perspectives on normative orders that interactive governance theory should emphasize and for which governance actions should account.

**JLP 64: 173-202**

# PURSUING LEGAL PLURALISM: THE POWER OF PARADIGMS IN A GLOBAL WORLD

Anne Griffiths

The Jubilee Congress of the Commission on Legal Pluralism took place at the University of Cape Town in September 2011, and celebrated thirty years of the Commission's role in understanding legal pluralism worldwide. Members have engaged in many debates over what constitutes legal pluralism and how it is to be perceived. From its inception in 1981, in Bellagio, Italy there was heated discussion about what to call law other than state law and how to identify its characteristics. Such debates continue today, and this paper highlights some arenas in which contestations over law and legal pluralism have particular salience. It highlights a number of domains in which the highly mobile and contingent nature of law is revealed, through the ways in which law is spatialized, representing multi-faceted dimensions of legal pluralism that are constantly in the making. Such a vision is at odds with the more traditional views of legal pluralism that are framed in terms of a state centred paradigm

# ABOUT THE CONTRIBUTORS

Giselle CORRADI is a Ph.D. candidate at the Human Rights Centre, Ghent University Law School, Belgium. Her research focuses on the relationship between human rights, legal pluralism and justice sector aid in sub-Saharan Africa, with case studies on Sierra Leone and Mozambique. She has previously published 'Human Rights Promotion in Post Conflict Sierra Leone: Coming to Grips with Plurality in Customary Justice', *Journal of Legal Pluralism* 60: 73-103 (2010). Contact: Giselle.Corradi@Ugent.be

Sue FARRAN is a Professor of Laws at Northumbria University. She received her legal education in South Africa and at Cambridge and for a number of years was a member of staff of the University of the South Pacific in Vanuatu where she remains an Adjunct Professor. Her research and publications focus on the Pacific region especially in respect of land, human rights and development. She is, among other things, author of *Human Rights in the South Pacific: Challenges and Changes* (2009) Routledge-Cavendish, London; co-author with D. Paterson of *South Pacific Perspectives of Property Law* (2004) Cavendish, London, and has recently edited a collection of papers for a special issue of the *Pacific Studies* journal 'Land and Law', December 2011. She is currently finalising a co-edited collection, with Don Paterson: *South Pacific Land Systems*, to be published by the University of the South Pacific. Contact: sue.farran@northumbria.ac.uk

Dorota Anna GOZDECKA is a Post-Doctoral Research Fellow at the Centre of Excellence in Foundations of European Law and Polity Research (University of Helsinki) and a Visiting Fellow at the Centre for European Studies (Australian National University). Her post-doctoral research focuses on theoretical aspects of multiculturalism and explores issues of growing religious and cultural pluralism of European societies in the European legal context. She is also a co-director of an international research project 'Post-Lisbon Integration: the Quest for a New European Identity'. The project focuses on constitutionalisation of key policy areas such as citizenship, free movement of persons, freedom, security and justice and fundamental rights in the context of ethnic, linguistic, cultural and religious diversity of Europe. Contact: gozdecka@mappi.helsinki.fi

Anne GRIFFITHS is professor and holds a personal chair in the Anthropology of Law at the School of Law at Edinburgh University. Her research focuses on anthropology of law, comparative and family law, African law, gender, culture and rights and juvenile justice. Her most recent publications include *The Power of Law in a Transnational World: Anthropological Enquires* (2009); *Spatializing*

*Law: An Anthropological Geography of Law in Society* (2009) and *Mobile People, Mobile Law: Expanding Legal Relations in a Contracting World* (2005) co-edited with F. and K. von Benda-Beckmann. Over the years she has held visiting appointments at various institutions including Senior Research Fellow, International Research Centre on Work and the Human Lifecycle in Global History (IKG), Humboldt University, Berlin (2010-2011), Distinguished Visiting Professor, Faculty of Law, University of Toronto, the Max Planck Institute for Social Anthropology, Halle/Saale, Germany, The International Institute for the Sociology of Law Oñati - Gipuzkoa, Spain. The University of Texas at Austin, School of Law and the Southern and Eastern African Regional Centre for Women's Law at the University of Zimbabwe. She is currently a member of the Executive Body of the Commission on Pluralism, a branch of the International Union of Anthropological and Ethnological Sciences, of which she was President from 2003-2009. Her current research, funded by the Leverhulme (2009-2010) is on the *Gendered Dynamics of Land Tenure in Southern Africa.* Contact Anne.Griffiths@ed.ac.uk.

Irene I. HADIPRAYITNO is a Researcher on Human Rights and the Right to Food in the Law and Governance Group, Wageningen University, Netherlands. She received her PhD in Human Rights and Development from the Faculty of Law, Utrecht University. She has published widely on topics related to the right to development, the right to food and food security and on social practices of negotiating human rights in the context of agricultural modernisation.

Amy R. JACKSON became interested in legal pluralism in the final year of her LLB degree at the University of Reading after spending a year on the ERASMUS year abroad program at Uppsala University, Sweden. The focus of the topic of her LLM dissertation at the University of Sussex was global legal pluralism. The title of her doctoral thesis, fully-funded by a studentship from the University of Reading and submitted in October 2011, is: *What is law? Unveiling a Subjective Legal Pluralism.* This research includes a qualitative empirical study to assess whether women living in Britain experience and construct the practice of veiling (such as wearing a *hijab* or *niqab*) as law. The influence of her research on black-letter law and religion lawyers became apparent when she was asked to chair the first panel on legal pluralism at the Law and Religion Scholars Network (LARSN) conference in May 2011. Contact: A.R.Jackson@pgr.reading.ac.uk

Svein JENTOFT is a sociologist and a professor at the Norwegian College of Fishery Science at the University of Tromsø, Norway. He has worked extensively on fisheries and coastal issues, including resource management and industrial organization in his native Norway as well as in other countries. Jentoft has published several books on the resource rights and livelihoods of indigenous peoples in Norway and in Nicaragua. His most recent book in English is *Poverty Mosaics. Realities and Prospects in Small-Scale Fisheries* (co-edited with Arne Eide), Springer (2011). His latest work also includes the governance of marine protected areas in Nicaragua and Spain. He is a co-editor and contributor to *Governability: Theory and Applications in Fisheries,* Springer, forthcoming. Contact: svein.jentoft@uit.no

Courtenay E. PARLEE is a doctoral candidate in Interdisciplinary Studies at the University of New Brunswick. She completed her Master's thesis on the clam industry while participating in the research undertaken through the Coastal Community University Research Alliance (Coastal CURA). Her work examined the consequences of the lack of effective dispute resolution in coastal and ocean management in Canada. She has presented papers at several national and international conferences, and is currently undertaking training in mediation and conflict resolution. Contact: courtenaye.parlee@gmail.com.

Oliver C RUPPEL is a Professor of Law, in the Departments both of Mercantile and of Public Law, Faculty of Law, University of Stellenbosch (South Africa). He lectures at various academic institutions worldwide as a Visiting Professor and currently serves as Coordinating Lead Author for Africa in the Intergovernmental Panel on Climate Change, Working Group II, housed at Stanford University. He was until 2010 one of 14 worldwide Founding WTO Chair holders. He held that Chair at the Faculty of Law, University of Namibia, Windhoek, where he also served as the Director of the National Human Rights and Documentation Centre. Contact: ruppel@sun.ac.za

Katharina RUPPEL-SCHLICHTING is a Senior Legal Researcher and the Director of the Windhoek based Legal Research and Development Trust of Namibia. A qualified lawyer and international legal consultant, she specialises in Public International Law, concentrating on International Environmental Law and Intellectual Property Rights. Contact: katharina.ruppel@googlemail.com.

Melanie G. WIBER is Professor of Anthropology at the University of New Brunswick. She is the author of *Politics, Property and Law in the Philippine Uplands* (1993 Wilfrid Laurier University Press), and is co-editor with Franz and Keebet von Benda-Beckmann of *The Changing Properties of Property* (2006 Berghan). For the past twenty-five years she has conducted research on natural resource management, including research on irrigation, farming and fisheries. She has served for many years on the Executive Body of the Commission on Legal Pluralism and is currently Editor-in-Chief of the *Journal of Legal Pluralism*. Contact: wiber@unb.ca.

# ACCESS TO JUSTICE IN PEMBA CITY: HOW EXPLORING WOMEN'S LIVED REALITIES WITH PLURAL LAW UNCOVERS PROGRAMMATIC GAPS

Giselle Corradi

## Introduction

What can justice sector aid in sub-Saharan Africa learn from women's lived realities with the law? The present contribution examines this question in the context of interventions that aim at improving women's access to justice[1]. In recent years, international development actors in sub-Saharan Africa have provided support for a series of initiatives that endorse this goal.[2] On the one hand, these actors supply technical and financial assistance for the incorporation into national law of international and regional women's rights conventions, such as CEDAW

[1] This work was supported by the Belgian Ministry of Scientific Policy in the framework of the programme 'Society and Future' 2007 [TA/00/17 AFTRALAW]. An earlier draft of this paper was presented at the Jubilee Congress of the Commission on Legal Pluralism 'Living Realities of Legal Pluralism', Cape Town, 8-10 September 2011.

[2] This is not to say that women's access to justice is an area of priority for justice sector aid in sub-Saharan Africa. For an appraisal of the extent to which justice sector aid in the region contributes to gender equality see Nyamu-Musembi (2005a).

© Copyright 2011 - Giselle Corradi.

and the Protocol on the Rights of Women in Africa. In order to comply with these standards, a number of activities are undertaken, such as legal reforms that eliminate discriminatory provisions from statutory law and the adoption of new legislation that protects the rights of women in specific areas, such as domestic violence. On the other hand, development actors address certain issues that are related to the implementation of women's rights. These include women's knowledge of the law as well as their capacity to claim their rights effectively. In this regard, women face particular obstacles since next to the physical, economic and socio-cultural barriers that make access to formal judicial institutions in Africa difficult in general, women are also likely to suffer ostracism in their communities and unequal treatment in court (Mukhopadhyay 2008). To alleviate this situation, justice sector aid funds initiatives such as legal literacy campaigns, capacity building for justice sector functionaries and the provision of legal aid and paralegal schemes by national bodies and/or local NGOs.[3]

In addition, the integration of pro-poor strategies within justice sector aid in recent years has meant that grassroots legal realities have begun to receive some measure of attention.[4] Next to the realisation that formal state justice is not accessible for most people in the region, development actors are increasingly considering how informal, non-state, traditional or customary justice forums can contribute to improving access to justice.[5] In this context, the relationship between legal pluralism and women's access to justice is seen as a Janus-faced phenomenon. Legal pluralism is deemed to enable access to justice since the absence of formal courts is compensated by the services provided by local instances of dispute processing. However, legal pluralism is regarded as an obstacle to women's rights since local forums often disregard the rights of women and rely on discriminatory norms, have a lenient attitude towards gender-based violence and are procedurally biased against women (UN Women 2011: 69). Against this backdrop, development

[3] See for example a range of World Bank grants in sub-Saharan Africa that focus on law, gender and poverty reduction (World Bank 2009) and the 'Women's Legal Rights Initiative' by USAID (USAID 2007).

[4] See DfID 2000; UNDP 2004; World Bank 2003: 45.

[5] There is no uniformity in the terminology employed by development actors. DfID and OECD-DAC use the term 'non-state' justice (DfID 2004; OECD-DAC 2007), UNDP refers to 'informal' or 'traditional' justice mechanisms (UNDP 2004), the World Bank speaks of 'customary' law systems (World Bank 2006: 156) and Danida of 'informal' justice (Danida 2010).

actors are beginning to support activities that bring the practices of these forums into line with women's rights, such as training for local justice providers and mechanisms for monitoring their operation (Chopra and Isser 2010; Kipfer-Didavi et al. 2005).

These interventions reflect the idea that legal processes can potentially contribute to gender equality and the empowerment of women, which are necessary conditions for the overall reduction of poverty, and eventually, the realisation of the right to development.[6] In this sense, the term 'access to justice' can be understood as a process in which a range of different interrelated factors combine to enable people to obtain a satisfactory remedy for a grievance (Wojkowska 2006: 30).[7] These include (i) the existence of a normative framework that upholds women's rights, (ii) knowledge of this framework by right-holders, (iii) the availability of justice forums where grievances can be presented, (iv) the treatment of cases by these forums in accordance with women's rights and (v) enforcement of decisions (ibid). Following an 'actor-oriented' perspective on gender and legal change, this paper interrogates how women's lived realities with the law can inform interventions that aim at improving such processes. Actor perspectives on gender and legal change pursue a grounded understanding of women's options and limits in negotiating gender relations within rule-generating and rule-upholding processes (Griffiths 1997; Hellum 1995; 2000; Hellum et al. 2007; Hirsch 1998; Nyamu-Musembi 2005b; Tsanga 2003). The individual woman and the girl-child are regarded as actors of change who mobilise different strategies of action in pursuing their goals (Hellum et al. 2007: xviii; Swidler 1986). However, this does not occur in a vacuum. As explained by Hellum: "The actor perspective does not imply that women and men are seen as totally free to change the rules affecting their social positions. (…) The focus of the analysis is therefore on different actors and their structurally limited possibilities to promote their aims and goals" (Hellum 1995: 19). It is from this viewpoint that the paper explores how access to justice

[6] This approach to international development is generally called 'legal empowerment', which denotes development strategies that seek to empower the poor through the use of the law (United Nations 2009). On the relationship between gender equality and poverty reduction see Morrison et al. (2007).

[7] As a human right, it can be found in Article 8 of the Universal Declaration, Article 6(1) of the European Convention on Human Rights, Article 25 of the American Convention, Article 7(1) of the African Charter on Human and People's Rights and Article 47 of the Charter of Rights of the European Union. See also Francioni (2007: 24-42).

interventions interplays with women's ability to draw on locally available legal resources.

For this purpose a case study was conducted in Pemba city, Mozambique. There are several reasons why Pemba city, the capital of Mozambique's most northerly province, Cabo Delgado, is a suitable site to study the relationship between women's perspectives on legal processes and interventions that aim at improving women's access to justice. In the first place, Mozambique is a country with a strong patriarchal socio-cultural order, in which women represent the poorest sections of the population (Tvedten et al. 2008: 5, 9). At the same time, Mozambique is grappling with serious obstacles in terms of access to justice (OSISA 2006: 121). As a result, both improved gender equality and improved access to justice can be found on the development agenda as means to fight poverty (GOM 2005). In addition, Cabo Delgado features the lowest indexes of human and gender development, as well as the largest discrepancy between human and gender indicators (UNDP 2008: 17; Tvedten et al. 2008: 15). In this context, a number of initiatives have been undertaken in Pemba city for the promotion of women's access to justice. Moreover, Pemba city presents a rich picture in terms of legal pluralism, with numerous state and non-state legal actors interacting in diverse ways. Finally, Pemba city offers a good opportunity to meet with women from different socio-cultural backgrounds, making it possible to explore the extent to which interventions have different implications for different groups of women (Griffiths 1997).

This case study is based on qualitative research carried out in August and September 2009 in Maputo and Pemba city and in September and October 2010 in Pemba city[8]. A first round of thirty-nine semi-structured interviews with international development actors, government officials, civil society organisations and local experts in Maputo allowed for the identification and discussion of trends in policies and interventions in the justice sector in Mozambique regarding legal pluralism and human rights. Based on this, Pemba city was selected as a suitable

[8] I am grateful to my supervisor, Prof. Eva Brems, for her continuous guidance and support. I also wish to thank all the interviewees who shared their time, views and experiences with me during the fieldwork in Mozambique. My thanks are also due to Angelo Matusse for his help in establishing contacts with state justice actors in Pemba city and to Esmeralda Mariano for her generosity in sharing material with me.

site to 'zoom in' on these issues at the local level. Second, eight local project implementers were interviewed in order to collect more information about interventions in Pemba and the local legal landscape. In addition, eighteen local justice providers (community court judges, community leaders, civil society organisations, legal practitioners and state justice providers) were interviewed in order to learn about their practices. The registers of the community court of Natite were also analysed, as well as the activity reports of 2008 of the community courts of Paquitequete, Natite and Cariacó. This was complemented by the observation of twenty-four mediation sessions at the local association 'Cabinet of Women's Legal Rights' (GDJM), one at a 'community police' and another at the 'Police Victim Support Centre for Women and Children Victims of Violence' (GAMCVV). Third, twenty-one semi-structured interviews with women who had resorted to (a) local instance(s) of dispute processing in Pemba city served the purpose of gathering women's perspectives on local legal processes. The findings from individual interviews were complemented by two focus group discussions with women from Paquitequete and Natite neighbourhoods on the kinds of conflict affecting women and their pathways to justice. The research did not cover specificities of Muslim women of Indian origin, a minority in Pemba city.

The paper is structured in five parts. Following this introduction, the second section describes the justice landscape of Pemba city in terms of the legal actors to whom women resort, their procedures, the types of case with which they deal and how they relate to each other. Part three depicts the kinds of strategies that have been supported at the national level and in Pemba city in order to improve women's access to justice and analyses how these relate to the justice landscape of Pemba. Section four examines the testimonies provided by different women in Pemba city regarding their perspectives on justice processes and their experiences with the law and explores how the latter are related to programmatic efforts. Finally, the conclusion summarises the main arguments of each section and links them together, at the same time showing the relevance of incorporating 'actor-oriented' perspectives on gender and legal change within justice sector aid.

## Women and the Justice Landscape of Pemba City

Pemba city is the capital of Mozambique's most northerly province, Cabo Delgado.[9] A coastal city on the Indian Ocean close to Tanzania, Pemba is

[9] The city has 138,716 inhabitants, of whom 49.5 per cent are women (INE 2007). Next to agricultural and informal economic activities, the city offers some formal

historically linked to the Swahili world and Islamic culture (Bonate 2009).[10] While specific figures for Pemba city are scarce, the province Cabo Delgado features particularly high levels of poverty and gender discrimination (Collier 2009). In a number of areas, the subaltern position of women is quite prominent. For example, illiteracy rates in the province are especially high amongst women, i.e. 88.5 per cent as compared to 60 per cent for men (Collier 2009: 25). The latter is associated with socio-cultural practices that inhibit girls from taking an equal part in education, including domestic responsibilities and early marriages (Tvedten et al. 2008: 12, 27). Moreover, sexual abuse, child motherhood and domestic violence are especially worrying in the northern provinces (Tvedten et al. 2008: 28, 29). According to available studies of gender relations in Pemba city, women tend to depend on their husbands and male relatives in respect of social and economic life strategies, while men increasingly combine multiple relationships and forms of family constitution, such as informal unions and religious or traditional marriages (Casimiro and Fonseca 2009). At the same time, widespread poverty in northern Mozambique makes it difficult for many men to maintain their roles as household heads (Tvedten et al. 2009: 6). In urban areas, where social pressure is more diluted, men more easily abandon their wives and children when they find another wife or lover, or they remain in polygamous unions while de facto not fulfilling their responsibilities towards all the wives (Tvedten et al. 2009: 28). In addition, women in this region are often dispossessed in cases of divorce or when the husband dies (Casimiro and Fonseca 2009).

In terms of justice options available to women, Pemba city displays a rich network of state and non-state legal actors and forms of normativity.[11] In contrast to most of the country, formal state justice is well represented in Pemba city, with the presence of district and provincial courts, the office of the prosecutor and the police, including special police centres for domestic violence. Regarding accessibility, district and provincial courts present general obstacles, such as

employment opportunities in the fishing sectors, transformation industries, banking and telecommunication services and the public administration (ROM 2002: 248).

[10] According to the 2007 Census, 72 per cent of the population in Pemba city are Muslim, 23 per cent are Catholic and the remaining 5 per cent adhere to other or no religion (INE 2007).

[11] For an analysis of legal pluralism in Mozambique in general see Meneses 2007, Santos 2006, Santos and Trindade 2003. For an analysis of legal pluralism and women's access to justice in Mozambique see Araújo 2005.

extended delays, as well as a number of barriers that affect poor and uneducated segments of the population in particular, such as litigation costs, language and the formality of procedures.[12] Nevertheless, the profile of female complainants recurring to these courts depends on the case. For example, cases involving minors, such as alimony payment, regulation of parental custody and recognition of paternal affiliation are often channelled through the office of the prosecutor, which operates expeditiously and is free of charge. Consequently, women from different socio-economic backgrounds resort to this institution when their ex-husbands have formal employment and hence a salary that can be confiscated for the payment of alimony.[13] By contrast, women from a better socio-economic background present cases at the formal courts, including labour disputes, dissolution of property on divorce and inheritance.[14]

In addition, the city counts on a number of state-sponsored legal services that operate either in collaboration or in parallel with the district and provincial courts. In the framework of national policies to combat domestic violence, the state created the 'Police Victim Support Centres for Women and Child Victims of Violence' (GAMCVV). These centres started operating in Pemba city in 2003. Since then, the volume of cases handled by the GAMCVVs has increased considerably. However, not all the disputes brought to the GAMCVVs involve domestic violence. In practice, women turn to the police with all kinds of grievances, including abandonment by their husbands and requests for payment of alimony. In these cases, the GAMCVVs provide counselling and mediation services. When domestic violence is the main grievance, the GAMCVVs' response depends on the case. Where there are serious physical injuries, the GAMCVVs request forensic examinations at the hospital and transfer the cases to the formal courts.[15] It is not uncommon, though, for complainants to go to these centres in search of an authority that can command their husbands to stop beating them but without intending to prosecute them. In such cases, women often withdraw their

[12] Formal state courts operate in the official national language, which is Portuguese. However, most people in Pemba speak Emakwa, Kimwani or Maconde. Only educated people master Portuguese fluently.

[13] Interview with the prosecutor of Pemba city, 1 October 2010; interview with an officer of the office of the prosecutor, Pemba, 22 September 2010.

[14] Interview with provincial court judge Beirão, Pemba, 29 September 2009.

[15] Interview with an officer of the GAMCVV, Pemba, 14 September 2009.

complaints when they understand the implications of prosecution.[16]

The city also hosts a branch of the 'Institute of Legal Representation and Assistance' (IPAJ), which is sponsored by the state to provide free legal aid to economically disadvantaged persons (Law 6/94). According to the local director, the cases brought to the IPAJ by female complainants are in the minority.[17] They mostly concern dissolution of property on divorce, alimony payment and payment delays in labour cases.[18] The IPAJ works with paralegals, who receive the cases, provide legal advice and attempt to mediate the disputes. Lawyers only intervene when a case needs to be transferred to the formal courts. In principle, the services of the IPAJ are free of charge, but the institute has to cope with the problem that some of its members request illegal fees (KPMG 2009: 30). A number of practising lawyers also offer their services in the city. However, considering that the average fee for a consultation amounts to about 37 USD, only women in a better socio-economic position can afford their services. When they do so, it involves cases of divorce, dissolution of property on divorce, inheritance and alimony payment.[19] Finally, though not directly associated with dispute processing, it is worth mentioning that there is a civil registration department in Pemba city, where parental affiliation and civil, religious and traditional marriages as well as marriage contracts can be registered. These registrations are particularly important for women in the context of producing proofs in the event of a divorce. However, the latter are difficult to obtain for various reasons, such as the high cost, i.e. about 50 USD, the delays and the reluctance of men to agree to register a marriage and the paternity of a child.[20]

At the level of non-state justice, Pemba has an even greater number of legal actors. The city is divided into 10 administrative units called neighbourhoods, which are further sub-divided into quarters and groups of ten houses. Each of these units is

[16] Interview with a local representative of Oxfam Intermon, Pemba, 7 October 2010.

[17] The bulk of cases handled by the IPAJ involve legal representation in criminal cases. Provincial Direction of the Justice Sector Cabo Delgado (2007: 2).

[18] Interview with Mr Alimusa, Pemba, 28 September 2010.

[19] Interview with legal practitioner Mr Mussirica, Pemba, 24 September 2010.

[20] Interviews with local women, Pemba, September/October 2010. See also Casimiro and Fonseca (2009: 3).

respectively presided over by a neighbourhood secretary, a chief of quarter and a chief of ten houses. These actors intervene in local conflicts when families and neighbours are not able to arrive at a solution on their own.[21] Often, senior members of the 'Organization of Mozambican Women' (OMM) provide advice in domestic disputes. The latter is done according to custom and common sense. In criminal cases, the neighbourhood structures work in close cooperation with the 'community police'. The latter are composed of volunteers from the neighbourhood, whose official function is to monitor crime in the community and provide liaison with the police. In reality, though, the community police represent yet another forum where conflicts are handled. Even cases for which they do not have jurisdiction, such as the rape of a minor, are 'solved' by the community police.[22]

Imams, their wives and church leaders also play a role in the non-state legal landscape of Pemba city. Their involvement as mediators in disputes depends on the role that religion plays in the life of the parties. When they intervene, it is often in the context of marital disputes, in which they try to reconcile the spouses. In this process, they resort to a combination of local customs and religious values rather than the strict application of religious or state laws.[23] Depending on the nature of a grievance or dispute, a traditional healer may also be involved at a certain point.[24]

---

[21] Interviews with local women and community leaders. Pemba, September 2009, September/October 2010.

[22] In these cases, the community police mediate the agreement of a compensation payment to the male custodian of the victim either by the perpetrator himself or by his family if he is a minor. The community police discourages the plaintiffs from taking these cases to the formal police. Observations at a community police forum, Pemba, 29 September 2010. The widespread character of this practice was confirmed at interviews with representatives from local civil society organisations. Interview with a local representative of the Human Rights League of Pemba (LDH), Pemba, 13 September 2009; interview with a local representative of Oxfam Intermon, Pemba, 7 October 2010.

[23] Interviews with Muslim and Catholic religious leaders from Natite and Paquitequete neighbourhoods. Pemba, 15 September 2009, 30 September 2010 and 5 September 2010. See also Casimiro and Fonseca (2009).

[24] When questioned about the role of traditional healers in disputes interviewees were rather reluctant to discuss the matter in detail but acknowledged that they are

In addition, each neighbourhood has a 'community court'. Created by the state but never regulated by law, these courts defy the state vs. non-state dichotomy.[25] The community courts are composed of predominantly male lay judges whose mandate is to mediate and seek reconciliation between the parties in minor criminal and civil cases by means of applying 'good sense and justice' (Law 4/92 art 2). In contrast to the operation of other neighbourhood leaders, these courts are legally entitled to impose small fines and community work as penalties, though they represent a voluntary forum so that enforcement of decisions depends on consensus and social pressure (Law 4/92 art 3).[26] Moreover, the community courts can transfer a case to the district court when no satisfactory agreement is reached at community level (Law 24/2007 art 86a). For this purpose, some community courts in Pemba city keep records and refer to state law in their rulings.[27] Community courts are easily accessible as they operate regularly in the neighbourhoods, charge fees that are affordable, i.e. about 3 USD, and conduct the proceedings in the local languages. A great majority of the cases they process involve women. These concern all kinds of domestic disputes called 'social cases', such as adultery, abandonment of the home by the husband, dissolution of property on divorce and inheritance, payment of alimony and witchcraft accusations. Systematic studies of the extent to which community courts in Pemba city respect the rights of women are not available. Nevertheless, the testimonies of community court judges indicate

consulted when women want to recover their husbands. Traditional chiefs (*regulos*) were not mentioned by interviewees as a local legal actor in Pemba city. When asked about their role, respondents said that their functions in the city do not cover dispute processing, as is the case in rural areas. Interviews with local women and community leaders, Pemba, September/October 2010.

[25] Originally, Law 12/78 established these courts as the lowest echelon of the popular justice system that was introduced after independence. With the political transition towards neoliberal democracy that followed the end of the civil war (1977-1992), these courts were withdrawn from the official justice system. The 'community courts' were then created by Law 4/92, but since then their operation has never been regulated.

[26] Nevertheless, in certain cases such as theft, the neighbourhood structures and the community courts collaborate with the community police for the enforcement of penalties, which includes illegal corporal punishments. However, this seems not to be the case when it comes to 'social cases' (see infra).

[27] Observations and interview at the community court of Natite, Pemba, 12 September 2009.

that this varies from court to court and from case to case. As will be explained in the next section, some community court judges participated in training on the Mozambican Family Law and in certain areas the decisions of these courts seem to be inspired by this law in favour of women. For example, in cases of dissolution of property on divorce or inheritance, some community court judges were reported as ruling that women are entitled to a share of the assets. This deviates both from the law and local practices. According to the former the division should be equal, but according to the latter women are virtually dispossessed. Nonetheless, community courts seem not to challenge the male-dominated model of social order. A case in point is the treatment of domestic violence, where community court judges were reported as requesting the husband to refrain from mistreating his wife while asking the wife to obey her husband.[28]

Finally, a range of civil society organisations provide free legal advice and mediation services. A local branch of the 'Human Rights League' (LDH) provides legal advice and representation in labour, civil and criminal cases that involve human rights violations. Moreover, they act as mediators in non-justiciable cases.[29] The 'Association Women and Development' (MULEIDE) has a similar mandate but with a specific focus on gender. In Pemba city, though, this organisation has seldom functioned as a legal advice centre and has mainly participated in legal awareness and civic education campaigns.[30] Finally, the 'Cabinet of Women's Legal Rights' (GDJM) plays a major role in dispute processing in Pemba city. Launched 1992 as an initiative of the OMM to shelter victims of domestic violence, the GDJM grew to become a popular mediation centre for domestic conflicts. This is largely the result of the charisma and authority of the coordinator, a woman of considerable social prestige and political power. In addition, the services of the GDJM are free of charge and the centre is open every day from Monday to Thursday. Overall, the work of the GDJM is similar to that of the community courts since it deals with the same kinds of cases and operates in a semi-formal manner, by mixing custom, common sense and state law as well as oral and written procedures. In contrast to the community courts, certain legal provisions, such as the equal division of assets on divorce, are consistently

[28] Interviews with community court judges from Natite, Cariaco, Paquitequete, Ingonane and Mahate, Pemba, 12, 15 and 16 September 2009.

[29] Interview with a local representative of the LDH of Pemba. Pemba, 13 September 2009.

[30] Interview with the local coordinator of MULEIDE, Pemba, 14 September 2009.

applied. However, gender equality is not always the guiding principle in the treatment of cases. Rather, the GDJM redefines proper masculine and female behaviour by combining the law and local norms. This favours women in some areas, but it also reproduces a patriarchal order in other ones.[31]

Regarding the relationships amongst these actors, the picture is quite complex. In most cases, grievances are first negotiated amongst the parties or with the involvement of close relatives. If this fails, the case is likely to be presented to the community structures, to the religious leaders, to the GDJM or at the community police. Should the community structures or religious leaders not succeed in facilitating an agreement, the case is generally transferred to the community courts. Whenever the latter cannot settle a case, they either refer it to the GDJM or to the GAMCVV or to the district court, depending on the dispute.[32] The GDJM may transfer a case to the district court or to the GAMCVV in cases of domestic violence, though in practice they rarely do so. In turn, the GAMCVV may refer the parties to the GDJM for reconciliation in cases where the complainant does not present serious injuries and she wishes to withdraw from prosecution. In civil cases, the GAMCVV may also suggest that a complainant seek advice at the IPAJ. Only a minority of disputes seem to be effectively pursued at formal judicial institutions, though direct recourse to the office of the prosecutor were reported to be frequent in cases of child support where the father has formal employment.[33] In cases involving better-off women, they may directly approach the IPAJ, the LDH or a lawyer. Appeals from the district courts lie with the provincial court. Appeals to the high court of appeal and the Supreme Court must be pursued in the capital city, Maputo. The following graphic illustrates this rich justice landscape:

---

[31] For example, women are reprimanded for not respecting male authority. Observations at the GDJM, Pemba, September/October 2010.

[32] The interviewed community court judges reported that cases of domestic violence where physical injuries are serious are transferred to the GAMCVV whereas 'social cases' are mainly transferred to the GDJM. Though community court judges reported that they transfer divorce cases to the district courts, representatives from local civil society organisations said that such disputes are rarely pursued at that level.

[33] Interview with the prosecutor of Pemba city, 1 October 2010; interview with an officer of the office of the prosecutor, Pemba, 22 September 2010.

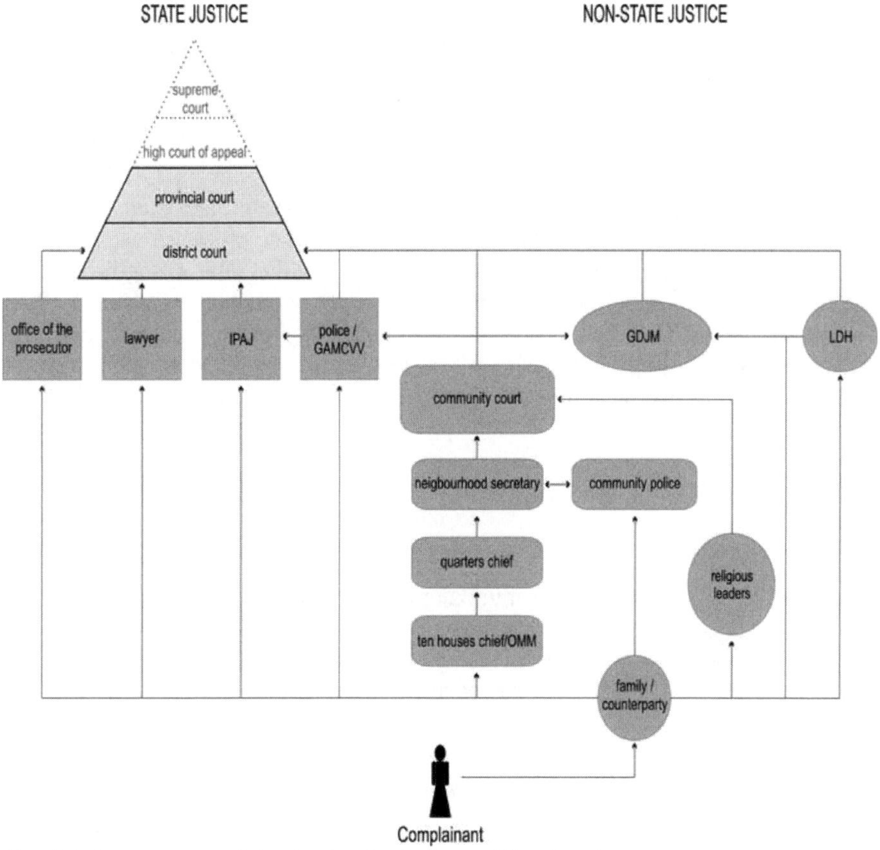


Graphic 1: women and the justice landscape of Pemba city

Despite the variety of legal actors that women may encounter on their pathways to justice, the extent to which female complainants are in a position to 'forum shop' should not be overestimated.[34] First, only better-off women or those whose husbands have formal employment seem to be able to engage with actors associated with formal judicial institutions, such as practising lawyers, the IPAJ or the office of the prosecutor. As a result, most women in Pemba city seem not to

[34] The term 'forum shopping' refers to the ability to navigate these legal instances strategically by calculating which forums will provide the most favourable response according to one's interests (von Benda-Beckman 1981).

have real access to state justice and statutory laws.[35] Second, none of the non-state instances to which most women refer seems to challenge patriarchal norms of social order.[36] At the same time, this is not totally surprising as these actors derive their legitimacy and means of coercion from a tacit social consensus about the appropriateness of their counselling and decisions. This context gives rise to processes of 'inter-legality', such as when community courts or the GDJM refer to state laws and written procedures as resources that reinforce their authority, particularly when they deviate from local practices that prejudice women.[37] In turn, the presence of formal judicial institutions in the city strengthens these actors' capacity to mobilise state law as a coercive means (Galanter 1981; Greenhouse 1985). The next section turns to the question of how national and local level strategies for improving women's access to justice relate to plural justice landscapes such as that of Pemba city.

## National and Local Strategies for Improving Women's Access to Justice

In recent years, a number of multilateral and bilateral agencies as well as international NGOs in Mozambique have provided support to governmental bodies and civil society organisations in devising and implementing strategies to improve women's access to justice.[38] At the national level, efforts have concentrated on

[35] For a discussion of the extent to which formal state courts uphold gender equality see WLSAMOZ (2001).

[36] This is not to suggest that women's complaints aim at challenging patriarchal norms of social order per se.

[37] The term 'inter-legality' refers to the mixture and interpenetration of elements from different legal orders (Santos 2002: 437).

[38] At the time the research was conducted, the main international development actors working on law and gender were the Embassy of Norway, the Embassy of The Netherlands, the Embassy of Sweden, UNIFEM, UNICEF, UNDP, Oxfam UK, Oxfam Solidarity, Action Aid and Save The Children. At the national level, the Ministry of Justice had a gender unit and important civil society organisations included Forum Mulher, Women and Law in Southern Africa, Associação de Mulheres de Carreira Juridica, Mulher Lei e Desenvolvimento, Liga dos Direitos Humanos de Moçambique and the Network for the Defense of Childrens Rights.

supporting advocacy and lobbying for advancing legislative reforms that would bring national laws into line with the National Constitution and the international treaties to which Mozambique is a signatory in the area of women's rights.[39] This resulted in two important pieces of legislation: the Law on Domestic Violence (Law 29/2009) and the Family Law (10/2004). The former makes domestic violence a crime and foresees that the aggressor be separated from the victim, but the text of the law that was finally approved has been strongly criticised for its many flaws (Arthur 2009). Amongst the main problematic issues, we find the provision in article 37 that the law be applied with consideration for the collective interests of the family, the lack of enforcement mechanisms for community work penalties and the lack of severe punishment of sexual abuse within marriage (Arthur 2009). Nevertheless, the law conveys considerable symbolic power by making domestic violence a public crime rather than a private affair.

The Family Law also represents an advance towards gender equality in several areas. Under this law, religious and customary marriages are recognised on an equal footing with civil marriages, allowing women to claim property rights on condition that the union is monogamous and registered (Law 10/2004 Art 16 and 17). In addition, the figure of the 'informal union' is created, which is defined as a singular and stable relationship between a man and a woman with the legal capacity to marry and who cohabit for at least one year without interruption (Law 10/2004 Art 202). As in the case of registered marriages, the legal regime for informal unions foresees the equal division of the property acquired during the union in case of divorce as well as an assumption of paternal affiliation. However, it does not prevent the parties from contracting a civil marriage with another person and though it does confer some maintenance rights upon the death of one of the partners, the law makes no provision for inheritance rights (Association of Women in the Media et al 2007: 23). Other areas that were modified by the Family Law include the introduction of the right of women to work without their husbands' consent (Law 10/2004 art 98), the provision that family assets are to be jointly administered by both spouses instead of the husband alone (art 102) and an increase of the minimum age of marriage from 14 and 16 years for girls and boys respectively to 18 years for both (art 24).

[39] The Constitution of the Republic of Mozambique upholds the principle of equality and non-discrimination in Art.35 and of gender equality in Art.36. In addition, Mozambique ratified CEDAW in 1993 and the Protocol to the African Charter on Human and People's Rights on the Rights of Women in Africa in 2005.

When looking at the initiatives undertaken in Pemba city with a view to implementing these laws, we find strategies on three fronts: first, improving the population's knowledge of the laws; second, enlarging the availability of forums to which women can have recourse for claiming their rights; and third, enhancing justice forums' knowledge of the law so that they decide cases accordingly. Regarding the first area, both pieces of legislation arrived in Pemba by means of civic education initiatives that were conducted by the 'gender working group' of the city, i.e. the LDH, GDJM, GAMCVV, MULEIDE and FOCADE (Forum of the Organizations of Cabo Delgado). In order to disseminate the laws, the gender working group organised different activities in the neighbourhoods, such as public lectures on the main aspects of the laws, group discussions at schools and radio programmes.[40] The GAMCVV also distributed folders at the neighbourhood administrative posts about their work as well as simplified versions of the law on domestic violence.[41] The GDJM provided information about their services through the radio as well. Concerning the availability of forums where women can claim their rights, international NGOs, such as Oxfam Solidarity Belgium and HIVOS, supplied financial support for the legal aid and mediation services provided by the LDH and the GDJM. In the area of domestic violence, the Ministry of the Interior opened two GAMCVVs in Pemba city. The creation of these specialised centres was a nationwide initiative motivated by the discrimination and prejudices that women victims of domestic violence suffered when reporting their cases at police stations.

In the area of enhancing justice forums' knowledge of the laws, a few activities were found too. At the level of state justice, the Centre for Legal and Judicial Formation (CFJJ), which provides national training for magistrates, incorporated a module on gender and human rights covering the laws (Arthur and Osorio 2009: 18). At the level of non-state justice, the project 'Support to the Citizen in Access to Justice', financed by the European Union and UNDP (2005-2009), supported the Human Rights Department of the Ministry of Justice to provide one-time training for some community court judges on the Family Law.[42] The community

[40] Interview with representatives from the gender working group of Pemba (MULEIDE, GDJM, LDH, GAMCVV, FOCADE), Pemba, 13, 14 and 15 September 2009.

[41] Interview with an officer of the GAMCVV, Pemba, 14 September 2009.

[42] Interview with a representative of the Human Rights Department of the Ministry of Justice, Maputo, 22 September 2009.

court judges of three neighbourhoods of Pemba participated in such a three-day training course in November 2007. During the training, discussions were held on how certain areas that are regulated by the Family Law were resolved in the community courts and subsequently the trainers explained how they should be resolved according to the new legislation. In addition, the community court judges who participated in the training course were requested to pass on this information to the judges of the other community courts of Pemba city, who had not been invited due to a lack of capacity to include them all. Finally, Oxfam Solidarity Belgium also organised collective training courses and exchange sessions about the topics addressed in these laws for the members of the gender working group.[43]

When looking at these initiatives, it is striking that local civil society organisations and their international partners drove most of them. The exception is the area of domestic violence, where the government set up the GAMCVVs, though these centres operate under serious structural constraints, such as deficits in their budgets and lack of autonomy to initiate legal processes (Arthur and Osorio 2009: 17).[44] As a matter of fact, the 'National Plan for the Advancement of Women' (2010-2014) acknowledges that domestic violence is a critical domain in promoting gender equality. Yet, national policies in the area of justice and legality foresee few concrete initiatives for improving access to justice for women. The 'National Plan for the Reduction of Absolute Poverty' (PARPA II 2006-2009) includes enhanced access to justice as one of the objectives for the justice sector under the first pillar on governance (GOM 2005: 80). However, none of the specific objectives mentioned under this rubric refers to gender. In turn, the second 'Strategic Integrated Plan for the Justice Sector' (PEI II 2009-2014: 83) has gender as one of its transversal issues, covering the development of gender policies in the justice sector, the reform of discriminatory legislation and the promotion of gender balance in decision-making positions. Nevertheless, transversal approaches to the promotion of gender equality in Mozambique have not been accompanied by enough tangible actions (Tvedten et al. 2008: 47). For example, despite obstacles to women's access to the formal courts there are no initiatives to improve the IPAJ's responsiveness in this area. Another important subject that remains poorly addressed is women's difficulties in registering their marriages and the paternal affiliation of their children (Casimiro and Fonseca 2009). Since most women in

[43] Interview with a representative of Oxfam Solidarity Belgium. Pemba, 14 September 2009.

[44] The Ministries of Justice and the Interior have traditionally been underfunded in Mozambique (OSISA 2006: 28)

Mozambique celebrate customary or religious marriages, in practice lack of access to registration means that most of them fall under the legal regime of informal unions, which affords them weaker legal protections (Monteiro 2007).

In addition, most interventions seem to engage only partially with the plurality of justice forums and normativities that are at play in Pemba city. Despite the role of community courts in processing a considerable share of local disputes and the fact that they were created by the state, no initiatives were found to provide them with operational support. Community court judges work ad honorem and receive little training and no funding for working materials, such as furniture, paper and stamps. Moreover, many community court judges regretted their weak articulation with the formal courts, the lack of communication with them and the poor follow-up of cases that they transfer to them.[45] The training that community court judges received on the Family Law was welcomed but it was only a one-time event involving a minimal fraction of the actors that women encounter on their pathways to justice in Pemba city.

Furthermore, the semi-autonomy of state laws, i.e. how state laws interplay with local normativities, is an area that deserves more attention (Moore 1973).[46] As was described in the previous section, local forums such as the GDJM and the community courts apply women's rights in a partial manner, thereby bridging the distance between the letter of the law and the patriarchal structures in which these forums and disputes are embedded. This implies that interventions need to deal with non-state norms too. In other words, those initiatives that aim at improving women's and justice forum's knowledge of the law need to move beyond legal and technical approaches and discuss the causes of asymmetrical gender relationships. For this purpose, sustained efforts are required in order to generate intra-community dialogue on gender relations and what women's rights might mean to women's concrete struggles (An Na'Im 1994). It also entails that these debates interrogate the subaltern position of women in society, while dismantling the ideologies that sustain the hierarchy of sexes (Tsanga 2003).

---

[45] Interviews with community court judges from Natite, Cariaco, Paquitequete, Ingonane and Mahate, Pemba, 12, 15 and 16 September 2009. Activity reports of the community courts of Natite and Cariaco for the year 2008, on file with author.

[46] According to Moore (1973: 720), social fields are characterised by their semi-autonomy. While they can generate rules and symbols internally, they are also vulnerable to rules, decisions and forces emanating from the larger world that surrounds them.

## Exploring Women's Testimonies

This section explores the testimonies of different women from Pemba city regarding their perspectives on legal processes and their experiences on their pathways to justice. What kinds of grievances emerge from these stories? What do they tell us about women's different strategies of action in response to them? How are the latter related to the justice landscape of Pemba city and those initiatives that seek to improve women's position in it? These accounts illustrate the many shapes of recurring themes while they hint at programmatic gaps.

### *'Women thank God'*

One of the main issues that surfaced in discussions with women about their experiences and views on local pathways to justice is the prominence of dyadic arrangements.[47] It is not uncommon for women in Pemba city to try to negotiate a solution with their counterparty and if this does not yield a positive outcome, to simply 'thank God'. This is often the case even if women know that there are alternatives.[48] This is exemplified by the case of Adelaida. At fifty-four, she works as a nurse and maintains her daughter aged twenty-five and her two grandchildren of nine and six. She divorced many years ago and her daughter is unemployed. The father of her grandchildren never wanted to register them and he refuses to provide any support. She talked about it with him and his family several times but in vain. She was recommended to go to the GDJM for counselling but she prefers

[47] According to Nader and Todd (1978: 8-11), the crucial variables in legal procedures are the number of actors involved and whether the outcome is voluntary or not. In unilateral arrangements the aggrieved party does not press a complaint, while he/she may continue or terminate the relationship with his/her antagonist or resort to self-help strategies. In dyadic arrangements, the two principal parties negotiate the settlement of their conflict by mutual decision. Triadic processes are differentiated by whether the intervention of a third party is voluntary or not (adjudication), and when it is voluntary, whether the outcome is decided by the parties themselves (mediation) of by the third party (arbitration).

[48] Individual interviews, Pemba, September/ October 2010; focus group with women from Paquitequete neighbourhood, Pemba, 20 September 2010; interview with a local representative of the Human Rights League of Pemba (LDH), Pemba, 13 September 2009; interview with a local representative of Oxfam Intermon, Pemba, 7 October 2010.

that justice be done by God.[49]

In other cases, women were reported as consenting to arrangements that were detrimental to them. Such responses were attributed to a lack of confidence that pressing a complaint would lead to a positive result. In this regard, many women regretted that men can pay to have a case decided in their favour while women cannot afford that.[50] Other women simply think that the forums they may refer to will not favour them. The case of Fatima is illustrative. She is twenty-two and does not work. After being traditionally married for four years, she got tired of her husband and told him that she wanted to divorce. Her husband sent her away from their house, keeping all their property. She accepted this. She knows the neighbourhood structures will agree with him because she was the one who requested the divorce.[51]

*...and some also press complaints*

At the same time, some interviewed women explained that things are changing with the presence of organisations such as the GDJM and the GAMCVVs, which encourage women to seek redress. According to a member of the OMM, "women used to suffer in silence, now they dare press complaints".[52] In this process, the exchange of experiences seems to play an important role. Consider the case of Maria. She was nineteen years old when she met her partner Domingo. They dated for a while until one day he gave a party with her family to recognise their union. However, he never built a house for the two of them, spent the night with her or left his belongings at the house of Maria's parents, where she lived.[53] Domingo was then forty and already had a wife. Ten years on, Maria has had two children with Domingo and is pregnant with a third. Maria and her children continue to live with her parents but she has never given up hope that Domingo would one day build a home for them. Every time she discusses the matter with him, he gets mad

---

[49] Individual interview, 28 September 2010.

[50] Focus group with women from Natite neighborhood, Pemba, 24 September 2010.

[51] Individual interview, 20 September 2010.

[52] Individual interview, 20 October 2010.

[53] These are all local signs conferring official status on a marital relationship.

and beats her. Her family tried to convince him too, but without success. Once she explained her situation to a friend, who recommended her to look for counselling at the GDJM. She presented her case there and attended a mediation session with Domingo, at which he promised to assume his responsibilities towards Maria and their children. He never did so. Then another friend of Maria who had been helped at the office of the prosecutor suggested that Maria go there. Maria's husband has a formal job with a transport company so the office of the prosecutor intervened and made him pay alimony for the children. Maria is satisfied with this outcome since Domingo is obliged to pay or he would go to jail. Though the alimony payment is not much, it helps her to send her children to school for she is unemployed. Nevertheless, what she really wants is to build a home for the children with Domingo.[54]

There are a couple of remarkable things about this case. In the first place, it reveals the relevance of a forum's capacity to enforce its decisions as a key element in access to justice. Maria's concerns about Domingo's duties towards her as his second wife were regarded as legitimate at the GDJM. That was not the case at the level of formal state justice. This places the GDJM normatively closer to the experience of Maria. However, the GDJM could not enforce the agreement. The office of the prosecutor would not offer any answers to Maria's frustrations as a wife, but it did have enough coercive power to make sure that Maria's children received their alimony. Not all women would have benefited from this, but Maria's partner had a formal job.

*Enforcement: the missing link?*

In a context where women are gaining confidence to press complaints, knowledge of forums that are accessible and have the reputation of defending women's interests may encourage women to seek redress for their grievances. At the same time, if these instances have limited means of guaranteeing compliance with their decisions, lack of enforcement may undermine women's trust in legal processes, even if women are satisfied with the outcome. This was the case for Carla, aged thirty-eight and working sporadically. She was married traditionally for three years and when she was five months pregnant her husband abandoned her. First, she waited to see if he would reconsider the situation when the baby was born, but he didn't. Then she decided to go to the GDJM, where the couple was invited for a

[54] Individual interview, 7 October 2010.

mediation session but her husband refused to go. He wanted to have the case solved by the community court. There, he recognised the paternity of the child and the community court determined that he had to pay her 18 USD per month alimony. Instead, he proposed to make a one-time compensation payment of 260 USD and thereby close the case once and for all. Everybody agreed, but so far he has not paid.[55]

Lack of enforcement is not only a barrier to accessing justice within those forums that mediate and rely on consensus. State justice also grapples with this issue in certain areas, as exemplified by the case of Mariana. Mariana is forty years old and works as an administrative assistant. She was traditionally married for eighteen years to João and had two children with him. Their relationship was a difficult one. João was very violent and would often beat her badly. Eventually, Mariana decided to divorce. Then, João sent Mariana and their two children away and kept their house for himself and his new girlfriend. After two years, he came back after Mariana. He threw down the front door of the apartment that Mariana was renting with her children and started beating her again. Mariana went to the police, who exhorted him to apologise. He would not do so and ended up in jail for a week. After that, he never disturbed Mariana and the children again. In the meantime, Mariana got in contact with a lawyer from her hometown, who helped her file her divorce at the district court. The district court decided that Mariana was to keep the custody of the children and that João had to pay alimony. In addition, the court ruled that Mariana was entitled to fifty per cent of the house, which was acquired in the course of their informal union. For a year and a half João would not pay alimony but the office of the prosecutor intervened and confiscated the amounts. From then onwards, João paid regularly. However, four years after the sentence was passed João continues to live in the house of which Mariana is half owner. In the meantime, he has married officially with another woman with whom he lives in that house. Mariana complained several times about it at the district court, but she did not get a satisfactory response.[56]

These testimonies suggest that while interventions focus on (i) the existence of a normative framework that upholds women's rights, (ii) knowledge of this framework by right-holders, (iii) the availability of justice forums where grievances can be presented and (iv) the treatment of cases by these forums in accordance with women's rights, *(v) enforcement of decisions* seems to be a key

---

[55] Individual Interview, Pemba, 3 October 2010.

[56] Individual Interview, Pemba, 4 October 2010.

area of concern for women in the process of accessing justice that remains out of sight. This is not to say that interventions in these four domains have been intensively carried out and are no longer necessary. On the contrary, these areas need to be reinforced. In the words of Maria, "I heard that women have rights...but what rights I don't know".[57] Nor does it mean that these four domains are irrelevant to the negotiation of gendered power relations. As a matter of fact, one crucial insight generated by the socio-legal scholarship is that law functions as a resource that can be mobilised for reproducing or contesting power relations (Lazarus-Black and Hirsch 1994; Starr and Collier 1989). In other words, women's ability to have recourse to a justice forum that upholds their rights contributes to counterbalancing male dominance. As explained by Mariana, "this new law on domestic violence is a good thing. Now it is no longer possible for men to just beat their wives cause they know that they can be punished... even if men have no respect, they are scared cause women can go to the police."[58] In turn, the capacities of these forums in terms of enforcement seems to play a role in the extent to which women can actually mobilise them as effective resources. At the same time, the lack of ability to enforce a decision may be an element in explaining why certain non-state forums apply women's rights only partially, as their rulings cannot deviate too much from what will be acceptable for voluntarily compliance. In that respect, Nader (2001) remarks that mediation and negotiation require conditions of relatively equal power amongst the conflicting parties in order to produce equitable outcomes. In a patriarchal context such as that of Pemba city, this implies that women's rights are often compromised.

Considering the justice landscape of Pemba city, enforcement means different things for different kinds of justice forum. While guaranteeing enforcement of state courts' rulings may require better case-load management, ensuring compliance with the decisions of non-state forums entails a whole other set of challenges that seem to go beyond justice processes themselves. Even if the existence of a legislative framework that upholds women's rights and formal judicial institutions in the city represents a resource to non-state justice providers for inducing compliance (Greenhouse 1985: 93, 94), in practice it seems that asymmetrical power relationships between men and women lead to impunity when men unilaterally decide not to respect their commitments. In turn, these realities need to be considered as part of a context where coercive mechanisms such as social pressure seem not always to operate as effectively. However, enhancing the

[57] Individual Interview, Pemba, 7 October 2010.

[58] Individual Interview, Pemba, 4 October 2010.

coercive powers of these forums by bestowing them with the authority to distribute retributive penalties does not seem to be an appropriate solution as this could lead to unchecked abuses of power (Stevens 2000).[59] Rather, this state of affairs seems to call for a 'transformative' approach to legal services addressing the social, cultural, psychological and political constraints that impede the actual implementation of women's rights (Tsanga 2003: 17). In other words, it requires a sustained commitment to change power imbalances in gender relations at different levels of society (Chopra and Isser 2010). A better articulation between state and non-state legal actors could represent a first step in this direction. This could allow not only for collaboration in enforcing fair decisions of non-state actors, but it could also open up spaces for dialogue and mutual learning amongst these forums.

## Conclusions

This paper started with the question of how women's lived realities with the law can inform development interventions in the area of women's access to justice. In each section, this question was addressed from a different angle, thereby revealing different parts of a partial answer. 'Women and the Justice Landscape of Pemba city' shows that despite the local availability of a rich network of justice actors, not all women have equal access to these instances. This illustrates the significance of non-state justice forums and norms in the lives of many women. The practices of some of these forums also indicate that processes of inter-legality bridge the distance between local patriarchal structures and women's rights. The latter is facilitated by the presence of formal judicial institutions in the city. This suggests that formal courts and state laws that uphold women's rights are relevant to improving women's access to justice, both directly and indirectly.

Subsequently, three issues were raised in the analysis of how national and local strategies for improving women's access to justice relate to the position of women in plural justice landscapes such as that of Pemba. First, considerable and sustained efforts are necessary in order to translate policy commitments into concrete actions that effectively enhance women's access to formal courts and state laws. Secondly, given the role of non-state justice in producing and reproducing gendered relations, interventions need to engage with these too. And third, such

[59] As a matter of fact, this is what currently happens when the community police dole out corporal punishments, though this seems not to be a practice for enforcing decisions in 'social cases'.

initiatives need to move beyond technical approaches that focus on the letter of the law. Instead, they need to explore how women's rights relate to the concrete concerns of women and they need to generate a public debate on asymmetrical gender relations.

Finally, the last section invoked the testimonies of different women about their lived realities with the law in order to uncover how their experiences relate to interventions. This exploration revealed that when a forum upholds women's rights in its decisions, enforcement is crucial too. Nevertheless, improved enforcement of decisions remains a programmatic gap at the level of both state and non-state justice. This, in combination with a culture of 'leaving justice to God', may undermine the process of building trust amongst women about claiming their rights. In addition, improving enforcement entails different approaches depending on the kind of forum. For state courts it may require more efficient case management whereas for non-state forums it rather points to the need to foster more equal gender relations in society. A better articulation between state and non-state justice forums was suggested as an element that could facilitate such processes of change.

Above all, this contribution illustrates how exploring women's lived realities with the law is essential in two ways. On the one hand, it contributes to understanding the kinds of process that interventions set in motion and the extent to which the latter contribute to the realisation of women's rights. On the other hand, it uncovers areas of intervention that remain unaddressed despite their potential to generate positive changes. As such, the paper shows the relevance of incorporating 'actor-oriented' perspectives on gender and legal change within justice sector aid.

## Glossary of Organizations

| | |
|---|---|
| FOCADE | Forum of the Organizations of Cabo Delgado |
| GAMCVV | Police Victim Support Centre for Women and Child Victims of Violence |
| GDJM | Cabinet of Women's Legal Rights |
| IPAJ | Institute of Legal Representation and Assistance |
| LDH | Human Rights League |
| MULEIDE | Association Women and Development |
| OMM | Organization of Mozambican Women |

## References

AN NA'IM, Abdullahi

1994 'State responsibility under international human rights law to change religious and customary laws.' Pp. 167-188 in Rebecca Cook (ed.), *Human Rights of Women. National and International Perspectives.* Philadelphia: University of Pennsylvania Press.

ARAUJO, Sara

2005 'Pluralismo jurídico e emancipação social: instâncias comunitárias de resolução de conflitos em Moçambique.' Presentation at the 11th General Assembly of CODESRIA, 'Rethinking African Development: Beyond impasse, towards alternatives', Maputo, 6 to 10 December.

ARTHUR, Maria Jose

2009 'Aprovação da lei sobre a violencia domestica praticada contra a mulher. Que resultados?' *Bulletin Outras Vozes*, November 2009, available at www.wlsa.org.moz, last date accessed 08/05/12.

ARTHUR, Maria Jose and Conceição OSORIO

2009 'Proposta para a criação do atendimento integrado no combate à violencia domestica.' Maputo, unpublished document on file with author.

ASSOCIATION OF WOMEN IN THE MEDIA, MOZAMBICAN ASSOCIATION OF WOMEN IN JUDICIAL CAREERS, ASSOCIATION OF RURAL WOMEN, ASSOCIATION FOR NUTRITION AND FOOD SECURITY, COMMITTEE OF THE WORKING WOMAN OF THE ORGANIZATION OF MOZAMBICAN WORKERS, HUMAN RIGHTS LEAGUE OF MOZAMBIQUE, ASSOCIATION WOMEN, LAW AND DEVELOPMENT, NETWORK FOR THE DEFENCE OF THE RIGHTS OF THE CHILD, and WOMEN AND LAW IN SOUTHERN AFRICA

2007 'Shadow Report: Stage of Implementation of the CEDAW in Mozambique.' Submitted for 38th CEDAW Session. Available at http://www.iwraw-ap.org/resources/pdf/Mozambique.pdf, last accessed 08/05/12.

BENDA-BECKMANN, Keebet von

1981 'Forum shopping and shopping forums - Dispute settlement in a Minangkabau Village in West Sumatra.' *Journal of Legal Pluralism* 19: 117-159.

BONATE, Liazzat

2009 'Transformations de l'islam à Pemba au Mozambique.' *Afrique Contemporaine* 3(231): 61-76.

CABO DELGADO PROVINCIAL DIRECTION OF THE JUSTICE SECTOR

2007 'Informação para o Portal do Governo.' Available at

http://www.cabodelgado.gov.mz/grandes-projectos/Direccao%20Provincial%20da%20Justica%20de%20Cabo%20Delgado.PDF, last accessed 08/05/12.

CASIMIRO, Isabel and Fatima FONSECA
2009 'Baseline Study Regarding the Impact of the Mozambican Family Law.' Available at http://issuu.com/oa-padare/docs/glr baseline policy report eng. tran oct. 2009 , last accessed 08/05/12

CHOPRA, Tanja and Debora ISSER
2010 'From "fixing" systems to supporting processes of change: rethinking women's access to justice in fragile states.' Paper presented at the International Conference on Access to Justice and Security, Non-State Actors and the Local Dynamics of Ordering, November 1-3, 2010, Copenhagen.

COLLIER, Edda
2009 *Perfil de Género em Cabo Delgado*. Maputo: Direcção Provincial da Mulher e Acção Social, Direcção Provincial das Finanças.

DANIDA (DANISH MINISTRY OF FOREIGN AFFAIRS)
2010 'How to Note: Informal Justice Systems'. Available at http://www.danidadevforum.um.dk/NR/rdonlyres/FE725502-ACF5-42C2-B677-C0D411AE2660/0/InformalJusticeSystemsfinalprint.pdf, last accessed 08/05/12.

DfID (UK DEPARTMENT FOR INTERNATIONAL DEVELOPMENT)
2000 'Justice and Poverty Reduction.' Available at http://www.gsdrc.org/docs/open/SSAJ35.pdf, last accessed 08/05/12.
2004 'Non-State Justice and Security Systems.' Available at http://www.gsdrc.org/docs/open/SSAJ101.pdf, last accessed 08/05/12.

FRANCIONI, Francesco (ed.)
2007 *Access to Justice as a Human Right*. Oxford and New York: Oxford University Press.

GALANTER, Marc
1981 'Justice in many rooms: courts, private ordering and indigenous law.' *Journal of Legal Pluralism* 19: 1-47.

GOM (GOVERNMENT OF MOZAMBIQUE)
2005 'Plan for the Reduction of Absolute Poverty 2006-2009 (PARPA II).' Maputo: Government of Mozambique, Ministry of Cooperation and Planning.

GREENHOUSE, Carol
1985 'Mediation: a comparative approach.' *Man*, New Series 20(1): 90-114.

GRIFFITHS, Anne
1997 *In the Shadow of Marriage: Gender and Justice in an African Community*. Chicago: University of Chicago Press.
HELLUM, Anne
1995 'Actor perspectives on gender and legal pluralism in Africa.' Pp.13-29 in Hanne Petersen and Henrik Zahle (eds.), *Legal Polycentricity: Consequences of Pluralism in Law*. Boston: Dartmouth Publishing.
2000 'Human rights and gender relations in post-colonial Africa: options and limits for the subjects of legal pluralism.' *Law and Social Inquiry* 25(2): 635-655.
HELLUM, Anne, Julie STEWART, Ali SARDAR, and Amy TSANGA
2007 *Human Rights, Plural Legalities and Gendered Realities: Paths are Made by Walking*. Harare: Southern and Eastern African Regional Centre for Women's Law and Weaver Press.
HIRSCH, Susan
1998 *Pronouncing and Persevering: Gender and the Discourses of Disputing in an African Islamic Court*. Chicago: University of Chicago Press.
INE (INSTITUTO NACIONAL DE ESTADISTICA)
2007 'Recenseamento Geral da População e Habitação.' Available at http://www.ine.gov.mz, last accessed 08/05/12.
KIPFER-DIVADI, Inez, Amy TSANGA, and Juliane OSTERHAUS
2005 'Bridging the Gap between Modern Legislation and Legal Reality: Working with Customary Legal Structures to Improve Women's Rights.' Available at http://www.gtz.de/de/dokumente/en-bridging-gap-costumary-law-womens-rights-2005.pdf, last accessed 08/05/12.
KPMG
2009 'Auditoria de Desempenho do Sector da Justiça. Final Report.' On file with author.
LAZARUS-BLACK, Mindie and Susan HIRSCH (eds.)
1994 *Contested States: Law, Hegemony, and Resistance*. New York: Routledge.
MENESES, Maria Paula
2007 'Pluralism, Law and Citizenship in Mozambique: Mapping the Complexity.' Report CES 291, Coimbra: Centro de Estudos Sociais.
MONTEIRO, Ana Cristina
2007 'Não reconhecimento da união de facto: uma forma de discriminação contra as mulheres.' *Bulletin Outras Vozes*, August 2007. Available at www.wlsa.org.moz, last accessed 08/05/12.
MOORE, Sally Falk
1973 'Law and social change: the semi-autonomous field as an appropriate

subject of study.' *Law and Society Review* 7: 719-746.

MORRISON, Andrew, Raju DHUSHYANTH and Nistha SINHA
2007 'Gender Equality, Poverty and Economic Growth.' Policy Research Working Paper 4349, Washington: The World Bank.

MUKHOPADHYAY, Maitrayee
2008 'Gender and Access to Justice in sub-Saharan Africa. Report on the KIT-CALS conference. 29-30 October 2008, Johannesburg, South Africa.' Available at http://www.kit.nl/net/KIT_Publicaties_output/ShowFile2.aspx?e=1530, last accessed 08/05/12.

NADER, Laura
2001 'The Underside of Conflict Management in Africa and Elsewhere.' *IDS Bulletin* 32(1): 19-27.

NADER, Laura and Harry TODD
1978 *The Disputing Process – Law in Ten Societies*. New York: Columbia University Press.

NYAMU-MUSEMBI, Celestine
2005a 'For or against Gender Equality? Evaluating the Post-cold War "Rule of Law" Reforms in sub-Saharan Africa.' Occasional Paper, United Nations Research Institute for Social Development.
2005b 'Towards an Actor Oriented Perspective on Human Rights.' Pp. 31-49 in Naila Kabeer (ed.), *Inclusive Citizenship, Meanings and Expressions*. London and New York: Zed Books.

OECD-DAC (ORGANIZATION FOR ECONOMIC COOPERATION AND DEVELOPMENT)
2007 'Handbook on Security System Reform, Supporting Security and Justice.' Available at http://www.oecd.org/dataoecd/43/25/38406485.pdf, last accessed 08/05/12.

OSISA (Open Society Initiative for Southern Africa)
2006 'Mozambique: Justice Sector and the Rule of Law.' Available at http://www.afrimap.org/english/images/report/Mozambique%20Justice%20report%20(Eng).pdf, last accessed 08/05/12.

ROM (REPUBLIC OF MOZAMBIQUE)
2002 'Folha Informativa dos Municipios.' Maputo: Ministerio da Administração Estatal. Pp. 245-251.

SANTOS, Boaventura de Souza
2002 *Towards a New Legal Common Sense*. Edinburgh: Butterworths Lexis Nexis.
2006 'The heterogeneous state and legal pluralism in Mozambique.' *Law & Society Review* 40(1): 39-76.

SANTOS, Boaventura de Souza and Carlos TRINDADE (eds.)
2003 *Conflito e Transformação Social: Uma Paissagem das Justiças em Moçambique*. Porto: Afrontamento.

STARR, June and Jane F. COLLIER (eds.)
1989 *History and Power in the Study of Law, New Directions in Legal Anthropology*. Ithaca and London: Cornell University Press.

STEVENS, Joana
2000 *Access to Justice in Sub-Sahara Africa*. London: Penal Reform International.

SWIDLER, Anne
1986 'Culture in action: symbols and strategies.' *American Sociological Review* 51(2): 273-286.

TSANGA, Amy
2003 *Taking Law to the People. Gender, Law Reform and Community Legal Education in Zimbabwe*. Harare: Weaver Press.

TVEDTEN, Inge, Margarida PAULO and Georgina MONTSERRAT
2008 'Gender Policies and Feminisation of Poverty in Mozambique.' CMI Report 2008: 13, Bergen: Chr. Michelsen Institute.

TVEDTEN Inge, Margarida PAULO and Minna TUOMINEN
2009 If Men and Women Were Equal, We Would All Simply Be People: Gender and Poverty in Northern Mozambique.' CMI Report 2009: 14. Bergen: Chr. Michelsen Institute.

UNITED NATIONS
2009 'Legal empowerment of the poor and eradication of poverty.' Report of the Secretary-General, 13 July 2009, A/64/133.

UNDP (UNITED NATIONS DEVELOPMENT PROGRAM)
2004 'Access to Justice: Practice Note.' Available at http://www.undp.org/governance/docs/Justice PN English.pdf, last accessed 08/05/12.
2008 'The Role of Information Communication Technologies in Achieving the Millennium Development Goals.' Mozambique, National Human Development Report, Maputo, Mozambique. Available at http://hdr.undp.org/en/reports/national/africa/mozambique/name,3367,en.html, last accessed 08/05/12.

UN WOMEN
2011 'In Pursuit of Justice, Progress of the World's Women.' Available at http://progress.unwomen.org, last accessed 08/05/12.

USAID (US AGENCY FOR INTERNATIONAL DEVELOPMENT)
2007 'The Women's Legal Rights Initiative Final Report.' Available at http://www.usaid.gov/our work/cross-cutting programs/wid/dg/wlr.html,

last accessed 08/05/12.
WLSAMOZ (WOMEN AND LAW IN SOUTHERN AFRICA MOZAMBIQUE)
2001 Familias em Contexto de Mudanças em Moçambique, Maputo: WLSAMOZ
WOJKOWSKA, E.
2006 'Doing justice: how informal justice systems can contribute.' Available at http://www.democraciaejustica.org/cienciapolitica3/sites/default/files/doingjusticeewawojkowska130307.pdf, last accessed 08/05/12.
WORLD BANK (INTERNATIONAL BANK FOR RECONSTRUCTION AND DEVELOPMENT)
2003 'Legal Services for the Poor Best Practices Handbook.' Available at http://www-ds.worldbank.org/external/default/main?pagePK=64193027&piPK=64187937&theSitePK=523679&menuPK=64187510&searchMenuPK=64187511&siteName=WDS&entityID=000090341 20050422154216, last accessed 08/05/12.
2006 'World Development Report, Equity and Development.' Available at http://siteresources.worldbank.org/INTWDR2006/Resources/477383-1127230817535/082136412X.pdf, last accessed 08/05/12.
2009 'Justice Sector Project Summaries Africa Region.' Available at http://siteresources.worldbank.org/INTLAWJUSTINST/Resources/JusticeSectorProjectSummariesAfrica.pdf, last accessed 08/05/12.

# LEGAL AND JUDICIAL PLURALISM IN NAMIBIA AND BEYOND: A MODERN APPROACH TO AFRICAN LEGAL ARCHITECTURE?

Oliver C. Ruppel and Katharina Ruppel-Schlichting

## Introduction

This article[60] is intended to give an overview on the various structures pertinent to the Namibian legal system as one vital example of legal and judicial pluralism in Africa. Legal pluralism has become a recognised concept all over our globalised world and it is deeply anchored in the Namibian legal system (Hinz 2007). However, as a world-wide observable phenomenon legal pluralism exists not within but also beyond legal orders (Ruppel and Winter 2011). As the concept of legal pluralism is continuously developing in the field of legal theory, it cannot be reduced to one clear, all-encompassing definition. What is clear however, is that

> [t]he wide field of law in its various local, global manifestations is more than just a 'law's empire': above all, it concerns dynamic and extremely complex and contested navigation patterns of rules and processes (Menski 2010: 443).

A broad variety of elements influence the applicable sources of law and thus, a legal system in its entirety. These influencing elements include religion, ethics, morality, society, government, globalisation and international law (Menski 2010:

---

[60] Our grateful thanks are due to Werner Mostert for his assistance in preparing this article for publication.

© Copyright 2011 - Sue Farran.

443). Different legal mechanisms may be applied for comparable situations (Griffiths 1986: 1-55). This is particularly true for the African, and in this case, the Namibian context, which will be elaborated in the following by focusing on applicable law and various dispute settlement fora. In this context, light will first be shed on the national level, before turning to the African regional level.[61] The article aims to reflect a 'modern approach' to African legal architecture. Modern in a sense that it not only focuses on legal pluralism on the national but also on the regional level, where the majority of the people is still governed by multiple legal and increasingly governed by multilayered political or economic regimes. Such complex systems of multi-level governance depend on the strength of interdependence between the regional, national and local levels. A view towards a more transnational pluralism thus offers not only an appropriate account of contemporary African legal reality but also reflects legal pluralistic insights beyond territorially-based application in an African legal environment.

## Southwest Africa - Namibia

The inhospitable Namib Desert constituted a barrier to European colonisation until the late 18th century, when traders and missionaries first explored the area. In 1878, the United Kingdom annexed Walvis Bay on behalf of the Cape Colony, while the rest of south western Africa would soon thereafter fall under German administration, henceforth to be known as German South West Africa. As a result of the Herero and Nama wars of anti-colonial resistance of 1904-1908,[62] Germany consolidated its hold over the colony, and prime grazing land passed to white control. German overlordship ended during World War I in the wake of South Africa's military occupation of the German colony.[63]

On 17 December 1920, South Africa took over the administration of South West Africa in terms of Article 22 of the 1919 Peace Treaty of Versailles (which incorporated the Covenant of the League of Nations) and a mandate agreement by the League Council. South Africa was mandated with the power of administration

[61] It should be noted that the numerous bilateral agreements to which Namibia is a signatory will not be discussed within the scope of this article.

[62] See also Ruppel (2009c, 2011b).

[63] See generally Ruppel and Ruppel-Schlichting (2011: 1-13).

and legislation over the territory.[64] Article 22 stated as follows:

> To those colonies and territories which as a consequence of the late war have ceased to be under the sovereignty of the States which formerly governed them and which are inhabited by peoples not yet able to stand by themselves under the strenuous conditions of the modern world, there should be applied the principle that the well-being and development of such peoples form a sacred trust of civilisation and that securities for the performance of this trust should be embodied in this Covenant. The best method of giving practical effect to this principle is that the tutelage of such peoples should be entrusted to advanced nations who by reason of their resources, their experience or their geographical position can best undertake this responsibility, and who are willing to accept it, and that this tutelage should be exercised by them as Mandatories on behalf of the League. The character of the mandate must differ according to the stage of the development of the people, the geographical situation of the territory, its economic conditions, and other similar circumstances. [...] There are territories, such as South-West Africa [...], which, owing to the sparseness of their population [...] or their remoteness from the centres of civilisation, or their geographical contiguity to the territory of the Mandatory, and other circumstances, can be best administered under the laws of the Mandatory as integral portions of its territory, subject to the safeguards above mentioned in the interests of the indigenous population.[65]

In 1946, the League of Nations was superseded by the newly formed United Nations. When the United Nations requested South Africa to place the territory under a trusteeship agreement it refused. In 1966 the South African mandate was officially revoked by the UN General Assembly.[66] Also in 1966 the South West African People's Organisation (SWAPO), under the leadership of Sam Nujoma,

---

[64] See www.state.gov/r/pa/ei/bgn/5472.htm, last accessed on 11 May 2012.

[65] Available at http://net.lib.byu.edu/~rdh7/wwi/versa/versa1.html ; last accessed on 11 May 2012.

[66] Ibid.

started to put pressure on the South African government, and took up an armed struggle to liberate Namibia. Political and social unrest within Namibia increased markedly during the 1970s, and was often met with repression at the hands of the colonial administration. The United Nations Institute for Namibia (UNIN) was established to educate Namibians for roles in an independent Republic of Namibia after the proposal was adopted by the United Nations General Assembly in December 1974. [67] In 1978, the UN Security Council passed Resolution 435 and authorised the creation of a Transition Assistance Group to monitor the country's transition to independence (Amoo and Skeffers 2008).

In April 1989 the UN began to supervise this transition process, part of which entailed supervising elections for a Constituent Assembly, which was also charged with drafting a constitution for the country. After more than a century of domination by other countries and a long struggle on both diplomatic and military levels, Namibian Independence was achieved and officially declared on 21 March 1990.

## Legal Pluralism

During the German colonial time, the strict segregation between 'natives' and 'non-natives' was a governing principle, which was also reflected in the plurality of existing laws and their isolated application (Sippel 2011: 203). Today Namibian law reflects the country's rich history. The law in place is the product of different sources: firstly, Roman law; secondly, the fusion of Roman law and Roman-Dutch customary law - hence the term Roman-Dutch law - which came in the wake of Dutch colonisation at the Cape of Good Hope; thirdly, from the early 19th century onwards English law asserted itself, leaving deep traces in Roman-Dutch law, after British hegemony in southern Africa had been established; and fourthly, indigenous customary law from time immemorial (Hinz and Santos 2002). Moreover, a broad spectrum of statutory laws and policies have been developed on the national level after Independence and the important role of international law has been anchored in Namibia's Constitution, as will be outlined below.

[67] The United Nations Institute for Namibia (UNIN) was an educational body set up by the United Nations Council for Namibia until 1990. It was based in Zambia's capital of Lusaka.

## The Constitution and International Law

The Namibian Constitution or the *Mother of All Laws*, as Namibians have come to call this legal instrument, is indivisibly linked to the founding of the Namibian state. The adoption of the Constitution came about after a three-decade-long struggle for Independence[68] and many more decades of colonial and military rule.[69] On 21 March 1990, Namibia became politically independent, with a basic legal framework drafted by the Constituent Assembly of Namibia. The Constitution was a result of joint efforts of and debates between the political parties represented in the Constituent Assembly, South Africa, the United Nations and the South West Africa People's Organisation (SWAPO) (Diescho 1994).

The Namibian Constitution has been hailed as one of the most democratic and liberal constitutions in the world (Schmidt-Jortzig 1991: 341-351). It shows a strong commitment to the rule of law, democratic government and respect for fundamental human rights and freedoms such as the protection of life, liberty, human dignity, equality, education, freedom from slavery, forced labour, and discrimination to name only a few rights enshrined in it. Furthermore, the Constitution contains mechanisms with regard to checks and balances between the three branches of government, the executive, the legislature and the judiciary. Principles of state policy, which guide the government's legislative processes, are provided in Chapter 11 of the Constitution. The Constitution enjoys hierarchical primacy amongst the sources of law by virtue of its Article 1(6). It is thematically organised into 21 Chapters that contain 148 Articles (Bukurura 2002: 57). The preamble of a constitution is an important tool for the interpretation of such document, because it reflects the general spirit of the drafter (Watz 2004: 21).

Article 144 of the Namibian Constitution incorporates international law explicitly as law of the land; it needs no legislative act to become so. International law is thus integrated into domestic law. National authorities and the judiciary in particular can, therefore, apply international law directly on the national level, before cases are taken to regional or international judicial or quasi-judicial bodies (Bangamwabo 2008: 168). However, international law has to conform to the Constitution in order to apply domestically. Whenever a treaty provision or other rule of international law is inconsistent with the Namibian Constitution, the latter

[68] On the struggle for liberation see Katjavivi (1988).

[69] For a detailed analysis of the background and origin of the Namibian Constitution see Diescho (1994), Erasmus (2002: 5-26).

will prevail.

In Namibia a treaty will be binding in terms of Article 144, if the relevant international and constitutional requirements have been met in terms of the law of treaties, and the Namibian Constitution. International agreements, therefore, will become Namibian law when they come into force for Namibia (Erasmus 1991). The conclusion of or accession to an international agreement is governed by Articles 32(3)(e), 40(i) and 63(2)(e) of the Namibian Constitution. The Executive is responsible for conducting Namibia's international affairs, including entry into international agreements. The President, assisted by the Cabinet, is empowered to negotiate and sign international agreements, and to delegate such power. It is required by the Constitution that the National Assembly agrees to the ratification of or accession to an international agreement. However, the Constitution does not require the promulgation of an international agreement in order for it to become part of the law of the land (Hinz and Ruppel 2008: 8ff). Further to Article 144, Article 96 of the Constitution promotes international cooperation, peace and security; it also exhorts respect for international law and treaty obligations, as a principle of state policy.

## Roman-Dutch and Common Law

The Namibian Constitution is special in several ways. Firstly, it was developed largely under the eyes and with the assistance of the international community. Secondly, the Namibian Constitution was certainly an experiment in southern Africa in putting an end to racial discrimination and apartheid (Watz 2004: 21). Namibia has not totally relinquished its South African legal legacy, however. Article 140 provides for legal continuity, stating that all existing laws prior to Independence are to remain in force until repealed by Parliament. This does not only mean that Roman-Dutch law continues to be the ordinary law of the land, but also that Namibia still has a considerable amount of pre-independence legislation.[70]

Roman-Dutch law is based on Roman law as it was applied by the courts of Holland and other provinces in the Netherlands; it was developed by writers such as Hugo de Groot and Simon van Leeuwen in the 17th and 18th centuries (du Plessis 1990: 40). Roman-Dutch law came to the Cape of Good Hope when the Dutch East India Company under its local Governor Jan van Riebeeck established

[70] See also Ruppel (2010a: 323-360).

a post for replenishing ships' supplies – today's Cape Town, in 1652. Roman-Dutch Law in South Africa was subject to further developments under the influence of particularly English law (du Plessis 1990: 49ff).

With the effect of Proclamation 21 of 1919, the Roman Dutch law developed by the South African courts became the common law of the territory, binding on the Namibian courts until Independence (Amoo 2008c: 69ff). This position was affirmed by Article 66(1) of the Namibian Constitution, which provides that

> both the customary law and the common law of Namibia in force on the date of Independence shall remain valid to the extent to which such customary or common law does not conflict with this Constitution or any other statutory law.

Common law refers to law and the corresponding legal system developed through court decisions and similar tribunals, rather than through statutory enactment. Common law is created and refined by judges: a decision in a case which is currently pending largely depends on decisions in previous cases and affects the law to be applied in future cases.[71] When there is no authoritative statement of the law, judges have the authority and duty to make law by creating precedent.

## African Customary Law

Despite the legal influence of the ex-colonial powers, a large number of Namibians still live under indigenous customary law (Hinz 2002: 69-89). It regulates marriage, divorce, inheritance and land tenure, amongst other things. Thus, customary law is a body of norms, customs and beliefs relevant for most Namibians. However, despite this relevance for the majority of the population, customary law has for a time been marginalised and even ignored owing to colonial rule. Customary law is a complex, dynamic system which has constantly evolved in response to a wide variety of internal needs and external influences (Hinz 2002).

Before the arrival of the colonists the indigenous populations have lived for generations according to their own distinctive laws. Customary law was passed on - orally - from generation to generation. Article 66 of the Namibian Constitution

[71] For further details on the common law in Namibia see Amoo (2008a: 62).

lays the foundation for the constitutional recognition of customary law. It states that both the customary law and the common law of Namibia in force on the date of Independence shall remain valid to the extent that such customary or common law does not conflict with the Constitution or any other statutory law. Section 3 of the Traditional Authorities Act[72] gives certain powers, duties and functions to traditional authorities and members thereof.

Currently there are 49 officially recognised traditional communities and most of them have their own customary laws and traditions: There are eight Oshiwambo-speaking communities, namely the Ombadja, Ombalantu, Ondonga, Ongandjera, Oukwanyama, Uukolonkadhi, Uukwaluudhi and Uukwambi; five communities in Kavango, namely the Ukwangali, Mbunza, Shambyu, Gciriku and Humbukushu; four communities in the Caprivi region, namely the Mafwe, Mashi, Masubia and Mayeyi. The remaining traditional communities can be devided into five different clusters, such as the Damara, the Ovaherero and Ovambanderu, the Nama, the San, the Batswana ba Namibia and the Bakgalakgadi (Ruppel 2010b: iii-iv).

It is the overall responsibility of traditional authorities to supervise and ensure the observance of the customary law of that community by its members. Customary law also plays an important role in the sustainable development of natural resources and the protection of biological diversity as it incorporates a broad knowledge of ecosystems relationships (Hinz and Ruppel 2008: 57-58, 2010).

While most of the customary rules have been transmitted orally from generation to generation, the process of ascertaining customary law in Namibia is on-going (Hinz and Namwoonde 2010). Article 66(1) puts customary law on the same footing as any other law of the country as far as its constitutionality is concerned. This means that customary law has to comply with the constitutional provisions, particularly Chapter 3, which contains fundamental human rights and freedoms. Certain conceptions related to human rights are from a customary law perspective sometimes still seen as 'Western' concepts (Menski 2010: 443; Hinz 2010a: 15) that interfere with cultural values. However, those aspects of customary law that are inhuman and discriminatory should not endanger the existence of customary law as a system of laws that governs the way of life of most Africans. The solution is not to abolish customary law, but rather to have such law reviewed. The abolition of customary law would mean erasing the modus operandi of various ethnic groups from the broad spectrum of Namibian society. Instead, one should

[72] No. 25 of 2000.

identify the sensitive aspects under customary practices (e.g. in regards to women and children)[73] that do not conform to the constitutional principles of equality, fairness, and justice, and apply law reform.

After all, the constitutional recognition of customary law protects it against arbitrary inroads, and places a legal duty upon national lawmakers to treat customary law like any other law as regards its repeal or amendment.[74] This dichotomy of laws makes the Namibian legal system an object of fascination to comparative lawyers as well as to legal ethnologists and sociologists (Ruppel 2009e).

## Judicial Pluralism

The Namibian court system also retains Roman-Dutch elements, inherited from South Africa along with elements of the African traditional (community) court system. The 'formal'[75] court system comprises the Supreme Court, the High Court, the magistrates' courts and the (traditional) Community Courts (Ruppel and Ruppel-Schlichting 2011: 8).

The courts are required to follow binding authoritative sources whereas those of persuasive authority may serve to convince a court to apply or interpret a legal rule in a particular manner. The sources of law in which they are usually consulted are statute law or legislation; judgements of the courts; international law (Article 144 of the Constitution); common and customary law (Article 66 of the Constitution) and to some extent legal writing (Ruppel and Ruppel-Schlichting 2011: 8).

The doctrine of *stare decisis* applies in Namibia, making the judgments of the superior courts one of the most important sources of the law. Literally *stare decisis* means 'the decision stands'. Obviously, when a court arrives at a decision, the parties to the dispute adjudicated will be bound by that decision. But what is the effect of such a particular decision on similar disputes arising in future? Is a court, when it has to settle another dispute of a similar or even the same nature bound by

[73] See research done on women and children by Ruppel (2008, 2009a).

[74] Cf Hinz (2002); Ruppel (2010d: 279f).

[75] For informal justice systems, cf Hinz and Mapaure (2010).

previous court decisions, or is it free to formulate its own principles and ignore a previous decision? Strict adherence to the doctrine of *stare decisis* would mean that courts are obliged to follow earlier decisions regardless of whether an earlier decision still makes sense. Therefore and for greater fairness and legal certainty, Namibian courts are bound by their own decisions unless and until they are overruled by a superior court. It is, however, conceivable that circumstances arise that would render it possible for a court to override its own legal opinion (Havenga et al. 2002: 8).

## The Higher Court Structure

The Supreme Court serves as the highest court of appeal and also exercises constitutional review of legislation. The seat of the court is in Windhoek. Prior to the attainment of nationhood in 1990 and the promulgation of the Constitution of the Republic of Namibia, which created an independent judiciary, the courts of Namibia were an extension of the judiciary system of South Africa (Amoo 2008b). Its appellate jurisdiction covers appeals emanating from the High Court, including appeals which involve interpretation, implementation and upholding of the Constitution and the fundamental rights and freedoms guaranteed thereunder (Amoo 2008c: 72). The Supreme Court is not bound by any judgment, ruling or order of any court that exercised jurisdiction in Namibia before or after independence. The Constitution further vests in Parliament the power to make legislation providing for the appellate jurisdiction of the Supreme Court. The Supreme Court is vested with unlimited appellate jurisdiction over appeals against any judgment or order of the High Court; and any party to any such proceedings before the High Court, if dissatisfied with any such judgment or order, has a right of appeal to the Supreme Court (Supreme Court Act No. 15 of 1990). Unlike, for example, South Africa, where there is a Constitutional Court, in Namibia the Constitution does not create a separate Constitutional Court per se, but the Supreme Court can constitute itself as a Constitutional Court (Amoo 2008a: 3).

The Supreme Court may exercise this jurisdiction *ex mero motu* (of the court's own accord) should it come to the notice of the court or any judge of that court, that an irregularity has occurred in any proceedings, notwithstanding that such proceedings are not subject to an appeal or other proceedings before the Supreme Court. A decision of the Supreme Court is binding on all other courts of Namibia and all persons in Namibia unless it is reversed by the Supreme Court itself, or is contradicted by an Act of Parliament, lawfully enacted in conformity with the principles of legislative sovereignty (Amoo 2008a: 3).

The High Court is a superior court of record and its jurisdiction is provided by both the Constitution and the High Court Act (No. 16 of 1990). The Constitution vests the High Court with both original and appellate jurisdiction, and all proceedings in the High Court are to be carried in an open court (High Court Act, section 13). It is situated permanently in Windhoek, and since 2009 also in Oshakati. Other than this, the court goes on circuit to venues including Gobabis, Grootfontein and Swakopmund.[76] The High Court derives its appellate jurisdiction to hear and adjudicate upon appeals from lower courts primarily from the Constitution (Article 80(2)). The court also has the power to confirm, amend, or set aside the judgment or order which is the subject of the appeal, and to give any judgment or make any order which the circumstances may require (High Court Act, section 19).

## The Lower Court Structure

The lower courts are responsible for administering justice. In terms of Article 78 of the Constitution, the lower courts form part of the judiciary, one of the three branches of the state. Lower courts are established in terms of Section 2(1) of the Magistrates' Courts Act (No. 32 of 1944). The bulk of the judiciary's work also takes place in the lower courts. There are thirty-two (32) permanent courts and more than thirty (30) periodical courts in Namibia (Amoo 2008c: 83). Lower courts are divided into a Regional Division and five administrative districts, namely Windhoek, Oshakati, Otjiwarongo, Keetmanshoop and Rundu. Each district has a seat for a regional court that presides on all criminal matters except high treason, but has no jurisdiction in civil matters (Amoo 2008c: 83).

The Magistrates' courts may be classified into regional, district and sub-district, division[77] and periodical courts[78]. Magistrates' Courts are courts of record[79] and

[76] Section 4 of the High Court Act provides that the seat of the High Court is to be in Windhoek, but if the Judge-President deems it necessary or expedient in the interest of the administration of justice, he or she may authorise the holding of its sitting elsewhere in Namibia.

[77] Section 2(f.) (2) (a)-(iv) of the Magistrates' Courts Act of 1944.

[78] Section 26 of the Magistrates' Courts Act of 1944; periodical courts are meant to serve the remote areas of the country, and as the name suggests, they are only held at intervals, when the volume of work in the area requires a court sitting.

their proceedings in both criminal cases and the trial of all defended civil actions are conducted in an open court.[80] The jurisdiction of the Magistrates' Courts in respect of causes of action is regulated by Section 29 of the Magistrates' Court Act, as amended.[81] The Magistrates' Courts have jurisdiction over liquid claims not exceeding N$100,000 and illiquid claims not exceeding N$25,000.[82] Magistrates' Courts are presided over by judicial officers, and advocates or attorneys of any division of the Supreme Court may appear in any proceeding in any court. All Magistrates' Courts have equal civil and criminal jurisdiction, except the regional Magistrates' Courts, which have only criminal jurisdiction (Amoo 2008c: 84). The territorial jurisdiction of a Magistrate's Court is the district, sub-district or area for which it is established; a court established for a district has no jurisdiction in a sub-district. Magistrates' Courts also have the jurisdiction to hear and determine any appeal against any order or decision of a Community Court.

According to sections 4-6 of the Traditional Authorities Act, there are 49 recognised traditional authorities in Namibia. These traditional authorities, as well as unrecognised traditional communities are governed by their customary laws and run traditional courts to decide upon matters brought before them (Hinz 2010b: 93). Community courts are a formal creation of the Community Courts Act (No. 10 of 2003), which also provides detailed procedures and requirements for the establishment and recognition of Community Courts in particular traditional communities. (For more details see Hinz 2010b.) The Community Courts are required to cater for all forms of proceedings exercised under customary law. The Act was drafted to give legislative recognition to and formalise the jurisdiction of the traditional (African) courts that render essential judicial services to members of traditional communities who subject themselves to their jurisdiction and the application of customary law. This formal recognition also brings the proceedings

[79] A court of record can be understood as 'a court whose acts and judicial proceedings are written on parchment or in a book for a perpetual memorial which serves as the authentic and official evidence of the proceedings of the court' (Amoo 2008c: 83).

[80] Section 5 of the Magistrates' Courts Act of 1944.

[81] Magistrates' Courts Amendment Act No. 9 of 1997.

[82] A liquid amount is fixed and certain and can – compared to an illiquid amount – be easily determined. *Maritime and General Insurance Co Ltd v Colenbrander* 1978 (2) SA 262 (D) at 264F.

of the erstwhile traditional courts within the mainstream of the judiciary in Namibia, and subjects their proceedings to formal evaluation and review by the superior courts (Amoo 2008c: 90). The Community Courts Act has, however, not yet been implemented, although it is in force. The office of the Ministry of Justice has pointed out that the delay in giving effect to the Act may be associated with a lack of funds for implementing the necessary infrastructure, as well as the lack of trained staff in the area of customary law (Hinz 2008: 78). It is yet to be seen when and how the Community Courts Act finally brings judicial scrutiny to customary law in Namibia. When this is done, it is expected that all Namibian courts will become even more mindful of the fact that the application of customary law is only valid to the extent to which it does not conflict with the Constitution or other statutory law.[83]

## The Ombudsman

One further mechanism to offer solutions for conflicts on the national level is the institution of the Ombudsman which was established in 1990 as a constitutional office by Chapter 10 of the Namibian Constitution and the Ombudsman Act No. 7 of 1990. The Ombudsman, an institution that can be classified neither as a traditional, nor as an informal justice system (Ruppel and Ruppel-Schlichting 2010), is designed to be an independent, impartial and neutral institution to keep a vigilant eye on the proper exercise of power and the protection of human rights. Broadly speaking, the Ombudsman in Namibia investigates complaints concerning violations of fundamental rights and freedoms and about the administration of all organs of Government. More precisely, the Office of the Ombudsman promotes and protects human rights, fair and effective public administration, and protects the environment and natural resources through investigations and the resolution of complaints.

## Namibia and the African Union (AU)

The historical foundations of the African Union originated in the Union of African States, an early confederation that was established by Kwame Nkrumah in the 1960s. The Organisation of African Unity (OAU) was established on May 25,

[83] As also observed by the Namibian Chief Justice Hon. Peter Shivute in his Preface to Hinz and Namwoonde (2010: ii).

1963. On 9 September 1999, the heads of state and governments of the OAU issued the Sirte Declaration (named after Sirte, in Libya), calling for the establishment of an African Union. The Declaration was followed by summits at Lomé in 2000, when the Constitutive Act of the African Union was adopted, and at Lusaka in 2001, when the Plan for the Implementation of the African Union was adopted. During the same period, the initiative for the establishment of the New Partnership for Africa's Development (NEPAD), was also established. The African Union was launched in Durban on July 9, 2002, by the then South African President, Thabo Mbeki[84], at the first session of the Assembly of the African Union. The Union's administrative centre is in Addis Ababa, Ethiopia and the working languages are Arabic, English, French, Portuguese, and Swahili. The African Union counts 53 member States with Morocco being the only African State that is not a member. Geographically, the African Union covers an area of 29,757,900 km² and for 2010, the United Nations Population Division estimated it to have a total population of 1,033,043,000.[85]

The Constitutive Act of the AU, to which Namibia is a party, provides that the African Union intends to function as Africa's premier institution and principal organisation for the promotion of accelerated socio-economic integration of the continent, which will lead to greater unity and solidarity between African countries and peoples. The AU envisages building a united and strong Africa and recognises the need to build a partnership between governments and all segments of civil society, in particular women, youth and the private sector, in order to strengthen solidarity and cohesion amongst the peoples of Africa. As a continental organisation, the AU focuses on the promotion of peace, security and stability on the continent as a prerequisite for the implementation of the development and integration agenda of the Union. To this end, a multitude of legal instruments have been adopted, inter alia, on the fields of human rights protection, economic issues, but also in the field of environmental protection (Ruppel 2011a: 55; for further details see: Viljoen 2007: 157; Ruppel 2009b; Visser and Ruppel-Schlichting 2008; Gawanas 2009; Keetharuth 2009). Some of these laws are binding upon Namibia.

The legal instruments under the umbrella of the African Union each have their

[84] Thabo Mbeki was the African Union's first President.

[85] Africa's entire population was estimated to be 1 033 043 000 in 2010, which includes the population of Morocco, estimated at 32 381 000. See http://esa.un.org/unpp/p2k0data.asp; last accessed 13 November 2010.

own provision on how disputes are to be settled. Alternative dispute resolution plays an important role in this regard since it is the favoured mechanism, as e.g. provided for in the African Convention for Nature Conservation. However, as a general rule, the African Court of Justice (ACJ) has the ultimate jurisdiction. The African Court of Justice, which is to be merged with the African Court on Human and Peoples' Rights, was established in 2002 (Hansungule 2009: 237). The Protocol establishing the ACJ was adopted in 2003 and will come into force after ratification by 15 AU member States. The Court is located in Arusha, Tanzania but has not yet become operational. The merged court will have jurisdiction over all disputes and applications referred to it which *inter alia* relate to the interpretation and application of the AU Constitutive Act or the interpretation, application or validity of Union Treaties, as well as human rights violations. To date, the African Commission on Human and Peoples' Rights, a quasi-judicial body established by the African Charter on Human and Peoples' Rights, is responsible for monitoring compliance with the African Charter on Human and Peoples' Rights.

By means of Article 144 of the Namibian Constitution international law explicitly becomes law of the land, needing no legislative act to become so. Article 144 mentions two sources of international law that apply in Namibia: general rules of public international law, and international agreements binding upon Namibia. The Constitutive Act of the AU and SADC Treaty (infra) constitute such international agreements which are binding in Namibia in terms of Article 144. The accession to such agreements is governed by Articles 32(3)(e), 40(i) and 63(2)(e) of the Namibian Constitution. The Executive is responsible for conducting Namibia's international affairs, including entry into international agreements. The President, assisted by the Cabinet, is empowered to negotiate and sign international agreements, and to delegate such power. It is required by the Constitution that the National Assembly agrees to the ratification of or accession to an international agreement. Namibia's national legal framework is therefore complemented by inter alia the laws and policies of the African Union and the Southern African Development Community.

## Namibia and the Southern African Development Community (SADC)

Namibia is a member of the Southern African Development Community (SADC). SADC was established in Windhoek in 1992 as the successor organisation to the Southern African Development Coordination Conference (SADCC), which was founded in 1980. SADC was established by the signing of its constitutive legal instrument, the SADC Treaty. SADC envisages

> [...] a common future, a future in a regional community that will ensure economic well-being, improvement of the standards of living and quality of life, freedom and social justice and peace and security for the peoples of Southern Africa. This shared vision is anchored on the common values and principles and the historical and cultural affinities that exist between the peoples of Southern Africa.[86]

SADC currently counts 15 states among its members, namely Angola, Botswana, the DRC, Lesotho, Madagascar, Malawi, Mauritius, Mozambique, Namibia, the Seychelles,[87] South Africa, Swaziland, Tanzania, Zambia, and Zimbabwe. SADCs objectives include amongst others the achievement of development and economic growth; the alleviation of poverty; the enhancement of the standard and quality of life; support of the socially disadvantaged through regional integration; the evolution of common political values, systems and institutions; the promotion and defence of peace and security; and achieving the sustainable utilisation of natural resources and effective protection of the environment.[88]

The Summit of SADC Heads of State and Government of SADC held in Sandton, South Africa, 16 - 17 August 2008 launched the SADC Free Trade Area (FTA) which is the first milestone in the regional economic integration agenda. The Summit recognised that free trade in the region would create a larger market, releasing potential for trade, economic development and employment creation. The SADC regional integration programme ambitiously provides that the establishment of the Free Trade Agreement[89] will be followed by a Customs Union by 2010, a

---

[86] SADC's Vision, available at http://www.sadc.int/index/browse/page/64; last accessed on 11 May 2012.

[87] The Seychelles was a member of SADC from 1997 to 2004 and rejoined SADC in 2008.

[88] These are some of the SADC objectives laid down in Article 5 of the SADC Treaty.

[89] While 12 member states (Botswana, Lesotho, Madagascar, Malawi, Mauritius, Mozambique, Namibia, South Africa, Swaziland, Tanzania, Zambia and Zimbabwe) have already ratified the SADC Protocol on Trade, Angola and the

Common Market by 2015, a monetary Union by 2016 and a single currency by 2018.[90] So far, the launch of the SADC customs union initially scheduled for 2010 has however been postponed due to the slow pace of implementation of the SADC. It is being observed that many countries are behind in harmonisation of regional standards and participation in terms of the SADC Trade Protocol.

The heterogeneity of SADC member states is not only reflected by surface area, population figures, size of the domestic markets, per capita incomes, the endowment with natural resources and the social and political situation, but also by the variety of legal systems applied in different member states. The legal systems of the world are commonly classified into various legal families or categories which describe the juristic philosophy and techniques shared by a number of nations with broadly similar legal systems by recognising the important relationship between law, history and culture. Over the centuries several main categories of legal systems have been described in the course of the world's legal history. Main categories include civil (or Romano-Germanic) and common law, socialist law (which has obviously forfeited relevance since the fall of the Iron Curtain) and several religious legal systems (Menski 2008).

African legal systems have always been an object of fascination to comparative lawyers as well as to legal ethnologists and sociologists, due to the broad variety of applied legal systems on the African continent. In the states of sub-Saharan Africa, the concept of legal pluralism is predominant. Despite the legal influences of the ex-colonial powers, a large number of Africans in SADC still live under indigenous customary law (Hinz 2002).

In view of the heterogeneity of legal systems within SADC but also with regard to a harmonious jurisdiction, it could be argued that in the long run the legal systems within the community should be unified (Latigo 2008). Of increasing significance for SADC member states will be the harmonisation of law working by the implementation and transformation of protocols and guidelines and aiming to reduce or eliminate the differences between the national legal systems by inducing them to adopt common principles of law. In terms of regional integration, the

---

Democratic Republic of the Congo (DRC) will join the SADC Free Trade Area (FTA) at a later stage.

[90] SADC Final Communiqué of the 28th Summit of SADC Heads of State and Government, held in Sandton, Republic of South Africa from August 16 to 17, 2008, www.sadc.int/index/browse/page/203; last accessed on 11 May 2012.

conformation of law is one central instrument to reduce normative barriers within the community. Unified law can indeed promote greater legal predictability and legal certainty, both essential for the investment climate and economic development in general. However, the extent and method of harmonisation is problematic as national positions and traditions have to be taken into consideration and, as a matter of fact, the differences that exist in respect of legal traditions in different countries of SADC must also be respected, even or rather especially in times of regionalisation and globalisation.

In terms of SADC Community Law, the SADC Treaty is the highest source of law within SADC's legal framework. In its Preamble, the Treaty determines, inter alia, to ensure, through common action, the progress and well-being of the people of southern Africa, and recognises the need to involve the people of the SADC region centrally in the process of development and integration, particularly through guaranteeing democratic rights, and observing human rights and the rule of law. The Preamble's contents are given effect within the subsequent provisions of the SADC Treaty. Chapter 3, for example, which deals with principles, objectives, the common agenda and general undertakings, provides that SADC and its member states are to act in accordance with the principles of human rights, democracy and the rule of law (Article 4(c)).

The SADC Protocols are the legal instruments by means of which the SADC Treaty is implemented. A Protocol comes into force after two thirds of SADC member states have ratified it. A Protocol legally binds its signatories after ratification. The implementation of the Protocol's provisions is the responsibility of the SADC member states (Article 14, SADC Protocol). The existing SADC Protocols include the following: Corruption; Culture, Information and Sports; Combating Illicit Drugs; Education and Training; Energy; Protocol on Extradition; Control of Firearms, Ammunition and Other Related Materials; Fisheries; Forestry; Gender and Development; Immunities and Privileges; Legal Affairs; Mutual Legal Assistance in Criminal Matters; Mining; the Facilitation of Movement of Persons; Politics, Defence and Security Co-operation; the Development of Tourism; Trade; Transport, Communications and Meteorology; and the Tribunal and the Rules of thereof (Ruppel and Ruppel-Schlichting 2012: 45).

The SADC Tribunal is the judicial body of SADC that has jurisdiction over disputes relating to the Protocol on the Tribunal and the Rules of Procedure thereof (Article 18, SADC Protocol). The establishment of the Tribunal was a major event in SADC's history as an organisation as well as in the development of its law and jurisprudence. The Tribunal was established in 1992 by Article 9 of the SADC Treaty. The legal provisions governing the SADC Tribunal are contained in the SADC Protocol on the Tribunal and the Rules of Procedure thereof (the Protocol), which entered into force in 2001. The Protocol comprises 39 Articles[91] and, among other things, establishes the Tribunal and clarifies its functions. According to Article 23 of the Protocol, the Rules of Procedure (the Rules) form an integral part of the Protocol. These Rules comprise 90 regulations governing, inter alia, the constitution and functions of the Tribunal; representation before the Tribunal; written, oral and special proceedings; and decisions.

The inauguration of the Tribunal and the swearing in of its members took place on 18 November 2005 in Windhoek, Namibia. The Council also designated Windhoek as the Seat of the Tribunal. The Tribunal began hearing cases in 2007. One of the first cases before the Tribunal was the case of Mike Campbell (PVT) Limited, challenging human rights violations by the expropriation of agricultural land in Zimbabwe by the government. (For more information see: Ruppel 2012, 2011c, 2009d, 2009f, 2009g, 2009h; Ruppel and Bangamwabo 2008.) In 2008 the SADC Tribunal in its final decision ruled in favour of Mike Campbell and 78 other white commercial farmers. The Tribunal held that the Republic of Zimbabwe was in breach of its obligations under the SADC Treaty. The ruling was considered to be a landmark decision, yet, Zimbabwe has so far refused to recognize the rulings of the SADC Tribunal. This unresolved issue of Zimbabwe's refusal to bow to rulings made by the Tribunal continues to haunt SADC. Only recently the SADC Tribunal was suspended until August 2012 while its role and functions and also the implications of a member state ignoring its rulings are reexamined. Interestingly, in March 2012 the African Commission on Human and Peoples' Rights decided to register and consider a complaint about the suspension of the SADC Tribunal. The claimants requested the African Commission to refer their communication to the African Court of Justice so it can order the SADC summit and its member states to lift, with immediate effect, the suspension of the tribunal, to reappoint the tribunal's judges and to give the tribunal the funding it needs to get on with its work.

[91] It has to be noted, however, that Articles 35 and 36 (ratification and accession, respectively) of the Protocol have been repealed by the Agreement Amending the Protocol on the Tribunal.

## The Tripartite Initiative

The fact that the process of regional integration in Africa is accelerating becomes even more evident when observing the following recent developments. In October 2008, the Heads of States of Governments of the member states of the SADC, the Eastern African Community (EAC) and the Common Market for Eastern and Southern Africa (COMESA) negotiated a communiqué of the Tripartite Summit of 22 October 2008 under which the Heads of State and Government representing the three regional economic communities agreed that the communities should merge into a single Customs Union beginning with a Free Trade Area in order to promote the rapid social and economic development of the region.[92] This is particularly remarkable given that the Free Trade Area covers all 26 countries of COMESA, EAC, and SADC. In December 2010, a revised Draft Agreement and Annexes, inter alia on Rules of Origin, Trade Remedies, and Dispute Settlement have been finalised and with the 2011 Second Tripartite Communiqué the respective Heads of State adopted the following developmental approach to the Tripartite Integration process that will be anchored on three pillars: Market Integration based on the Tripartite Free Trade Area (FTA); Infrastructure Development to enhance connectivity and reduce costs of doing business as well as Industrial Development to address the productive capacity constraints.[93]

According to the Communiqué, the Tripartite initiative incorporates almost half of the African Union with 600 million people and a Gross Domestic Product (GDP) of approximately US$1.0 trillion. A Tripartite Free Trade Area is envisaged by 2016. The negotiations are expected to take place in two phases, whereas in the first phase trade in goods, free movement of business people will be addressed; and in the second phase trade in services, intellectual property rights, competition

[92] Cf. First Communiqué of the COMESA-EAC-SADC Tripartite Summit of Heads of State and Government *COMESA EAC SADC TRIPARTITE*. 2008; available at http://www.comesa-eac-sadc-tripartite.org/sites/default/files/documents/Final%20Communique%20-%20The%20Tripartite%20Summit%202008.pdf; last accessed 19 October 2011.

[93] Cf. Second Communiqué of the COMESA-EAC-SADC Tripartite Summit of Heads of State and Government *COMESA EAC SADC TRIPARTITE*. 2011; available at http://www.comesa-eac-sadc-tripartite.org/sites/default/files/documents/Communique%20of%20the%202nd%20Tripartite%20Summit%20-%20English%20-%2012.06.2011.pdf/; last accessed 19 October 2011.

policy, trade development and competitiveness will be discussed. The outcomes of both phases have greatest significance for the environment in the single market and it will be seen if the Tripartite initiative will also bring prosperity to the people that have so far been left behind in Sub-Saharan Africa. Transforming society will require comprehensive legal, political, social, and economic reforms and development initiatives, such as investing more in education, public services, and infrastructure, enhancing participation in trade and protecting the environment for present and future generations. Moreover, it will be seen if the Tripartite initiative will push the regional integration agenda also to empower the poor and reduce pressures such as under-development, unemployment, environmental neglect, health emergencies, and strife (Ruppel and Ruppel-Schlichting 2012: 59).

## Namibia and the Southern African Customs Union (SACU) and Related Agreements

Having celebrated its 100th anniversary in 2010, SACU is the world's oldest customs union (Ruppel 2010c). SACU has five members, namely South Africa, Botswana, Lesotho, Namibia, and Swaziland. One objective of SACU is to facilitate the cross-border movement of goods between the territories of the Member States. The legal framework of the SACU is the SACU Treaty. The latter in its part eight on common policies provides for the development of common or harmonised policies and increased cooperation, in the areas of industrial development, agriculture and competition policy. However, at this stage, no common SACU policy is in place.

SACU has entered into trade agreements with third parties. In 2006 for example, SACU signed an FTA with European Free Trade Area (EFTA) states (Iceland, Liechtenstein, Norway and Switzerland), which came into force in 2008. As a first step towards the creation of a Free Trade Area between the *Mercado Común del Sur* (MERCOSUR) and SACU, SACU has signed a Preferential Trade Agreement (PTA) with MERCOSUR countries[94] in 2009. Trade liberalisation is the focus of this agreement and read together with its annexes, specific preferences are granted from MERCOSUR to SACU and vice versa. In 2008, SACU and the United States signed a Trade, Investment and Development Cooperation Agreement (TIDCA), in order "to promote an attractive investment climate and to expand and diversify

[94] Common Market of South America, consisting of Argentina, Brazil, Paraguay and Uruguay.

trade between SACU and the United States" (Article 1 of TIDCA). During the recent past, voices warning that SACU is in danger of being discontinued have become louder (Ruppel 2010c). Two crucial issues have moved to the centre of the debate. The first is the European Partnership Agreement (EPA) negotiation process, and the second the financial shortfall due to plunging revenues due to reduced imports amidst the global economic crisis which affected African economies by way of a drop in export values (McCarthy 2010). Currently, SACU is discussing possibilities on how to adapt to political and economic developments and addressing challenges such as a common negotiating mechanism, overlapping memberships, the institutional and policy framework, investment, competition and procurement. With regard to dispute resolution, the SACU Agreement establishes an ad hoc Tribunal to resolve any differences that might occur between or amongst member states (Articles 7(f) and 13). The Tribunal has not yet been established.

## Challenges

From the above it becomes clear that a myriad of laws are relevant for Namibia, on the local, national and regional levels. These sources of law evidently come from quite different and thus often inevitably conflicting sources (Menski 2010: 443, 2011: 149). On the national level, conflicts may arise for example between customary law and human rights law as provided for in the Constitution. One example for this out of many could be clause 24 on traditional marriages of the Combined Laws of the Kwangali, Mbunza, Shambyu and Gciriku which provides that

> [I]n the Kavango tradition, polygyny (having more than one wife at the same time) shall be permitted. A man shall be allowed to marry more than one wife, but a woman shall not be permitted to have more than one husband. (Hinz and Namwoonde 2010: 380)

Article 10 of the Namibian Constitution on equality and freedom from discrimination reads:

> (1) All persons shall be equal before the law
> (2) No persons may be discriminated against on the grounds of sex, race, colour, ethnic origin, religion, creed or social or economic status.

Article 66 (1) of the Namibian Constitution, the Supreme Law of Namibia, provides that

> [B]oth the customary law and the common law of Namibia in force on the date of Independence shall remain valid to the extent to which such customary or common law does not conflict with this Constitution or any other statutory law.

Article 8 on marriage and family rights of the SADC Protocol on Gender and Development states that

> States Parties shall enact and adopt appropriate legislative, administrative and other measures to ensure that women and men enjoy equal rights in marriage and are regarded as equal partners in marriage.

And, last but not least, Article 6 on marriage of the AU Protocol to the African Charter on Human and Peoples' Rights on the Rights of Women in Africa states that:

> Parties shall ensure that women and men enjoy equal rights and are regarded as equal partners in marriage. They shall enact appropriate national legislative measures to guarantee that [...]
>
> c) monogamy is encouraged as the preferred form of marriage and that the rights of women in marriage and family, including in polygamous marital relationships are promoted and protected.

The authors refrain from going into the details of this particular conflict at this stage. However, the example illustrates – admittedly stereotyping - the challenges that the concept of legal pluralism is facing in Namibia. This is not only true for the sources of applicable law, but also for the issue of jurisdiction of Namibian courts. Some of the cases that are being dealt with under customary law and before traditional courts may just as well fall into the jurisdiction of Magistrates Courts or the High Court.

On the regional level, the fact that many African states are members of various regional economic communities can be regarded as a hurdle in respect of the regional integration process (Viljoen 2007: 525). Except Mozambique, all SADC countries are at the same time members of at least one other trade agreement in the region. Eight SADC members are also members of the Common Market of Eastern and Southern Africa (COMESA), four countries, including Namibia, are members of SADC and the Southern African Customs Union (SACU), Swaziland is a member of SADC, SACU and COMESA, and Tanzania is a member of SADC and the East African Community (EAC). Various bilateral free-trade agreements as well as the membership of all SADC countries in the African Union (AU) may be regarded as obstacles to deeper integration in many respects. Such overlapping memberships are not only problematic in terms of duplication of work and costs, but also because a sub-regional customs union is envisaged by both COMESA and SADC, and double membership might result in conflicting tariffs. Moreover, overlapping memberships increase the number of applicable laws, inevitably increasing the risk of conflicting laws as well.

The question of concurrent jurisdiction of different judicial organs is another contentious issue with regard to multiple memberships which needs to be addressed. (For a more detailed discussion see Ruppel 2009d.) Namibia on the regional level 'only' falls under the jurisdiction of the judicial organs of SADC, SACU (if established) and the judicial bodies on the level of the African Union. However, the issue of overlapping or even conflicting jurisdiction of regional courts on the African continent may become a prominent one, especially for those countries that are members of more regional economic communities in Africa. For the time being, the consequence of overlapping jurisdiction is that a claimant may in fact choose to which judicial body a case is to be submitted,[95] as a competent court may not decline jurisdiction - the argument being that another court may as well be competent. In this context factors such as the cost of litigation, the organisational context in which the dispute would be decided, the entity which would decide the dispute, the advantages of the applicable law, who can initiate a complaint against whom, procedural advantages, the possibility of appeal, the remedies that can be obtained, the parties who are bound by an eventual ruling, and the consequences of non-compliance will be decisive (Pauwelyn 2004: 304).

Conflicts may of course also arise between national and international law. In this regard, it can be stated that the rule of exhaustion of national remedies, a rule that is normally being provided for by the laws of procedure of international courts, ensures that cases have to be dealt with on the national level first, before being heard by international courts; the latter may then decide on the question as to whether the national law in question is in line with community law.

[95] Referred to as 'forum-shopping': see Viljoen (2007: 502).

## Concluding Remarks

Namibia is a fascinating country, particularly in terms of legal and judicial pluralism. At the same time, it becomes clear, that such pluralism relevant for Namibia, on the local, national and regional level can be challenging. Namibian law reflects the country's rich history and the process of internationalisation. The law in place is the product of different sources, a mixture between imported and African law. Yet, sometimes the customary laws of the people do not fully reconcile human rights with their traditions and heritage. The challenge is, however, not to vitiate, but to find common ground between international law, human rights, customary law and practice in Namibia.

For that purpose the concept of legal and judicial pluralism needs further exploration and at the same time comparative law can help to reconcile the different types of law or legal traditions. The African legal architecture is gradually changing and it is therefore no longer self sufficient to only focus on legal pluralism on the local and national levels. Except Mozambique, all SADC countries are for instance at the same time members of the African Union and at least one other regional economic community in the region. The aforementioned implies that the legal mix of civil law, common law, roman-dutch law, customary law traditions must inevitably become more responsive to the (at times overlapping and concurrent) community laws (and jurisdictions) of the respective African and sub-regional economic communities. This holds particularly true in Namibia where the Constitutive Act of the AU and SADC Treaty constitute international agreements which are binding upon Namibia in terms of Article 144.

In conclusion, a view towards a more transnational pluralism is much needed in Namibia and beyond. Such view offers not only an appropriate account of contemporary African legal reality but also reflects legal pluralistic insights beyond territorially-based application of the law in complex systems of multi-level governance.

## References

AMOO, Sam K.
2008a *An Introduction to Namibian Law*. Windhoek: Macmillan.
2008b 'The Constitutional Jurisprudential Development in Namibia since 1985.' Pp. 39-57 in Nico Horn and Anton Bösl (eds.), *Human Rights and the*

*Rule of Law in Namibia.* Windhoek: Macmillan Education.
2008c 'The Structure of the Namibian Judicial System and its Relevance for an Independent Judiciary.' Pp. 69-98 in Horn and Bösl 2008.
AMOO, Sam .K. and Isabella SKEFFERS
2008 'The rule of law in Namibia.' Pp 17-38 in Horn and Bösl 2008.
BANGAMWABO, Francois X.
2008 'The Implementation of International and Regional Human Rights Instruments in the Namibian Legal Framework.' Pp. 165-186 in Horn and Bösl 2008.
BUKURURA, Sufian H.
2002 *Administration of justice in Namibia. Essays on constitutionalism and administration of justice in Namibia 1990–2002.* Windhoek: Out of Africa Publishers.
DIESCHO, Joseph
1994 *The Namibian Constitution in Perspective.* Windhoek: Gamsberg Macmillan.
DU PLESSIS, Lourens
1990 *An Introduction to Law.* 3rd Edition. Kenwyn: Juta.
ERASMUS, Marthinus G.
1991 'The Namibian Constitution and the application of international law in Namibia.' P. 94 in Dawid van Wyk, Marinus Wiechers and Romaine Hill (eds.), *Namibia: Constitutional and International Law Issues.* Pretoria: VerLoren van Themaat Centre for Public Law Studies, University of South Africa.
2002 'The impact of the Namibian Constitution on the nature of the state, its policies and society: the record after ten years.' Pp. 5-26 in Manfred O. Hinz, Sam K. Amoo and Dawid van Wyk (eds.), *The Constitution at Work: Ten Years of Namibian Nationhood.* Windhoek and Pretoria: University of Namibia Press and VerLoren van Themaat Centre for Public Law Studies, University of South Africa.
GAWANAS, Bience
2009 'The African Union: Concepts and Implementation Mechanism Relating to Human Rights.' Pp. 135-162 in Anton Bösl and Joseph Diescho (eds.), *Human Rights in Africa.* Windhoek: Macmillan.
GRIFFITHS, John
1986 'What is legal pluralism?' *Journal of Legal Pluralism* 24:1-55.
HANSUNGULE, Michelo
2009 'African Courts on Human Rights and the African Commission.' Pp. 233-272 in Anton Bösl and Joseph Diescho (eds.), *Human Rights in Africa.* Windhoek: Macmillan.

HAVENGA, Peter, Christoph GARBERS, Michele HAVENGA, W. G. SCHULZE, Kathleen VAN DER LINDE, and Trix VAN DER MERWE

2002 *General Principles of Commercial Law.* 4th Edition. Lansdowne: Juta Law.

HINZ, Manfred O.

2002 'Local knowledge and its legal protection,' unpublished Paper presented at the international trade law workshop of the International Development Law Institute, University of Stellenbosch, 24 June–12 July 2002. Windhoek, University of Namibia - Trade Law Centre for Southern Africa.

2007 'Recognition of legal pluralism in international human rights law: The application of human rights law in the context of a right to preserve and develop legal systems of a community's choice', unpublished paper presented at the expert meeting on human rights and traditional and informal justice systems in Africa: The right to fair trial and equality before the law, organised by the UN OHCHR and UNAM, Faculty of Law, Windhoek, 20 - 22 June 2007.

2008 'Traditional governance and African customary law: Comparative observations from a Namibian perspective. Pp. 59-87 in Horn and Bösl 2008.

2010a 'Justice for Justice and Justice for Peace: Legal Anthropological Observations on Traditional and Informal Justice Systems.' Pp. 3-23 in Hinz and Mapaure 2010.

2010b 'Traditional Courts in Namibia – Part of the Judiciary? Jurisprudential Challenges of Traditional Justice.' Pp. 93-114 in Hinz and Mapaure 2010.

HINZ, Manfred O. and Clever MAPAURE (eds.)

2010 *In Search of Justice and Peace. Traditional and Informal Justice Systems in Africa.* Windhoek: Namibia Scientific Society.

HINZ, Manfred O. and Emilia N. NAMWOONDE

2010 *Customary Law Ascertained. Volume I. The Customary Law of the Owambo, Kavango and Caprivi Communities in Northern Namibia.* Windhoek: Namibia Scientific Society.

HINZ, Manfred O. and Oliver C. RUPPEL

2008 'Legal protection of biodiversity in Namibia.' Pp. 3-58 in Manfred O. Hinz and Oliver C. Ruppel (eds.), *Biodiversity and the Ancestors: Challenges to Customary and Environmental Law. Case studies from Namibia.* Windhoek: Namibia Scientific Society.

2010 'Biodiversity conservation under Namibian environmental law.' Pp. 190-194 in Ute Schmiedel and Norbert Jürgens (eds.), *Biodiversity in southern Africa. Volume 2: Patterns and processes at regional scale.* Göttingen &

Windhoek: Klaus Hess Publishers.

HINZ, Manfred O. and SANTOS, Joas

2002 *Customary Law in Namibia: Development and Perspective*. 7th Edition. Windhoek: Centre for Applied Social Sciences.

HORN, Nico and Anton BÖSL (eds.)

2008 *Human Rights and the Rule of Law in Namibia*. Windhoek: Macmillan Education.

KATJAVIVI, Peter H.

1988 *A history of resistance in Namibia*. London: J Currey.

KEETHARUTH, Sheila B.

2009 'Major African Legal Instrument and Human Rights.' Pp. 163-232 in Anton Bösl and Joseph Diescho (eds.), *Human Rights in Africa*. Windhoek: MacMillan Education.

LATIGO, Alfred R.

2008 'Mainstreaming Regional Integration at national level.' Lusaka: UNECA Working Paper.

MCCARTHY, Colin

2010 'The global financial and economic crisis and its impacts on sub-Saharan economies.' *Trade Brief* 1. Stellenbosch: Trade Law Centre for Southern Africa.

MENSKI, Werner

2008 *Comparative Law in a Global Context: The Legal Systems of Asia and Africa*. Cambridge: Cambridge University Press.

2010 'Monsters, Legal Pluralism and Human Rights in Africa.' Pp. 443-456 in Hinz and Mapaure 2010.

2011 'Flying Kites in Africa: Legal Pluralism in a Plural World.' Pp. 141-158 in Ruppel and Winter 2011.

PAUWELYN, Joost

2004 'Going Global, Regional or Both? Dispute Settlement in the Southern African Development Community (SADC) and Overlaps with the WTO and other Jurisdictions.' *Minnesota Journal of Global Trade* 13(2): 231-304.

RUPPEL, Oliver C.

2008 *Women and Custom in Namibia. Cultural Practice versus Gender Equality?* Windhoek: Macmillan Education.

2009a *Children's Rights in Namibia*. Windhoek: Macmillan Education.

2009b 'The Protection of Children's Rights under International Law from a Namibian Perspective.' Pp. 53-100 in Oliver C. Ruppel (ed.), *Children's Rights in Namibia*. Windhoek: Macmillan Education.

2009c 'Koloniale Altlasten in Namibia und die Grenzen des Völkerrechts.'

*Allgemeine Zeitung* 12 August 2009, available at www.az.com.na/politik/koloniale-altlasten-in-namibia-und-die-grenzen-des-vlkerrechts.90-808.php; last accessed on 11 May 2012

2009d 'Regional Economic Communities and Human Rights in East and Southern Africa.' Pp. 275-319 in Anton Bösl and Joseph Diescho (eds.), *Human Rights in Africa*. Windhoek: Macmillan Education.

2009e 'The Ombudsman and Alternative Dispute Resolution. Facets of Legal Pluralism in Namibia,' unpublished conference paper presented at the conference on Legal Pluralist Perspectives on Development and Cultural Diversity, organised by the Commission on Legal Pluralism, Zurich, Switzerland, 31 August - 03 September 2009.

2009f 'The SADC Tribunal, Regional Integration and Human Rights: Major Challenges, Legal Dimensions and Some Comparative Aspects from the European Legal Order.' *Recht in Afrika* 2: 213–238.

2009g 'Das SADC Tribunal: Eine Juristische Zwischenbilanz.' *Allgemeine Zeitung* 5 February 2009 www.az.com.na/afrika/das-sadc-tribunal-eine-juristische-zwischenbilanz.80234.php; last accessed on 11 May 2012.

2009h 'The Southern African Development Community (SADC) and its Tribunal: Reflexions on Regional Economic Communities' Potential Impact on Human Rights Protection.' *Verfassung und Recht in Übersee* 42(2): 173–186.

2010a 'Environmental Rights and Justice in Namibia.' Pp. 323-360 in Anton Bösl, Nico Horn and Andre du Pisani (eds.), *Constitutional Democracy in Namibia. A critical analysis after two decades*. Windhoek: Macmillan Publishers.

2010b 'The Namibian Ascertainment of Customary Law Project and the Human Rights and Documentation Centre.' Pp. iii-vi in Hinz and Namwoonde.

2010c 'SACU 100: Reflections on the World's Oldest Customs Union.' *Namibia Law Journal* 2(2): 121-134.

2010d 'Women's Rights and Customary Law.' *Journal of African and International Law (JAIL)* 3(2): 259-300.

2011a 'International Environmental Law From A Namibian Perspective.' Pp. 33-78 in Oliver C. Ruppel and Katharina Ruppel-Schlichting (eds.), *Environmental Law and Policy in Namibia*. Windhoek & Essen: Orumbonde Press & Verlag Dr. A. Eckl.

2011b 'Kolonialunrecht in Südwest: Die völkerrechtliche und die politische Seite.' *Allgemeine Zeitung* 16 June 2011, available at http://www.az.com.na/politik/zwei-seiten-vlkerrecht-und-politik.128705.php; last accessed on 11 May 2012.

2011c 'Mike Campbell verstorben: Und das SADC Tribunal?' *Allgemeine*

*Zeitung* 20 April 2011, available at www.az.com.na/afrika/mike-campbell-verstorben-und-das-sadc-tribunal.125669.php; last accessed on 11 May 2012.

2012 'SADC land issues before the SADC Tribunal - A case for Human Rights?' Pp. 89-120 in Ben Chigara (ed.), *Southern African Development Community Land Issues. A New, Sustainable Land Relations Policy*. London: Routledge.

RUPPEL, Oliver C. and Francois X. BANGAMWABO

2008 'The Mandate of the SADC Tribunal and its Role for Regional Integration.' Pp. 179-221 in Anton Bösl, Willie Breydenbach, Trudi Hartzenberg and others (eds.), *Yearbook for Regional Integration*. Vol. 8. Stellenbosch, tralac, available at www.tralac.org/cause_data/images/1694/MRI2008WithCover20090415.pdf ; last accessed on 11 May 2012.

RUPPEL, Oliver C. and Katharina RUPPEL-SCHLICHTING

2010 'Between Formal and Informal Justice? The Mandate of the Ombudsman in Namibia.' Pp. 363-382 in Hinz and Mapaure 2010.

2011 'Namibia and its legal setup.' Pp. 1-13 in Oliver C. Ruppel and Katharina Ruppel-Schlichting (eds.), *Environmental Law and Policy in Namibia*. Windhoek & Essen: Orumbonde Press & Verlag Dr. A. Eckl.

2012 'Climate change and human security: relevant for regional integration in SADC?' Pp. 32-71 in Trudi Hartzenberg, Gerhard Erasmus and Andre du Pisani (eds.), *Yearbook for Regional Integration*. Vol. 11. Stellenbosch, tralac, available at http://www.tralac.org/files/2011/08/MRI-Yearbook-2011-Finalweb-20120419.pdf; last accessed 20 May 2012.

RUPPEL, Oliver C. and Gerd WINTER

2011 *Justice from within: Legal Pluralism in Africa and beyond. Liber amicorum Manfred O. Hinz in celebration of his 75th birthday*. Hamburg: Dr. Kovac.

SCHMIDT-JORTZIG, Edzard

1991 'The Constitution of Namibia. An impressive example of a state emerging under close supervision and world scrutiny.' *German Yearbook of International Law (Jahrbuch für Internationales Recht)* 34: 71.

SIPPEL, Harald

2011 'Each to His Own: Legal Pluralism in the German Colonies (1884-1914).' Pp. 193-1205 in. Ruppel and Winter 2011.

VILJOEN, Frans

2007 *International Human Rights Law in Africa*. Oxford: Oxford University Press.

VISSER, Wilmary and Katharina RUPPEL-SCHILICHTING
2008 'Women and Custom in Namibia - The Legal Setting.' Pp. 149-164 in Oliver C.. Ruppel (ed.), *Women and Custom in Namibia - Cultural Practice versus Gender Equality?* Windhoek: Macmillan Education.

WATZ, Frank L.
2004 *Die Grundrechte in der Verfassung der Republik Namibia vom 21. März 1990.* Göttingen & Windhoek: Klaus Hess Publishers.

# NAVIGATING BETWEEN TRADITIONAL LAND TENURE AND INTRODUCED LAND LAWS IN PACIFIC ISLAND STATES

Sue Farran

## Introduction

As in Africa and other parts of the world, islands in the South Pacific region experienced British colonial administration accompanied by the introduction of non-customary land laws and policies. In some cases colonial administrators took land which they deemed to be uncultivated or lying 'waste and idle' and claimed it for the Crown or later, the state. In other cases they reshaped customary institutions and structures in efforts to acknowledge local indigenous polities but at the same time understand them on their own terms. On independence and in the years just prior to and after independence, in many countries land which had been alienated to foreigners was restored to indigenous people, but the slate could not be wiped entirely clean of the colonial legacy. Indeed few countries rejected the colonial systems of laws and courts, so that even today, introduced laws and dispute resolution forums remain relevant and influential, despite the fact that in most Pacific island states over 80% of land is held under various forms of customary tenure. Persisting legal pluralism in respect of land, therefore offers opportunities to 'pick and mix' legal responses or develop new hybrid legal forms, and presents potential obstacles to those seeking to use land in new ways or harness its resources for development.

Alongside shifts from rural residency to urbanisation, from subsistence agriculture to cash-cropping and waged labour, there are other pressures both internal and external, to 'do' things with land, to make it more attractive for inward investment

© Copyright 2011 – Sue Farran.

and to exploit its resources commercially to generate income. There are demands for registration and demarcation of customary land interests, for the simplification of complex kinship rules which determine land rights, for greater individualization of land rather than communal access, and for the establishment of certainty through final court decisions rather than negotiated settlements which may be revisited and renegotiated. For some, both from within and without Pacific island countries, customary land tenure is seen as an obstacle to economic development, for others it is seen as essential for maintaining social stability and security and for ensuring the equitable distribution of resources in states where governance is weak and public provision virtually non-existent.

In considering how legal pluralism might be utilised to assist developing countries face the challenges of development in which land and its resources play a key role this paper moves away from the stagnant waters of theoretical debate to focus more on the ways in which "new, hybrid, or syncretic legal forms may emerge and become institutionalized" (von Benda-Beckmann and von Benda-Beckmann 2006: 19). Consideration of customary land tenure in those countries where it continues to be a significant feature of the legal landscape provides this opportunity.

Drawing on legal and anthropological research, this paper looks at contemporary examples of how Pacific islanders are negotiating the space between the two systems of customary land tenure and introduced land law, noting how the plural legal system provides an enabling environment.

The focus of this paper is on the Pacific island countries of Melanesia: Papua New Guinea, Solomon Islands and Vanuatu,[1] where, customary land tenure is the major form of landholding and traditional forms of social organisation and culture remain strongly influential. They are also countries experiencing rapid but unevenly distributed change and development which, while it can bring benefits to some, also threatens the livelihoods and social stability of others. Consequently adaptation strategies are required and where governments are weak, volatile, or under-resourced, people have to make these adaptations themselves.

[1] Fiji is also sometimes regarded as a Melanesian country but its customary culture and social organisation was strongly influenced by Polynesia due to its historical ties, especially with Tonga. New Caledonia although both Melanesian and in the Pacific region under consideration is not included here because it is not independent but remains an overseas territory of France.

Sue Farran

## The Context of Land and its Laws

The three island countries under consideration all came under the influence of British colonial rule in the course of the nineteenth century and with it, English common law.[2] They also shared the early-contact experience of land alienation to settlers - missionaries, traders and planters, which occurred initially with little restriction, and often with little formality. However, unlike the experience in some colonies, the existence of native land rights was recognised early on by the colonial administrators and by the last decades of the nineteenth century 'protective' measures had been put in place to prevent the wholesale alienation of land by indigenous people, and indeed to severely curtail indigenous land transactions. Although freehold titles granted to or acquired by non-indigenous settlers were generally upheld by the colonial administration and the Crown retained the right to acquire land where it was either deemed to be vacant and waste or where it was deemed to be necessary, by the time these countries became independent only very small percentages of land were held either by the state as public land, or under freehold title as private land.

Most land - around 95% in all three countries,[3] was held under customary land tenure and it may be this fact that led the respective governments of the newly independent states to leave unaltered the legal framework that underpinned many of the earlier colonial policies.[4] So for example, it is still the case that in the three

[2] Solomon Islands was not a colony but a protectorate, and Papua New Guinea (once united into one country of Papua) was a League of Nations Mandated Trust Territory (formerly a colony of Britain and Germany) and placed under Australian administration after 1918.

[3] In Papua New Guinea this is probably around 97%, in Solomon Islands this is about 90% and in Vanuatu around 98%. There are no accurate figures due to the lack of registration of land held under customary tenure.

[4] Some changes have of course been made. Freehold was abolished in Vanuatu at independence in 1980. In Solomon Islands, prior to independence in 1978, all freehold was converted into fixed term estates in the case of non-Solomon islanders and to perpetual estates for Solomon Islanders under the 1977 Land and Titles (Amendment) Ordinance. In Papua New Guinea, the Land (Tenure Conversion) Act 1963 authorised custom owners to apply to convert customary land into freehold. However ownership of freehold land is restricted by the Constitution and the Land (Ownership of Freeholds) Act 1976 to citizens, and it unclear how much land was converted in this way but it appears to be very little.

countries under consideration very little land is public land, prohibitions and controls on the alienation of privately held land to non-indigenous persons have been retained, and there are very limited forms of formal non-customary tenure - primarily, various forms of leasehold. It might therefore be argued that little has been done politically to eradicate the impact of colonial land legislation despite the fact that independence provided the opportunity to strengthen traditional land tenure forms, either implicitly or expressly. This inaction may also be due to the fact that colonial land systems only ever impacted partially on indigenous people in these countries. Colonial authorities had limited geographical and legal reach; parts of the population would not have engaged with any or very limited colonial administration and there were subjects, such as many aspects of family law that in turn impacted on customary land tenure, which fell outside colonial interest. Moreover, the imposition of separate legal regimes for administering justice to the native population meant that a diluted common law system was introduced, and even within this system, members of indigenous populations either did not participate in the development of the legal system or had very limited input until the period immediately prior to independence. Also significant was the enduring persistence of customary land systems throughout the colonial period, so that although not entirely unscathed at independence, reforming land tenure did not present a pressing issue for the early governments of these new states.[5] Consequently, contemporary land law is a mix of customary and non-customary law, both of which are formally recognised as sources of law, and neither of which can be said to emanate fully from the state, because in the case of customary law this is not homogenous in any of these countries, so there is no 'national' customary law, and in the case of non-customary land law, much of this was introduced prior to statehood or modelled on laws drawn from the Common Law of other former colonies.

This post-independence dualism of land governance, between customary laws and introduced land laws, might well have continued indefinitely were it not for the global environment in which even the smallest of Pacific islands exist; the tug of money, and the 'winds of change' which, while they may have shifted direction since they blew through the colonies in the 1960s, bring new aspirations, values and ambitions, not just for islanders but for those engaging with them. New forms

[5] Vanuatu might be regarded as exceptional in so far as all land was restored to customary owners at independence, although this was a process that had been commenced prior to 1980, and it did not mean the eradication of all non-customary forms of land tenure because existing freeholds were convertible to leaseholds.

of colonialism are reaching the Pacific and law and legal frameworks accompany them – just as they did in the nineteenth century.[6] Consequently the limited formal changes that have been introduced in land law post-independence have been largely directed at the commercial exploitation of land and/or its resources.[7] Failure of national governments either to clarify the scope and extent of customary law or to draw up national land policies has meant that for many Pacific islanders the only option has been to use the 'legal' tools that are to hand. So how are Pacific islanders in the twenty-first century navigating between their traditional land tenure systems and non-traditional introduced ones?

## Traversing Plural Systems

The traditional characteristics of land rights in Melanesia are that they are unregistered,[8] acquired through lineage and kinship links and are inalienable because present holders or beneficiaries of such rights are regarded as custodians of the land for future generations. In subsistence economies and among rural communities land represents a communal resource and association with the land reflects ties of ancestry and belonging as well as being important to identity.[9] Land and land rights have always been the focus of contestation, and the customary rules

---

[6] Merry and Brenneis have for example argued in their comparison of colonial Fiji and Hawaii that

> Law was a central mechanism in ... colonial endeavours ... critical to shaping colonial relations' and that its 'effect comes through its capacity to regulate (and)... in the resources it affords -or denies- communities for their own use in managing conflict and shaping local sociality ... legal arrangements affect the shape of social life and social inequalities (Merry and Brenneis 2003: 6-7).

[7] See for example, the Strata Titles Act 2000 in Vanuatu.

[8] This remains the case despite various attempts by colonial administrators to encourage the registration of land held under customary tenure.

[9] It has been said that "Land ... is what a mother is to a baby. It is with land that he defines his identity and it is with land that he maintains his spiritual strength." (Sethy Regenvanu, speaking of land in Vanuatu at the time of independence, quoted by van Trease 1987: xi).

that govern customary land tenure are open to conflicting interpretations and fluidity. While the persisting relevance and significance of this form of land tenure cannot be denied, the underpinning values associated with land are being challenged and are changing in many parts of the Pacific because the value of land in terms of its commercial potential is being realised. Also, in some countries and on some islands within countries there is considerable pressure on land, and securing land rights or rights to the benefits to be derived from land - for example, from logging or mining royalties, lease rental payments, government compensation pay-outs or other financial benefits -- is leading to new conflicts between custom claimants and the adoption of new strategies to manage land and disputes. There are therefore, both internal forces for change and external ones.

Externally, agendas for development funded by donor aid, have included expressions of concern that "communal land ownership has held back indigenous entrepreneurship in the Pacific as it has everywhere in the world" (Hughes 2003) and that communal landownership is "the principal cause of poverty" in countries such as Papua New Guinea (Hughes 2004). Among development concerns are that communal ownership inhibits mortgage borrowing which in turn prevents market development and leads to the under-utilisation of resources; that customary tenure is static and cannot adapt; that dealings with customary right holders are fraught with difficulties and uncertainties and are therefore unattractive to investors. Approaching land from a very different normative perspective these criticisms may be directed at the persistence of communal ownership and the plurality of uses and interests that may arise in respect of land; the lack of formal records; the procedures for determining who may represent the communal interest in land dealings or the forums for resolving disputes that arise. Ironically, some of these perceived obstacles are attributable to the formal legal system itself and legacy of various laws introduced under colonialism.[10] Some are attributable to fundamental flaws in understanding or accommodating different perceptions about the nature and value of land,[11] or in understanding the social framework in which land

[10] Among the development inhibitors identified for PNG for example Lakau included the plethora of different land laws (40+), many of which were outdated; the fact that customary land was not accommodated within these laws; a highly centralised land administration system and a failure to implement national land policy at the various different levels (Lakau 1991: 21).

[11] It has been said for example:

> Land 'in custom', is not simply the site of produce, it is the mainstay of a cultural vision of the world. Land is the heart of

interests are grounded.[12] Frustration with land development is not however limited to external agencies. Internally governments, individuals or particular groups may seek to develop their land or utilise it in non-traditional ways.

There are, consequently, several ways in which plural land systems are being 'bridged' or routes between the two are being facilitated or essayed. These include specific legislation which seeks either, to recognise and build on traditional features of customary land tenure or incorporate these in some way; formal dispute resolution mechanisms which seek to incorporate elements of traditional dispute resolution, or ways in which people themselves are navigating between systems in order to derive new benefits or accommodate changing objectives.

*Legislating for Hybridity*

Examples of the first response can be found in specific legislation passed by national parliaments. The response of national governments (often at the behest of or responding to the pressures mentioned above) to the perceived inadequacies of the existing legal framework has led to the introduction of new legal structures that attempt to straddle the plurality of values and structures that govern land. For example, in Papua New Guinea the institution of the Incorporated Land Group was introduced to provide a means whereby a customary land group could register as a corporation.[13] The aim was twofold: to facilitate the restoration of plantation land to customary owners under the plantation redistribution scheme and to encourage customary landowning groups to use their land in ways which would allow them to engage with a developing and changing economy. Increasingly membership of

> the operation of customary systems; it represents life, both materially and spiritually ... that is why Melanesian men and villages are so extremely sensitive about their land and why they are so deeply rooted in the soil (Bonnemaison 1991: 17).

[12] As stated in *Kalmari v Titus* [2011] VUIC 2: 'land is not a commodity. It cannot be sold or converted. It is, to many Ni-Vanuatus a virtual book which keeps the sacred stories of the origin of their tribes; it feeds and protects them; and displays evidences of their own identity as a clan within the society. It is one's fate. It encompasses one's past, present and future from generations to generations.'

[13] Following a Commission of Inquiry into Land Matters in 1973, the Lands Group Incorporation Act 1974 was passed.

these groups have been recognised a means of claiming entitlement to royalties either from logging – such groups are required under the Forestry Act 1991, mining, or cash-cropping, or entitlement to compensation for damage to land from the activities of extractive industries. Consequently, drawing on complex patterns of kin and lineage based land rights, membership is frequently challenged and changed with incorporated land groups being formed, fragmented and reconstituted, in order to participate in the monetary and other compensatory benefits derived from these extractive industries. Several changes to traditional lineage and kinship patterns are emerging. Although in principle land group membership is meant to map clan and group membership and be administratively controlled by government, in practice membership is often controlled by resource companies in association with those putting themselves forward as land group leaders. Further, rather than identifying the membership of customary social groups, the incorporated land group is determining membership as people put themselves forward to be included in order to reap the benefits.[14] At the same time, because traditionally a person may hold land interests over land scattered geographically and through different lines of the family, customary land tenure provides the means whereby an individual or the representative of a social unit may belong to more than one incorporated land group.

Similarly, also in Papua New Guinea, the introduction of a lease-lease-back scheme under sections 11 and 102 of the Land Act, 1996, which was intended to provide a framework for the leasing of land held under customary tenure for enterprise development, either as agricultural or business leases, has been utilised in a way that was probably not intended. Under the scheme customary owners acquire a formal, non-customary leasehold title to their land, which can be used for attracting mortgage finance for agricultural or business development purposes beneficial to the lease-holders. There is also the potential for sub-leases or assignments of the leases to be made to a third party who in turn may develop the land or use it for cash-cropping. The intention behind the device was that the State acquires the land by lease (without payment or compensation) and then leases it back to the person or persons, or the land group, from which it acquired the land or, with the agreement of the customary landowners, leases it to a third party

[14] In a number of places the recording of group genealogies has been done, in order to ascertain membership of the incorporated land group. Although this does not amount to registration of the land itself and has been held not to be evidence of title – *Re Hides Gas Project Land Case* [1993] PNGLR 309, it creates a closed list for future purposes.

business group or other incorporated body. During the period of the lease - which may not exceed 99 years, all customary rights in the land (except for those which are specifically reserved in the lease) are suspended. This is intended to be a voluntary process that customary landowners initiate and drive. While the lease-lease-back process has been used successfully in some parts of Papua New Guinea to develop large agricultural projects, especially in the oil palm sector, the process has proved less successful in encouraging custom owners to engage in their own development schemes and has been criticised as encouraging a 'rent-dependency' approach to land utilisation because customary owners have realised that a lease-back to a third party generates financial benefits without the risk that markets will fall or crops fail if they cultivate the land themselves. The scheme has also provide an opportunity for enterprising individuals, who already have political and traditional status - for example, chiefs, ministers, Big Men, to enter into lease-lease-back arrangements without the consensus or even knowledge of their group. In some cases the members of the customary land group are ignorant of either the lease or its significance. This misuse extends to central government where there has been abuse of the lease-lease-back process in circumstances where the Government has leased directly to large-scale extractive enterprises such as forestry, without distributing any benefits to the customary landowners.

Innovations in the legal framework to facilitate logging in Solomon Islands have also tried to bring customary rights holders and commercial extractive agencies together, although with varied success (Farran 2008). The Forest Resources and Timber Utilisation Act (the Forest Resources Act) 1999, which was implemented with Regulations on 29 February 2000, was brought in to replace the previous unsatisfactory legislation - the 1969 Forest Resources and Timber Utilisation Act. The new Act was intended to put in place a number of procedural steps to safeguard the relative interests of all parties while facilitating commercial logging for national and local benefit. Importantly the Act recognises customary rights to timber resources by providing that any company interested in logging must negotiate with the local owners. Although there are a number of apparent safeguards within the legal framework, the reality of timber extraction in Solomon Islands has been characterized by disputes, corruption, the emergence of new elites and the inequitable distribution of any benefits, as well as the unsustainable extraction of hardwood timber – it is estimated that if logging continues at the rate experienced over the past decade, the natural forest in Solomon Islands will be commercially exhausted by 2013 (ADB 2010: 29). Nevertheless, what is interesting about the Solomons' experience is that disintegration of central government in a period of civil and political unrest at the turn of the century, meant that not only did the executive and logging companies circumvent, ignore and short-cut the legal framework, but also that customary land owners took matters into their own hands, negotiating directly with logging companies. It has also been the case that logging, and the financial rewards attached to it, has provided a new milieu for the advancement of the traditional Melanesian 'Big Man' at local, provincial and central government level, so that traditional political status has been used to facilitate logging - through representation of custom owners and negotiation with logging companies, and has been enhanced by the new riches and power generated by logging contracts. Recognition of the customary owners in the legislation therefore, conferred a formal role on these but at the same time allowed traditional political structures to be manipulated so that some individuals could use customary forms of 'wantokism' and recognised forms of individual status to accumulate individual wealth, which while it might be subject to redistribution, would not necessarily go to all those who would be beneficially entitled in custom.

In Vanuatu it is not so much legislation that has changed land tenure, as the policy and practices of successive governments and especially Ministers of Lands, since the 1990s. As with other Pacific island countries, on independence the common law lease for a fixed period of time - up to a maximum of seventy-five years, was retained in Vanuatu, and secured in subsequent legislation. Although originally intended to encourage continued agricultural development by settlors who had lost their right to freehold in 1980, in recent years, especially through the last decade of the twentieth century and the first decade of this century, the approval of leases and particularly sub-leases of sub-divided leased land, has been much more liberal, resulting in a noticeable increase in the percentage of land alienated under leases to foreign investors either for residential purposes, for tourism or for commercial purposes. Recognition of this as a result of published field work in 2002 (Farran 2002), and subsequent awareness raising, informed resolutions emerging from a National Land Summit in 2006 (Tahi 2006). Although this has yet to yield positive results, it provided a platform for highlighting the challenges posed by changing land use, which in turn has manifested itself in localised strategies to use a variety of legal avenues for improving land security. Some of these will be considered below.

*Traversing a plurality of forms and forums*

Examples of the development of hybrid forums traversing plural legal systems for dispute resolution, can be found in the structure of courts and tribunals which hear and determine land issues and in the procedural forms which are adopted within these. In all three countries there is a degree of parallelism and cross-over between the forums that hear disputes over land governed by non-customary law and those that hear land held under customary tenure. Because the same parcel of land may be affected by inter-connected disputes, for example arguments over customary rights which impinge on arguments over who can grant a lease or receive financial benefits generated by the land, litigants move between these fora and in doing so adapt and adopt different ways of presenting arguments and substantiating claims.

In all three countries the formal courts - which are modelled on the English system of higher and lower courts, have jurisdiction to hear disputes regarding non-customary land. In Papua New Guinea, disputes about ownership or use of common law freehold, statutory freehold of converted customary land, and State owned land, are determined by the National Court, with appeal to the Supreme Court. In Solomon Islands, disputes about ownership or obligations of owners of perpetual or fixed term estates, and also about leases, are determined by the ordinary courts, i.e., the High Court and Court of Appeal, as are disputes about what land is public land, and disputes regarding the alienation of public land. In Vanuatu, disputes about ownership of government land, and disputes about non-customary dealings with customary land, are determined by the Supreme Court, with appeal to the Court of Appeal. Characteristic of these formal courts is the reliance on sworn evidence and oral testimony, strict procedural rules regarding the order of pleadings and the teleological aim of arriving at a final, binding ruling under which one party will be the winner and the other the loser. The process is adversarial and the parties may or may not be represented by lawyers who will often be strangers. Decisions, which are meant to be impartial and based only on the law, are made by judges who may, in the case of the appeal courts, be foreigners. The principles that influence the court will be previous decisions of the highest level of courts or the equivalent level if there is no higher court decision, and often the persuasive authority of decisions drawn from jurisdictions outside the region, such as England and Australia.

Within the formal system however, as indicated, separate dispute forums for customary land claims are also formally recognised - in whole or partially,[15] for

[15] For example, in Papua New Guinea disputes about ownership or use of customary land are often resolved by customary processes of: discussion; mediation; chiefly decisions, usually with the advice of elders, and occasionally force. Although these are recognised as legitimate processes in custom for determining disputes about land, and can be enforced by customary processes, they are not enforceable by the State, and often will not be regarded as conclusive by

example the Customary Land Tribunals of Vanuatu, the Customary Land Appeal Courts and Local Courts in Solomon Islands and the Land Courts in Papua New Guinea. Although these courts have separate jurisdiction the barrier between these fora and the ordinary courts is not absolute. In particular evidence derived from introduced land law may be put forward in customary land courts to support claims; for example, documents of contract and sale, or prior court decisions are used to support purported title to customary land or claims to land settled in custom. Alternatively, the ordinary courts may be involved in judicial review of the conduct of customary land courts or tribunals, or become involved because non-customary legal issues are being raised, for example the validity of a lease, the management or distribution of monies arising from the land, questions of succession or mortgage.

While a plurality of courts/tribunals hearing land disputes can lead to forum shopping it also reflects the different ways in which land is being used. For example, in Vanuatu while the ordinary courts have no jurisdiction to hear disputes relating to land held under customary tenure, they do have jurisdiction to hear any disputes regarding leases. So where the former land is leased then there may be issues that fall into the jurisdiction of two separate forums. Similarly, in Solomon Islands, the ordinary courts will not adjudicate customary land disputes but will adjudicate in timber rights disputes. So, for example, where there is a dispute regarding a timber rights agreement between different representatives of the customary land group, the High Court may grant an injunction to protect the logging company engaged in timber felling on the land, or may grant an injunction to order logging to cease, pending the outcome of the land dispute. Indeed it has been realised by the High Court that:

> in all of these cases involving logging on customary land, the propriety of the logging license cannot be entirely separated from issues of ownership of customary land. As those involved in the process of administering the law on forest and timber know, sensitive issues of custom do very much affect the procedure of obtaining a logging license on customary land in this country. Thus where the issue of ownership or other rights in custom over customary land is in dispute touching on the propriety of the logging license, a party cannot simply isolate the issues of custom and come to this (court) on the sole issue of the legality of the

---

the opposing parties, leaving open the possibility of further, future disputes.

license.[16]

Parties also realise that forum shopping can delay the resolution of a dispute – often for a number of years, which can be advantageous because the status quo may prevail pending a final outcome. In this way plural dispute fora can be exploited.

At the same time some of the features of distinct fora for hearing customary land matters are being lost through a process of hybridisation. For example, usually the procedures in the courts which hear customary land matters include modified formal rules of evidence so as to accommodate customary claims based on hearsay, oral evidence and narratives of genealogies. For example in Vanuatu, until 2000, land disputes affecting customary land were heard by the island courts.[17] Provision was made that each island court was to have at least "three justices knowledgeable in custom ... at least one of whom shall be a custom chief residing within the territorial jurisdiction of the court" (Section 3(1)),[18] and the courts were expected to "administer the customary law prevailing within the territorial jurisdiction of the court so far as the same is not in conflict with any written law and is not contrary to justice, morality and good order" (Section 10).[19] However, in determining land disputes (as in other matters) these courts are presided over by a magistrate, and as magistrates have become more professional and immersed in the non-customary law through university education and the practices and procedures of the magistrates courts, the island courts have been

[16] *Halu v JP Enterprise Ltd* [2003] SBHC 123.

[17] The establishment of these is provided for under the Islands Courts Act 1983, which confers on the Chief Justice the power to establish island courts by warrant.

[18] Prior to contact, 'chiefs' were not generally a feature of Melanesian social organisation but the colonial authorities found the role a useful one and promoted it to the degree that it is now an entrenched feature in Vanuatu (Bolton 1998). The existence of 'custom' chiefs and 'mission' chiefs (or condominium chiefs) confuses the land picture as explained in *Kalmarie v Titus* [2011] VUIC 2, which is considered below.

[19] There are also provision relating to orders of community work in lieu of fines or imprisonment and the power to order payment of compensation to victims, both of which find some resonance in customary practices. The legislation also provides that 'an island court shall not apply technical rules of evidence but shall admit and consider such information as is available' (Section 25).

increasingly influenced by state law, rather than customary law.[20] Although the island courts lost their land jurisdiction in 2000,[21] they have continued to hear a backlog of land cases and have been instrumental in the changing articulation of land claims.

In the two systems of courts different rules of procedure and evidence apply. For example, litigation involving leases which come before the formal courts - usually the Supreme Court, rely for evidence on documents of contract, registration, mortgage and so on. If custom is pleaded then it must be proved, it is not accepted as law,[22] and indeed it may be necessary to establish that the custom is one that is generally recognised rather than one that is merely local or particular to the plaintiff and/or defendant.[23] Disputes which come before the customary land tribunals on the other hand, or even the island courts, rely on oral evidence, much of it hearsay and unsupported. However, close analysis of what happens in courts where customary land disputes are being heard suggests that some litigants, and indeed those presiding over the court or tribunal, are adopting or adapting the language,[24] concepts and institutions of the introduced colonial system when litigating,[25] and presenting evidence in ways which have some characteristics of the formal courts. What is emerging therefore is a procedural hybrid in which certain aspects of the introduced, former colonial, land system is being merged with customary land tenure and vice versa.[26]

[20] For an assessment of the Island courts see Jowitt 1999; Weisbrot 1989.

[21] A new tier of courts was established under the Customary Land Tribunal Act 2001, "to provide for a system based on custom to resolve disputes about customary land" (Section 1). Although various customary practices are incorporated into the Act, in practice these tribunals have not been a success and are now under review.

[22] See more generally Zorn and Corrin Care 2002: 612, 638.

[23] The decisions of the courts are not consistent on this; for example, in the case of customary adoption it appears that different local customs are acceptable. However, fear of the rule of precedent may deter a judge from accepting an argument based on custom - see *Boe and Tage v Thomas* [1987] VUSC 9.

[24] For example, of 'ownership', 'occupation', 'rights': see Guo 2011.

[25] For example, the institution of the trusts is used quite commonly in Vanuatu and in Papua New Guinea by the incorporated land group.

[26] Reflecting Levi-Strauss's 'bricolage' theory cited by Westmark 1986: 131.

For example, in the Final Report of the National Land Summit it is stated in respect of the identification of legitimate custom landowners, that one of the problems was that there were "no clear custom rules available for chiefs to go by" (Tahi 2006: 24). Similarly, writing about the land tenure system of South Efate, Fingleton and colleagues have stated that "there is confusion about what is customary and how far kastom can form the basis for modern land tenure" (Fingleton et al. 2008: 29). However consideration of a recent case heard by the Island Court suggests that not only are there clear customary rules being articulated and recorded, but that evidence is being presented in non-customary ways. The case of *Kalmarie v Titus* [2011] VUIC 2, concerned a land dispute between the original claimant - Kalmarie, and ten counter-claimants. The Island Court Civil Procedure Rules section 8, states that the courts are empowered "to apply customary law of the area in dispute when determining customary ownership. However the decision must not stand against the spirit of justice, reality and good order." So, although the Constitution declares in Article 74 that "the rules of custom shall form the basis of ownership and use of land in the Republic of Vanuatu", acceptance of those rules is subject to "the spirit of justice, reality and good order". Two things flow from this: first establishing the custom rules – presuming that custom can be identified as 'rules', and then applying these in such a way as to comply with the caveat. In Kalmarie the applicable custom was that of North Efate (the island of the capital Port Vila). At the outset the court stated what the rules of this custom were:

> North Efate custom dictates that inheritance over customary ownership of land passes through patrilineal system. However the following are the exceptions:
> a) Matrilineal system if the only surviving descendant is a woman.
> b) PUMAS or custom will;
> c) Compensation;
> d) Adoption, (but the adopted person must be biologically related to the adopted family).

The principle that appears to emerge from the rules is that succession to land – and this is how claims are established, is patrilineal with some exceptions. This appears to be a clear statement of law. However, the court goes on to recognise that these rules do not exist in isolation but are closely associated with social organisation, which makes the application of the rules rather less clear. Customary land tenure is shaped by the management and allocation of rights and that depends on a system of chiefs, associate chiefs, family leaders and a local council of chiefs.[27] The Head Chief allocates a parcel of land to his assistant chief(s) who subdivides and allocates plots of that land to leaders of familis. The allocated lands become the properties of the receivers. However a tribute or tithe (*nasautong*) must be paid annually to the Head Chief. Thus, two customary aspects interact with the fairly clear principle: land powers associated with customary status, and observance of custom. The court refers to this payment as a 'custom lease' although formally there is no such thing and in practice it has the characteristics of a rent or tribute rather than a lease, but the phrase is an interesting example of hybridity across forms and language.

In establishing rights under the stated principle the court expected claimants to show:

1. That their tribe began on the land. And that there are descendants of the same tribe; going back through generations as far as he/she could.
2. That they are knowledgeable in the past and present cultural practices of the area in dispute; and
3. That they are confident with the boundaries of the land in dispute.

The Island court is not required to apply "technical rules of evidence but shall admit and consider such information as is available" (Section 25 of the Island Court Act, CAP 167), and each claimant is entitled to call five witnesses who are meant to submit a written statement on which they can then be cross-examined. Corroboration of evidence goes towards building a 'probable' case, which is the

[27] This is set out in the Kalmarie judgement and can be summarised as follows:1. Head Chief: Controls manages and protects lands in the interest of his people. The Head Chief appoints an Assistant Chief or head of each tribe/clan/Naflac (Naflac is a group identified by a common totem); 2. Assistant Chief(s): assists the Head Chief in the management of the land. He/they performs specific custom duties such as being: Warriors, Munuwei or custom spirit/clever/witch, messenger, etc. The brothers and/or brothers-in-law of the Head Chief hold this position and are answerable to the Head Chief; 3. Leader of Family, who is immediately under the Assistant Chief. He is responsible for the family affairs in a unit or household. These leaders are answerable to the Assistant Chief; 4. Council of Chiefs, which is a group of Assistant Chiefs chaired by the Head Chief of the village to discuss and make decisions in all matters for the good governance of the community.

burden of proof. This evidence focuses on genealogies, knowledge and identification of boundaries, recollection of cultural events and practices. However, it has been recognised in the Island Courts that most evidence is hearsay, often incomplete and sometimes framed at the request of one of the claimants. In the case of *Family Sope Imere (Mele Village) v Mala* [1994] VUIC 2, the present Chief Justice (then a magistrate) referred with approval to a decision of the Supreme Court (which at the time had appeal jurisdiction of customary land cases) in which it had been stated:

> When there is a conflict in tradition, custom story about land, one side of the story must be right and the other side must be wrong. This does not mean that both parties are no honest in their belief, both may be honest in the belief, however in cases like this, the behaviour or the way in which evidence is given in court may help reach the truth. Therefore, the best way to test custom history or tradition is to refer back to the happenings of the recent years as presented in the evidence, and consider one of the history given in court which that would most probably be close to the truth.[28]

In determining probability of truth demeanour under cross-examination – rather than the respect afforded in custom to status, becomes important, and although not essential, supporting documentary evidence is becoming increasingly relied on, especially documented family trees and sketch maps of boundaries and physical evidence of events or landmarks, such as photos and artefacts, or permanent markers for custom graves on the land such as concrete slabs (mission graves are discounted as are decisions of the Joint Court under the condominium).[29] In the *Kalmarie* case, for example, the presiding magistrate commented with approval on the 'comprehensive' family tree of the tenth counter-claimant, which linked him to

[28] *Malas Family v Songoriki Family*, [1986] VUSC 12.

[29] *In Family Sope Imere (Mele Village) v Mala* [1994] VUIC 2, it was stated: 'The court would like to clarify the fact that Joint Court Judgement on registration of the disputed area, is not binding to the court in any way, Joint Court decisions were based on the legal basis of land ownership of the white settlers. Furthermore, as a result of those decisions, rights of the native land owners were taken away. The Joint Court decisions took place [long] ago, because at that time the Condominium Government of New Hebrides failed to consider the views of the custom owners'.

four of the other counter-claimants, and noted with similar approval that the fifth counterclaimant "has put tremendous effort in presenting this case before us".[30] Indeed in presenting his evidence to establish his ancestors' spiritual and cultural attachment to the land his evidence seems - somewhat improbably, to have dated back to 1330. The credibility of his claim rested on several factors: his ability to show the court traditional sites and cultural attachment to the place in dispute, through traditional stories and sacred places within the land; the transplant of place names from place of origin to place of residence; the retention and practice of certain construction skills; and paper evidence in a French book describing the movements of islanders in which there was cross reference to persons and events relied on by the claimant. Despite his convincing evidence, however, this claimant was unsuccessful. The crux of the matter was whether absenteeism - by the claimant's ancestors, from the land was a matter to which the court should have regard. In a previous case it had been held that long possession could not prevail over customary ownership even of absentees,[31] and a line of reasoning adopted in the Solomon Islands,[32] that the concept of acquisition of ownership by adverse possession, or loss of rights through failure to bring an action after the elapse of a certain period of time, were incompatible with custom. However, in Efate, the island council of chiefs has drawn up a document of customary law: the Vaturisu Customary Land Laws. Ironically, impetus for this was as a result of the resolutions of the National Land Summit, referred to earlier, and the failure of the national government to take any steps to more clearly articulate what customary law, referred to in the constitution, was to apply to land. This statement of laws, contrary to the previously outlined position, stipulates that "customary ownership of land on Efate is determined by physical occupation which can be realistically proven going back at least 6 generations of the descendant of the original occupier utilising the land in question". This clearly departs from the prior position but is arguably a pragmatic solution that draws from the customary tradition of establishing genealogies while seeking some form of certainty, especially on Efate, which as the capital island has long had a history of immigration and land occupation.

---

[30] Similarly, with the eleventh claimant the presiding magistrate observed: 'This claimant has done a marvellous work of art and research'. Although perhaps more in line with the customary narration of claims, most of this was rejected as being historical relating to stories of origin rather than the piece of land in question.

[31] *Manie v Kilman* [1988] VUSC 9, where the Chief Justice said: 'long possession cannot prevail over the true custom ownership of the land'.

[32] *Buga v Ganiferi* [1982] SBHC 4.

Looking at the evidence presented and challenged in the 2011 Kalmarie case, also suggests a shifting dynamic. A number of the witnesses were elderly, and many had gaps in their knowledge. Given the changes taking place in Vanuatu, it is also probable that over the next decades the type of evidence that can be presented by witnesses will change. Knowledge of traditional practices is being lost. Many urban dwellers do not have close links with their ancestral lands and may seldom visit. Although many bodies are returned for burial in their ancestral lands, increased urbanisation means that ties with these lands are increasingly attenuated, especially among younger people. Landmarks are changed and changing, either due to natural occurrences or because of changes in land use and cultivation. In a changing media environment, oral histories may be lost and some indigenous languages have already disapperared, and therefore place names have already been lost or are endangered. Where custom is reduced to writing then that process too, may change the custom - as with the statement of laws of the Vaturisu. These changes are just part of a larger, although fragmented picture of the ebb and flow of plural legal systems.

*Navigating with a Purpose*

This process goes further and brings us to the third way in which plural systems are being experienced. At a pragmatic level people are adapting and adopting legal forms and frameworks to meet their own objectives. Woodman has suggested that the customary law observed by the courts and that observed in social practice may be different (Woodman 2001). However, I would suggest that the 'transformation' to which he refers to describe the process that occurs when "a body of norms which has been observed as part of the social order and enforced outside and independently of any modern state institutions is then adopted and enforced by the courts and other institutions of a state" (Woodman 2001: 27), can operate in reverse. In other words, Pacific Island people are adopting the body of norms and their manifestations (or elements of them) that are observed in the courts and formal legal system, and incorporating these in ways that have consequences for social ordering. Guo, for example, in her research among the Langlanga in Solomon Islands found that narratives of lineage were being adapted to meet evidential requirements acceptable to the courts hearing land claims, so that 'law' had become a genre of discourse appropriated by people to frame their relationship with land and incidentally their relationships with each other because land and kinship are social inseparable. She refers to this co-evolution of the local and the legal as creating a new "legalscape" (Guo 2011). While the law is regarded as only one aspect of this shaping and reshaping of peoples' relationship with land, which itself is subject to constant modification as strategies are tried and tested in court, and succeed or fail, the process of litigation provides a creative forum for adaptation.

In Vanuatu, my own research into narratives of land claims suggests a similar selective process for the presentation of evidence to support kinship and origin claims, whereby the strength of evidence is measured by corroborative narrative of events and geographical knowledge, as well as hard-copy evidence, and the number of generations back that can be convincingly named (Farran 2010). There is a tendency towards a simplification of lineage histories with the exclusion or inclusion of certain kinship ties depending on their utility as evidence that is both comprehensible and acceptable to the court. Extended networks of kin are excluded unless they can usefully link to co-claimants (as demonstrated in the Kalmarie case considered above), and the narration of boundaries is reduced to sketch plans. Indeed a reading of land dispute cases coming before the island courts or more recently, the customary land tribunals suggests that the 'obscurity' and 'complexity' of customary land tenure may be a myth propagated by those seeking to develop the land or to avoid the complexities of understanding how the system works. In this way aspects of customary land tenure can be used as a shield - by those resisting development, or misused by those seeking to circumvent the interests it protects. Alternatively there are those who can see the advantages and disadvantages of customary land tenure and those of other land tenure forms and manoeuvre accordingly.

This process of interlegality or interaction between two systems[33] is illustrated by the manipulation of lease registration in Vanuatu. In Vanuatu only leases are subject to registration. There is no system of registration of customary interests in land, and even the registration of leases does not directly provide any indication of customary ownership. Indeed many custom land owners are suspicious of proposals for any such registration believing that this may be a means whereby the Government (or foreigners approved by the government) will take away their land. However, some ni-Vanuatu see registration of leases as advantageous. In field studies undertaken in 2010,[34] researchers found that in some cases registration was

[33] This is a term used by Svensson 2005: 74.

[34] These were field studies undertaken on two separate islands, Epi and Tanna, by a World Bank Programme *Jastis blong Evriwan* (Justice for the Poor). The reports of their research can be found on the World Bank site http://web.worldbank.org/WBSITE/EXTERNAL/TOPICS/EXTLAWJUSTICE/E

viewed in a positive light because it afforded an unchallengeable right to the land and thereby conferred a security of title that was not available under customary tenure. The use of registration in this way can apply to formerly alienated land where continuing disputes since independence have meant that registration of any pending leases has been delayed. Registration can also be used to secure new leases (over non-alienated customary land) where there are or may be customary disputes. In such a case registration of a lease will effectively trump any unwelcome customary claims, at least for the duration of the lease because of the indefeasibility of title conferred by registration. Tactics for securing such leases vary. In some cases the present occupants may take it upon themselves to go to the capital and register a lease in favour of other members of the family, or may approach the Minister of Lands with a request to exercise his power to grant leases over disputed lands,[35] even where the land is subject to pending court actions or the conflicting claims have been ruled on.[36] In this way registration of a lease may be used to secure present occupancy in the face of threatened dispute – particularly where land is being occupied and used by 'incomers' even if they have been there for several generations, or to secure mortgage finance over the land for development purposes such as tourism, or to facilitate sub-division, or to silence or bring to an end a long running dispute which has not been resolved by the various customary and non-customary forums. Women may also use leases to secure rights for themselves in patrilineal societies or to secure rights for their children if such rights seem precarious, perhaps because of family breakdown or land shortages.

Growing awareness of the advantages of leases for securing their own rights to land has also been demonstrated by a greater willingness to challenge leases registered to others and the case law suggests that increasingly registration of leaseholds itself is being challenged by those whose claims to customary land predate any registration. Often these challenges are triggered when the monetary

XTJUSFORPOOR/0,contentMDK:21172707~menuPK:3282963~pagePK:210058~piPK:210062~theSitePK:3282787,00.html#Vanuatu, last accessed on 9/06/12.

[35] Under the Land Reform Act 1980. This Act, which was originally intended to apply to land that had been alienated prior to independence continues to be used even where land that has never been alienated is in dispute.

[36] Although the exercise of the Minister's powers in the face of court rulings or where he knows litigation is pending have been challenged this continues to happen. See V*alele Family v Touru* [2002] VUCA 3, and the Resolutions of the National Land Summit 2006.

value of land becomes apparent in the course of lease negotiations or thereafter. The system of registration is being used therefore, not only to secure leases for lessees - thereby fulfilling its intended (state) purpose, but also to assert customary claims against lessees and sometimes against those who granted the lease, or to secure customary land rights within the customary structure. These dynamics of change in plural legal systems are not state-led - although they may be directly or indirectly state-endorsed, or the outcome of any conscious policy, but rather the result of people using the plurality of legal tools available to them to secure desired ends.

In some cases even unsuccessful colonial policies appear to be being re-invented by indigenous people. For example, in Papua New Guinea, Goddard has written about the re-drawing of kinship narratives to support land claims among the Motu-Koita people who live near the capital Port Moresby and who have increasingly come to feel marginalised and under-compensated for the urban sprawl on their traditional lands (UNESCO 2001; Goddard 2010). This has led to an increase in litigation in the formal and informal courts as the commercial value of land becomes more important (although land alienation has been experienced by these people for over one hundred years). This is turn has had two consequences: it has influenced land discourse and practice among villagers, and it has changed legal constructions of custom. Notably, Goddard asserts that "patrilineal idioms which were once only a small part of the consideration of rights to land use among the Motu-Koita are becoming transformed into legal rules" (Goddard 2011). This shaping of kinship rules has come about because of the legal preference for consistency when courts engage with customary land claims, in a legal environment in which courts accept oral history, legends and mythology as legitimate evidence in the investigation. Attempts to engage with the vicissitudes of oral narratives and understandings of customary land holding were made in the colonial period, notably by Land Commissioner Bramell.[37] A preference was given to interpreting kinship structures as unilineal (patrilineal) which was both pragmatic - because colonial administrators dealt only with men, and less complicated than taking into account various other possibilities.[38] Despite its

[37] This resulted in a document: 'Native Land Custom' composed by J.C. Bramell in 1964.

[38] Although Goddard points out that Bramell did record the 'cognatic' element noticed by anthropologists (Goddard 2011), Bramell also acknowledged that 'land custom' did not remain constant and that the word 'ownership' was not an altogether appropriate interpretation of local traditional understandings of

colonial antecedents which might have been rejected by now, Goddard suggests that the version of custom now being used in the land court demonstrates the process of a gradual transformation of a patrilineal idiom into a rule, as "customary behaviour becomes increasingly subjected to Western juridical principles".

By contrast, Eves writing about the Lelet people - also in Papua New Guinea, has indicated how a shift to long term crops, notably coffee, has motivated some villages to move away from customary plural inheritance rights to land, to focus on unilineal rights, here matrilineal rights, in order to rationalise the number of possible claimants over the land whose claims might disrupt the long tenure needed for coffee cultivation. Legal, and consequently kinship changes are being proposed by way of village constitutions abolishing certain land claims, notably patrifilial claims (Eves 2011). Perhaps paradoxically, the present land tenure reforms are not dissimilar from those proposed during colonial times. Then and now the proposed reforms posed a threat to the flexibility and fluidity of customary land tenure systems and potentially threatened to undermine social relationships. This might still happen and if the proposed reforms succeed communities may become more fragmented and new forms of land conflict could arise. Nevertheless, this selective adjustment to the kinship underpinnings of customary tenure marks a conscious effort to adapt the former because of changes in land use being brought about by development - here mono cash crops which require long-term security of tenure for a limited number of people.

## Conclusion

What do these shifts in the accommodation of different forms of land tenure in the Pacific region tell us about legal and cultural pluralism? Merry has suggested that "state law penetrates and restructures other normative orders through symbols and through direct coercion" and, at the same time, that "non-state normative orders resist and circumvent penetration or even capture and use the symbolic capital of state law" (Merry 1988: 881). There is some evidence to suggest that this is happening is these Pacific island states. It is also clear that the law relating to land is illustrative of Moore's theory of semi-autonomous social fields in which a legal system may have "rule-making capacities, and the means to induce or coerce compliance; but it is simultaneously set in a larger social matrix which can, and

landholding, and he recognised that the introduction of a cash economy had affected Motu-Koita approaches to land-use.

does, affect and invade it, sometimes at the invitation of persons inside it, sometimes at its own instance" (Moore 1978: 56). Clearly in Melanesian countries to suggest that customary and state law are two separate systems in a plural whole or are the antithesis of each other is over-simplistic, as is distinguishing between law and other forms of social ordering especially in the context of land. Nor is it helpful to seek a hierarchy of normative orders when so much land is held under customary tenure or to suggest that there is a clear dichotomy between the colonial past and the post-colonial present. Pacific Island people are navigating between tradition and modernity every day, and for some this involves reshaping the legal landscape. The pattern is piecemeal with the result that new hybrids are adding to, rather than reducing, the plural framework. Arguably, however, it is because of this plurality that this navigation is possible.

## References

ASB (ASIAN DEVELOPMENT BANK)

2010 *Solomon Islands 2010 Economic Report*. Manila. Asian Development Bank.

BENDA-BECKMANN, Franz von and Keebet von BENDA-BECKMANN

2006 'The dynamics of change and continuity in plural legal orders.' *Journal of Legal Pluralism* 53–4: 1-44.

BOLTON, Lissant,

1998 'Chief Willie Bongmatur Maldo and the Role of Chiefs in Vanuatu.' *Journal of Pacific History* 33: 179-195.

BONNEMAISON, Joël

1991 'Magic Gardens in Tanna.' *Pacific Studies* 14(4): 71-90.

*EVES, Richard*

*2011 'Puzzling Over Matrilineal Land Tenure and Development in New Ireland, Papua New Guinea.'* Pacific Studies *34: 350-374.*

FARRAN, Sue

2002 *Myth or Reality: Case Study of Land Tenure in Efate*. Vanuatu: University of the South Pacific Law School.

2008 'Timber! Felling the Future of the Solomon Islands.' *Australian Property Law Journal* 16(2): 109-128.

2010 'Law, land, development and narrative: a case-study from the South Pacific.' *International Journal of Law in Context* 6: 1-21.

FINGLETON, Jim, Anna NAUPA and Chris BALLARD

2008 'Village Land Trusts in Vanuatu: "One Common Basket"'. Pp. 21-24 in

*Making Land Work*. Vol. 2. Canberra: Commonwealth of Australia.

GODDARD, Michael

2010 'Heat and history: the Motu-Koita and Moresby'. Pp. 19-46 in Michael Goddard (ed.), *Villagers and the city: Melanesian experiences of Port Moresby, Papua New Guinea*. London: Sean Kingston Press.

2011 'Bramell's Rules: Custom and Law in Contemporary Land Disputes Among the Motu-Koita of Papua New Guinea.' *Pacific Studies* 34: 323-349.

GUO, Pei-Yi

2011 'Law as discourse: Land Disputes and the Changing Imagination of Relations Among the Langalanga, Solomon Islands.' *Pacific Studies* 34: 223-249.

HUGHES, Helen

2003 'Aid has Failed the Pacific.' *Issue Analysis* 33: 1-32. Centre for Independent Studies.

2004 'Can Papua New Guinea Come Back from the Brink?' *Issue Analysis* 49: 1-2. Centre for Independent Studies.

JOWITT, Anita

1999 'Island Courts in Vanuatu.' Working Paper 3. *Journal of South Pacific Law* 3: http://www.vanuatu.usp.ac.fj/journal_splaw/Working_Papers/Jowitt1.html. Last accessed 8/06/12.

LAKAU, Andrew

1991 *State Acquisition of Customary Land for Public Purposes*. Lae, Papua New Guinea: Dept. of Surveying and Land Studies, Papua New Guinea University of Technology.

MERRY, Sally Engle

1988 'Legal pluralism.' *Law & Society Review* 22(5): 869-896.

MERRY, Sally Engle and Donald BRENNEIS

2003 'Introduction.' Pp. 1-34 in Sally Engle Merry and Donald Brenneis (eds.), *Law and Empire in the Pacific: Fiji and Hawaii*. Santa Fe, School of American Research Press.

MOORE, Sally Falk

1978 'Law and social change: the semi-autonomous social field as an appropriate subject of study.' Pp 54-81 in Sally Falk Moore *Law as Process: An anthropological approach*. London, Boston: Routledge & Kegan Paul.

SVENSSON, Tom

2005 'Interlegality, a process for strengthening indigenous peoples' autonomy: the case of the Sámi in Norway.' *Journal of Legal Pluralism* 51: 51-77.

TAHI, Steven

2006 Final Report: National Land Summit. Port Vila, Vanuatu: Government of the Republic of Vanuatu.

UNESCO (UNITED NATIONS EDUCATIONAL, SCIENTIFIC AND CULTURAL ORGANIZATION)

2001 *Partners in Coast Development: the Motu Koitabu people of Papua New Guinea*. Paris: UNESCO.

VAN TREASE, Howard

1987 *The Politics of Land in Vanuatu*. Suva: University of the South Pacific.

WEISBROT, David

1989 'Custom, Pluralism and Realism in Vanuatu: Legal Development and the Role of Customary Law.' *Pacific Studies*. 13(1): 65-98.

WESTMARK, George

1986 'Court is an arrow: legal pluralism in Papua New Guinea.' *Ethnology* 25(2): 131-149.

WOODMAN, Gordon R.

2001 'Customary Law in Common Law Systems' *IDS Bulletin* 32(1): 28-34.

ZORN, Jean and Jennifer Corrin CARE

2002 'Barava Tru': Judicial Approaches to the Pleading and Proof of Custom in the South Pacific.' *International and Comparative Law Quarterly* 51: 611-639.

# CAUGHT BETWEEN DIFFERENT LEGAL PLURALISMS: WOMEN WHO WEAR ISLAMIC DRESS AS THE RELIGIOUS 'OTHER' IN EUROPEAN RIGHTS DISCOURSES[134]

Amy R. Jackson and Dorota A. Gozdecka

## Introduction

> I feel it is an obligation upon Muslim women to wear the jilbab, although there are many other opinions.[135]

Issues concerning law and religion and the wearing of religious garments in Europe stand at the forefront of the current human rights discourse. In this paper, by concentrating on the situation of Islamic dress practices in Europe, we question how the position of the religious 'other' can be conceptualized amongst the plurality of intersecting legal and normative orders regulating areas pertaining to religion and identity. We examine diverse methods and approaches of legal

[134]A version of this paper was presented at the Jubilee Conference of the Commission on Legal Pluralism in Cape Town, 8-10 September 2011.

[135] Shabina Begum quoted in BBC News. 'School Wins Muslim Dress Appeal.' 22 March 2006. Available online at: http://news.bbc.co.uk/1/hi/education/4832072.stm.

© Copyright 2011 - Courtenay E. Parlee and Melanie G. Wiber.

pluralists to the occurring legal and normative conflicts in cases concerning the wearing of these religious garments in Europe.

The various types of Islamic dress include: women wearing garments such as a *hijab* (headscarf), *niqab* (face veil), *jilbab* (a long coat like garment which covers the body except the hands and face) and *burqa* (a garment worn over daily clothing, along with a *niqab* and *hijab*). Women wearing these garments in Europe have been prohibited from doing so on the basis of the argument that the garments infringe constitutional principles, such as secularism. As a result a Swiss national, Lucia Dahlab, Turkish nationals Leyla Sąhin, Sefika Kőse and French national Belgin Dogru have all brought claims of infringements of their right to manifest their religion under Article 9 of the European Convention on Human Rights (ECHR).[136] The European Court of Human Rights (ECtHR) held that institutional policies that prohibit the wearing of *hijabs* in schools and universities were compliant with democratic principles and met requirements of proportionality and necessity.[137] Recently, domestic legislation in countries such as France and Belgium began to explicitly prohibit wearing of religious garments covering the

[136] Note that claims have also been brought under other legal provisions. In the United Kingdom (UK), for example, under discrimination provisions provided by Regulation 3 of the Employment Equality (Religion or Belief) Regulations 2003 (SI 2003/1660) superseded by section 19 of the Equality Act 2010, in effect 1 October 2010. See the Employment Tribunal cases of *Azmi v Kirkless Metropolitian Borough Council*, Employment Appeal Tribunal, Appeal No. UKEAT/009/07/MAA (2007), in which the Tribunal held that the refusal of the Headteacher and Governors of a primary school to allow a teaching assistant to wear a *niqab* was not a form of direct discrimination on the grounds of her religious beliefs; and *Bushra Noah v Sara Desrosiers (Trading as Wedge),* ET 2201867/ 2007, in which it was held that, whereas a hairdresser's refusal to employ a woman who wore a *hijab* was not a form of direct discrimination (because any employee covering their hair would have been treated in the same way), it was a form of indirect discrimination (because the requirement for employees to display their hair in the salon amounted to a provision that put the claimant's religion at a disadvantage).

[137] In the cases of *Dahlab v Switzerland*, *Sąhin v Turkey*, *Şefika Köse and 93 Others v Turkey*, and *Dogru v France*, the ECtHR expressed its view on the relationship between a *hijab* and other principles of European democracy, such as gender equality.

face.[138] These prohibitions may result in further claims being brought before the Court and further conceptualisations of the occurring conflicts.[139]

We contend that the existing Court judgments upholding such prohibitions rely on only one method of approaching legal pluralistic conflicts. The Court only takes into account constitutional legal pluralist approaches to the problems of rights (Besson 2008, 2009a, 2009b, 2011; Sweet 2009), which overemphasise constitutional conflicts and lead to institutional interpretations of terms such as secularism. Meanwhile, social-scientific (Griffiths 1986) and anthropological (Moore 1973) notions of legal pluralism, which focus on the conflicts between state-law and other normative orders (for example, cultural and religious), are neglected in the Court judgments. We ascertain that although these accounts of legal pluralism are divergent they ought to be viewed as supplementary. The current judicial interpretations result in women who wear Islamic dress being caught in a gap between institutional interpretations of constitutional principles and studies that focus on the conflict between personal perceptions of normativity and state-law. The gap between studies of institutional and socio-legal pluralisms appears to be vast and the individual[140] can easily disappear behind larger institutional frameworks

[138] For example, in France Article L141-5-1(V) of the Education Code regulates, in accordance with the principle of *laïcité*, the wearing of symbols or clothing denoting religious affiliation in schools and colleges (in effect 2 September 2004). The public wearing of the *burqa* was prohibited in France on 13 July 2010 see BBC News, 'French MPs Vote to Ban Islamic Full Veil in Public', 13 July 2010, available at: www.bbc.co.uk/news/10611398. It prescribes fines of approximately £119 for women who break the law and a one-year jail term for men who force their wives to wear a *burqa*. Furthermore, the public wearing of the *burqa* was prohibited in Belgium on 29 April 2010: see *Daily Mail*, 'Belgium Bans Burkas', 30 April 2010, p. 41.

[139] In September 2011 two French women, who continued to cover their faces by wearing a *niqab* in public, were issued with fines. Their aim was to exhaust local remedies in order for their case to be admissible for the ECtHR, as stipulated under Article 35(1) ECHR. See BBC News, 'France Imposes First *Niqab* Fines', 22 September 2011, available at: www.bbc.co.uk/news/world-europe-15013383.

[140] For the purposes of this paper, we refer to the liberal notion of the "individual" primarily as rights bearer or legal subject. Following Vakulenko (2007) and literature cited therein, we argue that studies of subjectivity (which, in conjunction with legal pluralist studies, we call 'subjective legal pluralism') and those with an intersectional focus (such as that advocated for by critical legal pluralists) illustrate

(Frerichs 2010).

In this paper, our aims are to: first, begin bridging the gap in the existing literature between institutional and socio-legal notions of legal pluralism. Second, encourage future analyses by judges and researchers on the relationship between the state, cultural and religious groups and their members to acknowledge that a plurality of legal pluralisms exists and ought to be simultaneously addressed. The paper is structured in three parts. The first part focuses on how women who wear Islamic dress in Europe are constructed as the religious 'other' in ECtHR judgments such as in the cases of *Dahlab v Switzerland* (*Dahlab*), *Sąhin v Turkey* (*Sąhin*), *Şefika Köse and 93 Others v Turkey* (*Şefika Kőse*), and *Dogru v France* (*Dogru*) and how they are subsequently juxtaposed with the necessity of protecting the constitutional order of a Member State. The second focuses on different ways of conceptualising legal pluralism. These include transnational, constitutional and socio-legal approaches. Furthermore, it analyses the consequences of these diverse theoretical responses for the emergence of some, but denial of other, types of rights pluralism. In the final part of the paper, we consider a suggestion for a more contextualised pluralistic resolution of these conflicts of law.

We argue that it is necessary to re-contextualise the analysis of rights in this situation and place the rights bearer (or legal subject) at the centre of future pluralistic discussions in this important area of culture, religion, gender, politics and law. A more contextualised legal analysis of diverse legal and social implications can help to avoid one-sided solutions, such as those focusing on general constitutional notions, and achieve a better balance in which identity, belief and diverse legal orders are taken into consideration.

## I. The Religious 'Other' Against a Constitutional System – Asymmetry of the Position

The cases of *Dahlab, Sąhin, Şefika Kőse* and *Dogru* were concerned with whether prohibitions on a *hijab* for a teacher at a Swiss state school; a student at a Turkish university; students of secondary schools in Turkey; and a girl in secondary school

the futility of constructing the individual as atomistic, detached and 'relentlessly self-interested'. Instead, studies of different social influences illustrate that structural and communal influences are always subsumed and internalised in the individual (Vakulenko 2007: 186).

who wore a headscarf during physical education classes in France, infringed the applicants' rights to manifest their religion under Article 9 ECHR. In all of the cases ECtHR constructed a negative image of the *hijab* as a symbol that is non-compliant with the values of European democracy. Beginning from the case of *Dahlab* the ECtHR held that:

> The applicant's pupils were aged between four and eight, an age at which children wonder about many things and are also more easily influenced than older pupils. In those circumstances, it cannot be denied outright that the wearing of a headscarf might have some kind of proselytizing effect, seeing that it appears to be imposed on women by a precept which is laid down in the Koran and which, as the Federal Court noted, is hard to square with the principle of gender equality. It therefore appears difficult to reconcile the wearing of an Islamic headscarf with the message of tolerance, respect for others and, above all, equality and non-discrimination that all teachers in a democratic society must convey to their pupils. (*Dahlab*: para.1.)

We argue that this type of reasoning constructed the image of women who adopt Islamic dress code as the religious 'other'.[141] As shown above, a prohibition on wearing a *hijab* was juxtaposed with principles of tolerance and respect for others. This interpretation constructed a generalised image of Islam and equated the applicant's religious perceptions of normativity with intolerance and discrimination. As Motha argues, equal liberty of a woman to practice her religion has been put into opposition with her emancipation (Motha 2007: 144-145). Evans has also observed the problem of stereotypical images of the religious dress practises of women in the Court's reasoning (Evans 2006: 71-73). Stereotypical images promote a vision of religion and normativity as 'foreign' and in a negative sense strongly concentrated on 'otherness'. Gunn suggests that such 'otherisation' is caused by the fear of secularists

[141] We use the term 'othering', 'other' and 'otherisation' in accordance with the terminology used in social sciences and which emphasises exclusion from what is considered the standard. In the context of religion, 'otherisation' in the European context refers primarily to traditions alien to a particular nation state's religious tradition(s). Depending on the traditional place of a religion in a nation state's legal system, religious (or non-religious) adherents of non-traditional religion (or non-religion) are often legally marginalised. Law is either shaped in a way which leads to 'otherisation' or is applied in a way which leads to it.

that a headscarf interferes with the image of a secular Europe and therefore it becomes the first line symbol in a battle over what is perceived as the dangers of Islamism (Gunn 2005: 27).[142] Marshall underlines that there exists an assumption that Islam, in particular, is patriarchal and against gender equality (Marshall 2008: 187). Meerschaut and Gutwirth similarly observe that the ECtHR frequently holds an essentialising view of Islam in its jurisprudence. First, the Court sees Islam as static and always incompatible with the Convention; and second, it always views Islam as interventionist (Meerschaut and Gutwirth 2008: 447-448). For these reasons, 'fearful symbols' (Gunn 2005) are simply juxtaposed with values of equality. The view of equality is however very narrow as Rebouché argues. She asserts that the analysis is too narrow, because 'it fails to adequately weigh the implications of repressive state conduct - in the name of secularism - on women' (Rebouché 2009: 733). Such juxtaposition can impact upon the believer's own perceptions of garments such as a *hijab* and classify believers as undemocratic without due attention to differences between them and their self-perception of inter-normativity. As Vakulenko contends, even though no evidence of interventionist Islamist pressure on the applicants was produced, their agency became obscured by overwhelming structural forces and as a result religion, as a part of the identity of an individual, was ignored in favour of a perception of religion as a homogeneous organising principle of society (Vakulenko 2007: 192).

As a result of the otherisation of religious individuals and the equation of religion with institutional, rather than identity related notions, we argue that decisions concerning headscarves focus upon constitutional aspects of prohibitions. Institutional perception of Islam is simply juxtaposed with the constitutional principle of secularism and a wide margin of appreciation, in regulating matters of law and religion, is frequently invoked. Accordingly, the ECtHR decided that the case of *Dahlab* was manifestly ill-founded due to the potential proselytising effect of the garment which justified intervention of the state. The Court underlined that:

> [...] the Federal Court held that the measure by which the applicant was prohibited, purely in the context of her activities as a teacher, from wearing a headscarf was justified by the potential interference with the religious beliefs of her pupils at the school and the pupils' parents, and by the breach of the principle of denominational

[142] Further arguments on the oppositional relationship between Islamic and Western values exposed by the wearing of religious garments, such as *hijabs*, are made by Joppke (2009) and Todorov (2010).

> neutrality in schools. (*Dahlab*: para.1.)

Given that no complaint from the parents was ever brought against the applicant, Lucia Dahlab, the ECtHR's dismissal of the case was primarily based on the protection of denominational neutrality of the state as a preventive method of securing potential beliefs of others. In *Sąhin*, again by applying the doctrine of the margin of appreciation, a prohibition on the wearing of a *hijab* in a Turkish university was found to be compliant with the constitutional principle of secularism and therefore did not constitute infringement of Article 9. Here the Court referred even less to the applicant's rights and extensively elaborated on the Turkish constitutional principle of secularism and the entitlement of local authorities to preserve the principle:

> Having regard to the above background, it is the principle of secularism, as elucidated by the Constitutional Court, which is the paramount consideration underlying the ban on the wearing of religious symbols in universities. In such context, where the values of pluralism, respect for others and, in particular, equality before the law of men and women are being taught and applied in practice, it is understandable that the relevant authorities should wish to preserve the secular nature of the institution concerned and so consider it contrary to such values to allow religious attire, including, as the present case, the Islamic headscarf. (*Sąhin*: para.1.)

Similarly, in the case of *Şefika Köse* the ECtHR upheld the prohibition on wearing headscarves in Muslim state-funded Imam-Hatip Secondary Schools. It relied similarly on the domestic constitutional principle of secularism:

> In conclusion, the Court finds that the restriction in issue and the related measures were justified in principle and proportionate to the pursued aims of protecting the rights and freedoms of others, preventing disorder and preserving the neutrality of secondary education. (*Şefika Köse*: para.1.)

Analogically in *Dogru* the Court once more refused to examine compliance of secularism with freedom of religion as entrenched in the Convention and instead emphasised that in the French context when the applicant was forbidden to wear a headscarf while attending physical education classes:

> [...] the purpose of that restriction on manifesting a religious

> conviction was to adhere to the requirements of secularism in state schools, as interpreted by the Conseil d'Etat in its opinion of 27 November 1989 and its subsequent case-law and by the various ministerial circulars issues on the subject. (*Dogru*: para.1.)

Consequently, reference to a 'wide margin of appreciation', and concern over preservation of constitutional principles of the state, created a form of legal reasoning that focused on larger institutional frameworks such as constitutional order and left the identity and autonomy aspect of freedom of religion on the margins. Focusing on general notions such as secularism, democracy and tolerance these judgments artificially reduced discussion of identity related aspects of religion and the rights bearer's own perception of religious normativity. Subsequently a religious individual now equated with 'other' non-democratic and structural religions became juxtaposed with another institutional structure, namely constitutional and 'democratic' secularism. Therefore, in finding a balance between secularism and religion the arguments of the applicants regarding *their own* religious precepts were simply overlooked: considered irrelevant. In positioning the individual against institutional and constitutional notions the Court, for instance in *Şefika Köse,* simply considered it 'sufficient to note that both the parents and the pupils were informed of the consequences of not obeying the rules' (*Şefika Köse*: para.1.). This type of reasoning creates a problematic asymmetry between an individual and the national system that prevents the ECtHR from elaborating on the interaction between gender, religion and identity (Vakulenko 2007: 190). Motha ascertains that autonomy lies at the foundation of emancipatory politics in a heterogeneous society (Motha 2007: 145). When autonomy is universalised and standardised it generates a specific type of subjectivity and the emancipatory project turns against itself.[143] For example, juxtaposing the wearing of a *hijab* with values (such as gender equality, tolerance and a standardised image of a citizen in a democratic society) results in a denial of autonomy of the rights bearer (see the quotation from the *Dahlab* judgment, above). In her dissenting opinion in *Sąhin*, Judge Tulkens also emphasised that what was essentially lacking from the debate on religious dress are the actual voices of women who wear these garments themselves (*Sąhin* judgment: para. 11). For this reason, European Governments and Courts should take into account the complex reasons why women choose to cover their heads and/or bodies.

---

[143] Bhandar, for example, argues that the liberal ideologies of secularism and multiculturalism, both employed as techniques by political states to govern the differences between people, generate their own particular type of subjectivity: a liberal individual who is ostensibly Christian (Bhandar 2009).

To summarise, the ECtHR has upheld decisions made by public institutions which have banned a *hijab* from being worn. The decisions discussed in this section of the paper focused on the institutional aspect – the maintenance of the secular tradition and the right of the ECtHR to interfere in the constitutional tradition – rather than the complex relationship between autonomy, heteronomy and a woman's own perception of *her* body and identity and the reasons behind *her* behaviour, which *she* believes to be dictated by another normative order other than state-law.

## II. Different Conceptualisations of Legal Pluralism

We argue that the unwillingness of the ECtHR to provide a clear articulation of whether the foundations of the constitutional system are in fact compliant the requirements 'necessary in a democratic society', aspects which the Court weighs simultaneously, stem from its decisions being based on considerations prevalent in transnational and constitutional pluralist ideas concerning the multiplicity of intersecting legal orders. In the following sub-sections, we contend that because of a constitutional (or institutional) pluralistic focus, and the marginalisation of socio-legal studies, no attempt to contextualise rights and the position of rights bearers in their specific legal, historical and social context is presently undertaken (Vakulenko 2007).

### *A. Transnational and Constitutional Pluralist Approaches to Rights*

Transnational and constitutional pluralists are primarily concerned with the coexistence of external legal orders interfering with the state legal order, for example, the human rights norms created by supranational and international legal systems. Following the Habermasian analysis of cosmopolitan justice (Habermas 2001), the theory of European constitutional pluralism focuses upon the tensions between national and *inter* and *supra*national normative orders and the functioning of the post-national community(ies) (Fine and Smith 2003). European human rights theorists are increasingly interested in the relationship between international human rights and domestic human rights as well as human rights and domestic democracy (Besson 2011: 33). And even though human rights play a pivotal role in searching for new models of supranational governance, the dominant approach in analyses of European rights pluralism is primarily constitutional and institutional. European rights theorists analysing European legal orders attempt to describe and classify the plurality of different constitutional and rights orders in diverse ways, but primarily do so through the perspective of the mutual influence between these orders. In the pluralist interpretation of the relationship between legal orders, individuals are seen by European legal pluralists as a part of imagined communities (Anderson 1991) – national and international (Nash 2003) - rather than rights bearers. In the analyses of European rights pluralism, rights bearers are absorbed by imagined community(ies) representing larger constitutional and legal frameworks. As a result legal orders such as systems of human rights protection are seen as interacting orders (Besson 2009a). Typically then, these theoretical arguments focus primarily upon the polarization between international constitutionalisation of human rights standards and their pluralisation: in other words, coherence and fragmentation of legal orders and human rights approaches.

For example Sweet argues that international regimes, such as the EU or ECHR, naturally create tensions between systems (Sweet 2009). In fact, these tensions can, and normally do, generate norms that gradually become constitutional and thus legitimate. The fact of pluralism can never be extinguished and the pluralist-constitutional dichotomy is only a different way of describing the same variable. Eventually constitutional pluralism generates a body of *jus cogens* norms, which among others, argues Sweet, include basic human rights norms. In other words, appropriate contextualisation and interpretation of freedom of religion, for example, happens over time as a result of tension between national and international orders and necessarily bears costs such as controversial judgments.

Besson, on the other hand, puts primary emphasis on the question of legitimacy of human rights norms in a condition of legal pluralism (Besson 2008). Besson questions perspectivist approaches in which every order has its own perspective and its own solutions for the pluralism of norms. In her account, any monist approaches to international regimes are unwarranted due to their limited democratic pedigree. Coherence, argues Besson, is far from logical consistency and therefore coherence between fundamental rights and other fundamental values guaranteed by national normative orders, the ECHR and other international human rights instruments, is not enough to resolve conflicts of law (Besson 2009a). Therefore, the close relationship between human rights and democracy requires legalisation of human rights being created in each given political community. That requires, given the current state of the international community which lacks appropriate legitimacy, legalisation of human rights primarily at the domestic level. International human rights then, argues Besson, can be regarded as human rights only if they match in a minimal way an existing set of domestic human rights (Besson 2011: 40).

Having similar concerns in mind, Joseph Weiler in his commentary concerning another case dealing with religious symbols, this time crucifixes, argues that:

> The European Court of Human Rights is not an Oracle. It is a dialogical partner with the Member States Parties to the Convention, and the legitimacy and persuasiveness of its decisions resides both in their quality and communicative power. The ECtHR is simultaneously reflective and constitutive of the European constitutional practices and norms. When there is a diverse constitutional practice among the Convention States - and there certainly is in this area - the Court needs to listen, not only preach, and to be seen to be listening. (Weiler 2010: 1, commenting on *Lautsi v Italy*.)

These fears of unwarranted interference in a domestic constitutional order by international courts such as the ECtHR results in what Carrozza calls being caught on the dual horns of affirming unity and respecting diversity (Carrozza 1997-1998: 1217-1237). Greer and Williams affirm that the ECtHR has been perplexed by the problem of delivering both individual justice and constitutional justice. As constitutional justice, the authors understand delivering justice through primary constitutional principles: 'democracy', 'priority of rights', 'the rule of law', 'proportionality' and 'margin of appreciation' (Greer and Williams 2009: 467-470). With the emergence of the EU's rights regime, possible conflicts between unity and diversity have increased and so have possibilities of interpretation. Greer and Williams observe the emergence of the EU's institutional justice interpretation, which seeks justice for an institution rather than for individuals (Greer and Williams 2009: 478).

Due to the concerns for legitimacy and democracy of international human rights, the ECtHR's judgments in matters such as regulating religious garments, focus on a 'wide margin of appreciation' as a safe balancing principle. Individual justice becomes secondary and instead we find a simple reference to constitutional systems of the Member States. Rejection of individual conduct contradictory to these principles is left without due analysis and rather than examine whether the constitutional principles infringes upon rights of individuals and therefore in unwarranted ways impacts upon their belief, autonomy and identity, the analysis is reversed. The question that the Courts dealt with was not whether Turkey, France and Switzerland infringed freedom of religion of the applicant but whether the applicants infringed the constitutional principles, with which the ECtHR did not find itself legitimate to interfere.

*B. Missing Insights in the European Rights Discourses – Socio-Legal Perspectives*

Alongside constitutional and transnational legal pluralists, socio-legal pluralists also present an image of law as a multiplicity of interacting normative orders. However, their focus is directed frequently towards the analysis of intersections between state-law and other normative orders, such as religious law (Sandberg 2011).[144] In their analysis the concerns are not related to preservation of a legitimate human rights order but instead focus on the legitimacy of the state order to interfere with other normative orders structuring the identity of legal subjects.

The current sub-section considers three legal pluralist analyses of the leading UK case on religious dress *R (on the application of Begum) v Headteacher and Governors of Denbigh High School* (*Begum*). Since the case was never brought to the ECtHR, the discussion did not oscillate between preservation of state-law and its relationship with the ECHR norms but rather focused on the applicant and the question of whether the alleged exclusion of a student for breaching the school's uniform policy by wearing a *jilbab* infringed her right to manifest her religion under the Human Rights Act 1998. (This Act largely incorporates the ECHR into English state-law.) In contrast with the concern as to whether a constitutional principle shall be sufficiently respected and whether territorial divisions between constitutional and international law are maintained, socio-legal pluralists focus on illuminating the multiplicity of other normative conflicts and their impact upon the autonomy of the believer. The three legal pluralist analyses focused upon in the current sub-section are: first, social-scientific legal pluralism; second, a notion of legal pluralism that is sensitive to the cultural and religious diversity of normative orders; and finally, critical legal pluralism.

First, social-scientific legal pluralists tend to question which normative order(s) have jurisdiction over a particular legal subject in a situation at a given time. Drawing upon Griffiths' (1986) descriptive definition of legal pluralism, several laws can be seen to be operating in the particular situation that occurs in *Begum*. These are: *state-law* is apparent in the various court judgments of the case; *human rights law* on which Shabina's claim was based; institutional policies (notably the *uniform policy*) of Denbigh High School; and the *religious laws* Shabina viewed as obligating women to wear a *jilbab*. As well as illuminating the existence of a multiplicity of laws in this situation, a social-scientific legal pluralist analysis of

[144] Sandberg calls 'internal' spiritual laws made by religious groups themselves 'religious law' (Sandberg 2011: 10).

*Begum* details the particular interactions between the various normative orders (Jackson 2010). This analysis includes consideration of whether, and how, normative order(s) are incorporated into state-law.[145] For example, the decision upholds a weak element of pluralism by allowing schools discretion over their own uniform policies.[146] The overlapping relationships between different normative orders are illuminated by the social-scientific legal pluralist approach and the impact of the overlaps for situating the legal subject in particular rather than artificially reduced structural context is underlined.

Second, scholars such as Shah criticise Griffiths' legal pluralist approach for failing to account for the cultural and religious diversity of normative orders (Shah 2009). In comparison with Griffiths' image of law as the self-regulation of normative orders, Shah contends that Chiba's dynamic notion of the three-level system of law (which consists of official law, unofficial law and legal postulates) conceives a dynamic relationship between official and unofficial law (Chiba 1986). Menski extends Chiba's three-level system of law in his 'kite model' (Menski 2009).[147] Bhamra affirms that Menski's kite model illustrates that law is "the product of a variety of sources and processes that go beyond the nation-state" Bhamra 2011: 93. Bhamra provides a full account of Menski's kite model in Bhamra 2011: Chapter 9). When people encounter situations of legal pluralism they are not passive recipients of legal regulations; rather, they are active agents who actively choose to adopt a particular law from the multiplicity of rules that exist. Menski and Pearl further formulate a notion of hybrid laws, such as '*Angrezi*

---

145 One example is incorporation of certain rights under the ECHR into English state-law, for example, Article 13(2) of the Human Rights Act 1998 incorporates Article 9 of the ECHR into English law.

146 Following the reasoning of the ECtHR in the *Sąhin* case, which applies the doctrine of margin of appreciation in relation to the accommodation of religious dress by state parties, it was held that the school was given power by Parliament to decide on the appropriateness of its own school uniform policy.

147 Menski further described his model in a plenary session entitled 'Legal Pluralism and the Search for the "Right Law": Law as Kite Flying' at the Jubilee Congress on Legal Pluralism 8-10 September 2011, hosted by the University of Cape Town, South Africa. In his model Menski identifies four main sources of law: the state, society, natural and international law. He likens the push-and-pull factors of these sources of law to be like a flying kite. Absent from Menski's kite model, however, is the position of the legal subject.

*Shari'a*' law (Menski and Pearl 1998). Following this conception, the dynamism of official and unofficial law is revealed as legal subjects adapt their customary traditions into the regulations found in English law. A legal subject is perceived to be an active agent who chooses to follow both English law and their traditional customs simultaneously. In relation to the inter-normative conflicts created in cases such as *Begum,* Shah illustrates how this is generated by the struggle between the legal postulates of modernity and uniformity, on the one hand, and individual legal agency, on the other (Shah 2005: 177-179). Whereas the first is strongly affirmed by state-law, the second is relied upon by the applicant.

In liberal democratic societies, all citizens have a general duty to obey state-law, even though they may not agree with a particular policy. Any person who decides to break the law will be subject to judgment and the punishment which the state imposes. In his work Ssenyonjo considers the normative conflict(s) that surround the religious dress practices of women who wear a *hijab, jilbab, niqab* or *burqa* in Europe (Ssenyonjo 2008). In the search for appropriate solutions he refers to two perspectives of Islamic scholars. The first view is that Islamic religious dress practices are a strict religious obligation that applies to all women regardless of the laws of the state in which they reside. Under this view, passing a law which prohibits the wearing of a *hijab*, *jibab*, *niqab* or *burqa* interferes with women's freedom of religion and forces them to disobey *Allah*. The second view held by Islamic scholars recognises the obligatory nature of covering but argues that this is not obligatory in a non-Islamic state. Ssenyonjo refers to the statement of al-Azhar Muhammad Sayyid Tantawi to the French Minister of Internal Affairs (Nicholas Sarkozy), in 2003, that:

> The veil is a divine obligation for Muslim women [...] No Muslim ruling or ruled, has the right to oppose this obligation. However, this obligation is valid if Muslim women live in a Muslim state. Yet if they find themselves in a non-Muslim state (like France, for example) and their rules want to adopt law in opposition to the veil, it is their right. (Ssenyonjo 2008: 214).

Framed in the discourse of rights, Ssenyonjo states that Tantawi's argument is based upon his interpretation of the verses of the *Qur'an*, so that a woman who is prohibited by state-law from following the dress practices her religion commands should not fear divine punishment. Following this argument, in non-Islamic secular societies, such as Turkey or France, there is no religious obligation for a woman to cover. Ssenyonjo then goes on to state that the "obligation to wear the *hijab*, in a non-Islamic state which respects freedom of religion or belief, should be generally observed" (Ssenyonjo 2008: 164). Therefore, in non-Islamic societies that respect freedom of religion and belief, such as the UK, women should be allowed to follow their obligation to cover. Prohibitions of religious dress in these states are not justified, unless there is a special ground that justifies interference with one's religious beliefs (as provided under Article 9(2) ECHR).

Nevertheless, both Shah's and Ssenyonjo's approaches risk being overly simplistic: any approach that is sensitive to the cultural and religious diversity of *normative orders* can be criticised for essentialising human experiences of these orders and communities.[148] The communities and their boundaries might appear unsurpassable and homogenous. Scholars such as Al-Hibri, for example, observe that the religious practice of covering the head and/or body by a woman is not simply a religious *or* a cultural practice, rather a merger of both these realms (Al-Hibri 1999). Malik also illustrates the need to move from "single axis" descriptions, in terms of culture, *or* religion *or* gender, to pluralistic articulations (Malik 2008). She discusses the cases of *Sąhin* and *Begum* to illustrate how women who wear a *hijab* or a *jilbab* receive gender inequality in state-law's narrative. As part of the UK-based feminist judgments project, Malik agrees with the dissenting opinion of Judge Tulkens in *Sąhin* that an analysis is needed of the perspective of women who adopt Islamic dress practices (Malik 2010). Malik argues that, rather than creating a conflict for the respondent in cases, such as *Begum*, between the applicant's choice of religious dress as a member of a particular branch of Islam and her choice of preferred school as a British citizen and a member of the wider community, state-law should enable both the recognition of her culture as well as her religion and right to access education (or employment): both are public goods which are also important for her autonomy. While there is much to be credited by Malik's approach, which places Shabina at the centre of the House of Lords' decision, she does not consider Shabina's own narrative or how she experienced wearing a *jilbab* as law.

Finally, in order to overcome the potential essentialisation of personal experiences, critical legal pluralists such as Kleinhans and Macdonald challenge assumptions that confine an image of law to simply legislation interpreted by state institutions or to the self-regulation of normative orders (Kleinhans and Macdonald (1997).

[148] In order to overcome this criticism, Bano captures the narrative accounts of British Pakistani Muslim women to document what they make of the claims of *shari'a* councils, in relation to divorce proceedings, in their own lives (Bano 2008).

Instead, they imagine law as autobiographical: what *is* law, in a particular situation, is found in the human imagination and is captured in the narrative accounts of people (Macdonald 2002). On the one hand, scholars such as Melissaris question whether a pluralistic approach that locates law within the subjectivity of people can "say anything meaningful about the concept of law" (Melissaris 2009: 5). This is because every person, out of approximately the seven billion in the world, will have their own ideas about what law *is*. On the other hand, Kleinhans and Macdonald affirm that their notion of critical legal pluralism does not undermine the concept of law, instead it is:

> [...] a call for a more intense scrutiny of the legal subject conceived as carrying a multiplicity of identities [...] It takes as its starting point the assumption that all hypotheses of normativity merit consideration from a legal point of view. (Kleinhans and Macdonald 1997: 40)

Macdonald convinces us that "rules are only as good as the reasons behind them" (2002: 86). For this reason, law is also phenomenological. In the broad sense, philosophical phenomenology can be defined as the analysis and description of everyday life - the life world and the associated states of consciousness of human beings (Sokolowski 2000: 2).[149] Phenomenology stresses the importance of analysis and interpretation of the structure of conscious experiences of the relationships of human agents. A phenomenological study of law reveals the importance of reasons behind establishing law-inventing and law-abiding behaviours of the state, cultural and religious groups and their members.[150]

Empirical research conducted with a random sample of women who wear a *hijab* or a *niqab* in the UK indicates that these participants are aware that their human rights may be infringed by any prohibition of these religious practices (Jackson

[149] Critical legal pluralists follow the dialectical-phenomenology of the Hegelian tradition (for an introduction see Taylor 1985), rather than the transcendental-phenomenology established by Husserl (for an introduction to this approach see Sokolowski 2000), or the methodological approach of hermeneutic-phenomenology proposed by Schutz (1962).

[150] In comparison to the approach proposed in this paper, Reinarch conducted a phenomenological study of positivist law. He uses a phenomenological approach to reveal the essence of the structure of civil law by engaging in descriptions of a claim, an obligation and a promise. (Reinarch 1983)

2011). For example, participants in the study stated that "there are human rights as well...the Universal Declaration of Human rights...is a very solid basis on which they [European states' infringements of the right to religion] can be challenged" (Mona, a post-graduate student from Pakistan who wears a *hijab*). Another participant commented that "I don't think that they [European governments] have a right to tell us how to practice our religion" (Raani, an undergraduate student born in the UK, whose parents originate from Pakistan and who wears a *hijab*). However, one study participant, Cynthia (a contractual negotiator for a finance company, who wears a *hijab*, and whose family originates from Mauritius) stated that even if she were to take her employers to court, if they were to introduce a prohibition of the garment at her place of work, she felt that the court would find in favour of her employer. On this point another study participant, Ghazala (who wears a *hijab* and is a nursery nurse from Algeria) asserted that "I would stop, to be honest with you, I wouldn't carry on [working there]; the work is not my life, the religion is my life". Forcing or prohibiting women to wear a *hijab*, *jilbab*, *niqab* or *burqa* is equally limiting to a woman's liberty.

Building upon the arguments made in the previous section, what is omitted in the ECtHR's analysis in the cases such as *Dahlab, Sąhin*, *Şefika Kőse* and *Dogru* are the normative perspectives of the legal subject (or rights bearer) themselves.

## III. Encouraged and Discouraged Forms of Legal Pluralism – Internal and External Perspectives

Bearing in mind the divergent legal pluralist analyses of rights illustrated above, we ask the question how the diverse legal pluralist theory impacts upon the fact of the legal pluralism of rights, which we understand to be the fact of coexistence of diverse legal and normative orders regulating rights, for instance state law, international law, European law, religious law, custom, legal postulates and other forms of law distinguished in scholarship. In the section below we illustrate how certain types of rights pluralism are slowly acknowledged as acceptable while others are systematically discouraged. We also examine what these developments mean for freedom of religion in particular.

Despite the importance of socio-legal studies for the intersectional (Vakulenko 2007) positioning of legal subjects and in spite of socio-legal pluralists' pleas for more culture-sensitive, context-specific and autonomy-related approach to rights mentioned above, European courts such as the ECtHR either carefully omit or specifically reject forms of internal legal pluralism. Meerschaut and Gutwirth illustrate that the ECtHR explicitly rejects legal pluralism of different legal regimes within state-law as contrary to human rights (Meerschaut and Gutwirth 2008). In the case of *Refah Partisi (the Welfare Party) and Others v Turkey,* for example, the Court elaborated that "a difference in treatment between individuals in all fields of public and private law according to their religion and belief manifestly cannot be justified under the Convention" *(Refah Partisi*: para. 119*)*. In this judgment the Court explicitly rejected a form of internal legal pluralism, meaning multiplicity of different legal orders within a territory of the same state (Maduro 2007; Kleinhans and Macdonald 1997). The Court emphasised that this type of pluralism is contrary to the principle of equality and may lead to unjustified discrimination.

At the same time, however, forms of external legal pluralism have become a reality of European rights regimes. External legal pluralism we understand to be pluralism created by regimes stemming from outside of the legal order of a state (Maduro 2007). Institutional, constitutional and competence driven interpretations of human rights are slowly becoming a reality of European human rights regimes. In the European legal space, external human rights pluralism stems from the existence of at least three mutually influencing rights orders. These are: first, the constitutional traditions of European states; second fundamental rights protection based on the EU normative order, including the Charter of Fundamental Rights (EU Charter), and third, international law protection stemming from the ECHR.[151] We argue that European Courts, including both ECtHR and ECJ thanks to their constitutional and institutional interpretation, create external forms of legal pluralism of human rights. Overlaps and conflicts between the constitutional and international rights and their implication for women who cover their heads and bodies are illustrated here by the cases that emerged before the ECtHR. More interestingly, however, strong forms of external pluralism are created by jurisprudence concerning the relationship between European human rights stemming from the ECHR and fundamental rights stemming from the EU Charter.

The cases of *Yassin Abdullah Kadi and Al Barakaat International Foundation v. Council of the European Union and Commission of the European Communities*

---

[151] Another possible overlap of human rights protection systems that may develop further pluralisation of rights standards stems from non-regional international human rights documents. For example, in the latest periodic report concerning Turkey CEDAW focused on possible consequences of headscarf bans and exclusion of women that such a ban may lead to (UN 2010).

(*Kadi*) before the ECJ, and *Bosphorus Hava Yollari Turizm ve Ticaret Anonim Sirketi v. Ireland* (*Bosphorus*) before the ECtHR, as well as multiple cases referring to "wide margin of appreciation" accept uneven and interwoven force of diverse interacting legal regimes. In other words external legal pluralism of rights is not discouraged. Concerns for independence of legal regimes and "territory" of influence of international, European and constitutional law in regulating a person's basic rights have lead gradually to the coexistence of different rights regimes (Greer and Williams 2009).

In the case of *Kadi,* the ECJ emphasised the importance of former Article 6 (now Article 2) in protection of fundamental rights and expanded the competence of the Court to review compliance as entrenched in the Treaties. However, the approach to rights remained Europe-centred and based upon the idea of compliance with EU constitutional principles and fundamental rights rather than international human rights obligations (Besson 2009b). Gráinne de Búrca criticised the pluralist interpretation of European and international law despite greater significance given to rights (de Búrca 2009). Pluralist reading, according to de Búrca, underlined the internal and external autonomy of the EU legal order, which may encourage other systems to assert their local constitutional norms as a barrier to enforcement of international law. In other words, the ECJ encouraged the assertion of local understandings of human rights and their particular constitutional priorities over international law. If the Court sustains its current approach, the Community order will continue to be governed by the Community order itself. In the case of international law obligations permeating to the EU order, it will still be the EU norms and internal fundamental rights understanding that will be seen as taking priority over international law (Besson 2009b: 252). For women adopting religious dress practises, this type of rights pluralism may generate problematic situations when permissible forms of covering become regulated differently when in employment relations with EU institutions and in other relationships between the rights bearer and the state.

Finally, in the case of European legal orders a different constellation in the relationship between the EU and ECHR may give rise to a certain asymmetry of rights. The question of the revision of the Community's obligations in the light of human rights standards came under judicial scrutiny in the case of *Bosphorus* before the ECtHR where an equivalence of a rights test was developed. In the case, the ECtHR dealt with questions of jurisdiction over provisions of Community law. The key issue in the case was whether Ireland infringed the provisions of the ECHR by application of Community law. Upon analysis the ECtHR found the protection of rights provided by the Community law 'equivalent' to that of the Convention system

(*Bosphorus*: para. 165). However, in agreement with Douglas-Scott, we see it as necessary to emphasise that the equivalence test was very general and focused on the overall evolution of ECJ fundamental rights rather than the actual circumstances of the case and the actual approach to particular rights (Douglas-Scott 2006). The presumption of equivalence is therefore criticised for creating a potentially privileged position for EU law before the ECtHR without actual review of the standard in question (Sumner 2008). Following van den Berghe, if the EU's fundamental rights are automatically presumed to protect rights in the same way as the ECHR does, two standards of interpretation of rights obligations may occur (van den Berghe 2010). The first one will be applied to the Member States and the second one, based on the assumption of equivalence to the EU; this may lead as a result to inequality in treatment. Equivalence presumption may diversify the European understanding of rights in the name of autonomy of various normative orders. In the case of religious dress practices of women, this type of asymmetry may mean that the rights obligations of member states and EU organs could be outlined differently. If any norms under the EU system concerning the religious dress practices develop, they might be automatically presumed as 'equivalent' to those of the ECtHR.

Multiple combinations of equally effective systems with differently understood and selectively applicable concepts of freedom of religion may occur in European rights systems leading to visible differences in treatment. Thus, a multiplicity of legal orders may apply in, for instance, a situation of a Muslim civil servant working in an EU institution who decides to start wearing a *niqab* leading to possible difference in treatment at work. In this case, the freedom to wear such a garment could be defined and limited differently if applicable in connection with EU law, when understood as freedom of religion under the ECHR and in the constitutional system of the particular state. The ECJ has not yet considered religious dress practices in its case-law, but this issue may arise before the ECJ in the area of employment relations and fall under the Employment Equality Directive (Council Directive 2000/78/EC). Due to problems of enforceability such as limited *locus standi* and limited area of competences to which the fundamental rights norms of the Charter apply (Gozdecka 2012) it might take time before such a case is brought before the ECJ. However, should such a case arise, it would define the number of possible rights overlaps in the context of religious garments.

These diverse rights constellations create an external European legal pluralism of rights stemming from considerations of autonomy of legal orders, which may lead to internal pluralism and to difference in treatment. Unlike with internal legal pluralism, however, external pluralism contextualises rights by their placement closer to imagined rather than relevant legal and political communities - European and national. These communities being far from the rights bearer's own community are likely to have different concerns than the questions of autonomy, heteronomy, majority, minority, subjectivity and identity in the conflict of rights such as freedom of religion. Having in mind the complex nature of rights such as freedom of religion it appears unjustified that external legal pluralism of human rights appears possible, whereas internal legal pluralism is discouraged. Given the complex reasons behind practices such as wearing *hijab* or *jilbab*, it appears more legitimate to contextualise rights by placing them closer to communities relevant for rights bearers. Categorisation of internal pluralism as 'undemocratic' as in the *Refah Partisi* case, and equation of Islam as 'undemocratic' as with the cases concerning religious garments, appears less convincing given the growing external pluralism of European human rights.

We argue that this development is misguided and leads to the situation of a deadlock in interpretation of rights such as freedom of religion. In the context of religious garments, rights bearers are caught between a plurality of potentially competing understandings of human rights none of which takes into consideration the applicants' own understanding of rights and normative obligations. If the current diverse interpretation of human and fundamental rights in combination with equivalence standards but without regard to deep conflicts of other normative orders encountering state law is sustained, many different normativities concerning religious dress practises may arise and bring about what Motha calls a "civil war" of different heteronomies encountering autonomy (Motha 2007: 155). In order to avoid such intransigent war of different heteronomies we argue that European rights pluralism requires contextualisation which could be based upon adopting the forms of analysis applied by socio-legal pluralists. Institutional legal pluralist analyses of interactions between different legal orders are not sufficient to cover the multiple levels of inter-normativity faced by religious believers.

## IV. Towards Greater Contextualisation of Rights – Combining Transnational, Constitutional and Socio-Legal Perspectives

As illustrated by the findings from an empirical study conducted with women who wear a *hijab* or *niqab* in the UK (Jackson 2011), people are constantly pushed and pulled in various directions due to their normative commitments. Within these situations, however, there exists a space within which a person can interpret the way his or her commitments make sense for them. A person holds a consciousness and creative capacity to overcome possible normative conflicts between, for example, gendered, cultural, religious and Western values. Some normative conflicts may prove difficult to resolve, as they result in a position of deadlock.[152] A deadlock position between two or more laws is generated for a variety reasons. One example of such a conflict is the situations encountered by applicants or claimants wanting to wear a *hijab* or *jilbab* and work, or attend a school or university. In such cases, although the courts are provided the authority to decide these conflicts, judges do not appear to take into consideration the aspects of inter-normativity that cause applicants to be caught between different forms of pluralism. Whereas external forms of legal pluralism are increasingly accepted and given consideration, internal forms are explicitly discouraged. Nevertheless, as we have shown and as Kleinhans and Macdonald observe, law (including state-law) is not homogenous:

> There will always be a plurality of unofficial legal orders competing with each other and with State law. And State law itself is multiple. This latter multiplicity is both internal and external [...] In other words, for legal pluralists, State law itself typically comprises multiple bodies of law, with multiple institutional reflections and multiple sources of legitimacy. (Kleinhans and Macdonald 1997: 31-32)

Divergent approaches of legal pluralists generate diverse responses to the problem of conflict of laws. European legal pluralists focus upon the conflict of institutional legal orders. However, as stated above, this is likely to result in the omission of the relevant perspectives of the rights bearer (or legal subject) in the space where legal and normative orders intersect. Following Macdonald we contend that "[t]he best response to the inevitable existence of informal [law] is not to suppress it...[r]ather, the best response is to give it a productive institutional outlet" (Macdonald 2002: 28). In this final part of the paper we argue for a more contextualised approach to the conflicts of laws in the situations concerning women who follow Islamic dress practices.

However, we do not understand contextualisation as legalisation of rights by their placement closer to a domestic state law system, as for instance argued by Besson (2011) or by reference to an even wider 'margin of appreciation' as Weiler (2010) does, nor by greater reliance on constitutional principles as argued by Greer and

[152] The result of, and other possible ways to overcome, an impossible compromise stemming from the deadlock position is discussed elsewhere (Sandberg and Jackson n.d.).

Williams (2009). Such conceptualisations take into consideration only one side of inter-normativity and do not sufficiently conceptualise the position of a rights bearer (or legal subject) in situations where constitutional conflict pertains to the area of basic rights relevant for autonomy and identity. Frerichs observes the problem of abstract conceptualisation of "fictional" units such as nations, regions, normative orders and other functional systems in the European legal pluralist discourses (Frerichs 2010). Functional collectives identified by transnational legal pluralists, underlines Frerichs, work "behind the backs" of individuals who are unable to identify with them. Trying to integrate the two perspectives, Frerichs proposes a cobweb model of pluralisms consisting of concentric circles joined by radii. Seen from the centre, the cobweb of pluralisms represents the rights bearers (or legal subjects) perspective. The concentric web circles represent territorial collectives and functional systems, whereas the radii in the cobweb illustrate pluralisation and constitutionalisation.

While, the question of how these three perspectives interact remains rather open in Frerichs work, we argue that it may serve as a useful and valuable model in better contextualizing human rights. In conflict of laws, including practices affecting identity and autonomy, we argue that it is necessary to look at normative conflicts, not merely through a systemic and institutional lens. We must examine how people make sense of diverse obligations and how their autonomy and identity are impacted by the coexistence of diverse legal and normative obligations. Frerichs's cobweb model opens up a possibility of a more comprehensive approach to the conflict of rights by focusing the analysis both on the constitutional and institutional aspects as well as the perspectives of the rights bearers.

Following Meerschaut and Gutwirth we argue that:

> [...] a multiplicity of human rights, constitutional principles and interests are interwoven in the matter of legal pluralism - some overlapping, some competing. When balancing these rights and interests in relation to the accommodation of religious law, one should contextualise. Balancing Islamic law and religious freedom on the one hand, and secularism and equality on the other is far too reductionist and simplistic. The issue of accommodation of Islamic law is not an issue of general and abstract statements but it demands careful attention to practice and understanding of Islamic law. Such balancing is thus not about 'the' sharia or 'the' Islam or 'the' secular republic. [...] Human agency plays a crucial role in the conception and development of Islamic laws. (Meerschaut and

Gutwirth 2008: 464)

Human rights pluralism becomes a reality of our time as Kinley notices (Kinley 2012). A growing need to secure democratic legitimacy of rights and the necessity of taking diverse dimensions of rights into consideration reveals the inherent indeterminacy of human rights and their necessary openness to some degree of differential application. Due to this indeterminacy, human rights will naturally be "bendable" and open to pluralistic interpretations. The central problem of rights pluralism becomes its manageability in a way where the potential of rights is retained. A plurality of legal pluralisms can, according to Kinley, be manageable only by sketching certain roughly drawn limits that should not be crossed. These limits in Kinley's account, include among others the potential of rights for empowerment of rights bearers (or legal subjects) and they cannot be empowered if their identity and agency is not viewed as an integral part of legal pluralistic equations (Kinley 2012).

## Conclusion

As illustrated by the reasoning in the ECtHR cases such as *Dahlab*, *Sạhin, Şefika Köse* and *Dogru* the European rights discourse does not adequately discuss the lived reality of pluralism. In these cases women who wear a *hijab* are caught between multiple of approaches towards these garments. These include, for example: different forms of dress expected from the perspective of their faith; different expectations of dress when working or studying at an institution, such as a state school or university, and yet other expectations of dress when walking down the street.

In Europe, the reaction to garments such as *hijabs* provides an example that the depth of normative conflicts of rights may not be limited to procedural and functional conflicts between state and inter-state normative orders. The conflict may go deeper and touch upon the very core of our notion of "freedom". In our analysis of various normative pressures on women wearing *hijabs, niqabs* and *jilbabs*, we have shown that normative overlaps become most apparent when they incorporate perspectives of rights bearers: a perspective otherwise overlooked by an institutional interpretation of legal conflicts.

In this paper, our primary goals were to first, begin bridging the gap between studies of transnational, constitutional and socio-legal pluralisms and their respective areas of concern - external and internal pluralism of rights; second, encourage future analyses by judges and researchers on the relationship between the state, cultural and religious groups and their members to acknowledge the plurality of legal pluralisms that exists; and finally, contextualize rights by considering a person's understanding and autonomy related to inter-normative conflicts. Having in mind the dichotomy of analysing pluralisms, observed by Frerichs, we have attempted to shift the focus of analysis from functional and institutional to a perspective that pays attention to legal subjects' accounts. Whereas we do not aim to exhaust possibilities of re-construction, we approach the plurality of pluralisms from the centre of Frerichs' cobweb. In the case of basic rights of pivotal importance, such as freedom of religion, it is not enough to search for institutional legitimacy. By removing rights bearers from the center and approaching rights pluralism only institutionally we may cross the roughly sketched lines that Kinley draws when he speaks about the "bendability" of boundaries of rights (Kinley 2012).

For the reasons outlined in this paper, we suggest more contextualised analysis of rights focusing on relevant rather than imagined communities. Such analyses could be conducted if the perspectives of rights bearers (or legal subjects) remain in the center of discussions concerning institutional inter-normativity. In the case of freedom of religion, it is necessary to investigate *both* how this freedom is influenced by diverse normative orders and how people make sense of being the irreducible site of inter-normativity. This is achieved by taking into account socio-legal methodologies such as qualitative methods of data gathering. What is currently missing from the European rights discourse on the topic of Islamic dress practices is the belief that rights bearers have autonomy and the creative capacity to construct their own *unique* identities. Since we suggest, that more contexualised versions of European legal pluralist analyses be undertaken, the question remains: Is it possible for judges and researchers analysing the relationship between law and society to combine institutional and socio-legal perspectives of legal pluralism as we propose? Or, are these perspectives incompatible or opposing ways of theorising (or approaching) infinite scenarios of legal pluralism?

## Legislation and Cases

European Convention on Human Rights and Fundamental Freedoms (1950) ETS No 5.

Charter of Fundamental Rights of the European Union, *Official Journal of the European Union*, C 303/1.

*Bosphorus Hava Yollari Turizm ve Ticaret Anonim Sirketi v. Ireland* [2005] ECHR 2005-VI.

*Dahlab v Switzerland* [2001] ECHR 2001-V.

*Dogru v France* [2009] 47 ECHR.

*Lautsi v Italy* [2009] ECHR and Grand Chamber judgment [2011], Application No. 30814/06.

*R (on the application of Begum) v Headteacher and Governors of Denbigh High School* [2007] 1 AC 100; [2006] UKHL 15; [2006] 2 WLR 719; [2006] HRLR 21 (HL).

*Refah Partisi (the Welfare Party) and Others v Turkey* [2003] ECHR 37.

*Sąhin v Turkey* [2005] 44 ECHR 5

*Şefika Köse and 93 Others v Turkey* [2006] ECHR 20

*Yassin Abdullah Kadi and Al Barakaat International Foundation v. Council of the European Union and Commission of the European Communities*, Joined Cases C-402/05 P and C-415/05 P.

## References

AL-HIBRI, Aziah Y.

1999 'Is Western Patriarchal Feminism Good for Third/World Minority Women?' Pp. 41-46 in Susan Okin Miller et al. (eds.) *Is Multiculturalism Bad for Women? Susan Okin Miller With Respondents*. Princeton: Princeton University Press.

ANDERSON, Benedict

1991 *Imagined Communities: Reflections on the Origin and Spread of Nationalism*. London and New York: Verso.

BANO, Samia

2008 'In Pursuit of Religious and Legal Diversity: A Response to the Archbishop of Canterbury and the 'Shar'ia Debate' in Britain'. *Ecclesiastical Law Journal* 10: 282–309.

BESSON, Samantha

2008 'How International is the European Legal Order?: Retracing Tuori's Steps in the Exploration of European Legal Pluralism'. *Journal of Extreme Legal Positivism* 5: 50-70.

2009a 'Whose Constitution(s)? International Law, Constitutionalism, and Democracy'. Pp. 381-407 in Jeffrey L. Dunoff and Joel P. Trachtman, *Ruling the World? Constitutionalism, International Law, and Global Governance*. Cambridge: Cambridge University Press.

2009b 'European Legal Pluralism after Kadi'. *European Constitutional Law Review* 5: 237-264.

2011 'Human rights and democracy in a global context: decoupling and recoupling'. *Ethics and Global Politics* 4(1): 19-50.

BHAMRA, Meena K.

2011 *The Challenges of Justice in Diverse Societies: Constitutionalism and Pluralism*. London: Ashgate.

BHANDAR, Brenna

2009 'The Ties that bind: Multiculturalism and Secularism Reconsidered'. *Journal of Law and Society* 36(3): 301-326.

BÚRCA, Gráinne de

2009 'The European Court of Justice and the International Legal Order after *Kadi'*. *Harvard International Law Journal* 51(1): 1-51.

CARROZZA, Paolo G.

1997-1998 'Uses and Misuses of Comparative Law in International Human Rights: Some Reflections on the Jurisprudence of the European Court of Human Rights', *Notre Dame Law Review* 73(5): 1217-1237.

CHIBA, Masaji (ed.)

1986 *Asian Indigenous Law in Interaction with Received Law*. London: KPI.

DOUGLAS-SCOTT, Sionaidh

2006 'Bosphorus Hava Yollari Turzim Ve Ticaret Anonim Sirketi v. Ireland'. *Common Market Law Review* 4: 243-254.

EVANS, Carolyn

2006 'The "Islamic Scarf" in the European Court of Human Rights. M*elbourne Journal of International Law* 7: 52-73.

FINE Robert and Will SMITH

2003 'Jürgen Habermas's Theory of Cosmopolitanism'. *Constellations: An International Journal of Critical and Democratic Theory* 10(4): 469-487.

FRERICHS, Sabine

2010 'Constitutional Ideal Types in the Global Age: A Sociological Review'. Pp. 69-88 in Kaarlo Tuori, and Suvi Sankari, *The Many Constitutions of Europe*. Farnham/Burlington: Ashgate Publishing.

GOZDECKA, Dorota A.

2012 'Human rights, fundamental rights and the common constitutional traditions in the protection of religious pluralism and diversity in Europe – a study in the democratic paradox. *Finnish Yearbook of International Law* 2010(1): 169-190.

GREER, Steven and Andrew WILLIAMS

2009 'Human Rights in the Council of Europe and the EU: Towards 'Individual', 'Constitutional' or 'Institutional' Justice?' *European Law Journal* 14(4): 462-481.

GRIFFITHS, John
1986 'What is Legal Pluralism?' *Journal of Legal Pluralism,* 24: 1–55.
GUNN, Jeremy T.
2005 'Fearful Symbols: The Islamic Headscarf and the European Court of Human Rights.' *Strasbourg Consortium: Freedom of Conscience and Religion at the European Court of Human Rights,* available at: http://www.strasbourgconsortium.org/document.php?DocumentID=3846 , accessed on 30 April 2012.
HABERMAS, Jürgen
2001 *The Postnational Constellation: Political Essays*. Cambridge, Mass.: MIT Press.
JACKSON, Amy
2010 'A Critical Legal Pluralist Analysis of the *Begum* Case'. *Osgoode Hall LawSchool Comparative Research in Law and Political Economy Research Paper Series,* Research Paper No. 46/2010: 1-25.
2011 *What is Law? Unveiling Subjective Legal Pluralism*. PhD Thesis, University of Reading.
JOPPKE, Christopher
2009 *Veil: Mirror of Identity*. Cambridge: Polity.
KINLEY, David
2012 'Bendable Rules: The Development Implications of Human Rights Pluralism'. Pp. 50-65 in Brian Z. Tamanaha, Caroline Sage and Michael Woolcock (eds.), *Legal Pluralism and Development: Scholars and Practitioners in Dialogue*. Cambridge: Cambridge University Press.
KLEINHANS, Martha-Marie and Roderick A. MACDONALD
1997 'What is a Critical Legal Pluralism?' *Canadian Journal of Law and Society* 12(2): 25-46.
MACDONALD, Roderick A.
2002 *Lessons of Everyday Law*. Montreal: McGill Queen's University Press.
MADURO, Miguel Poiares
2007 'Interpreting European Law: Judicial Adjudication in a Context of Constitutional Pluralism'. *European Journal of Legal Studies* 2(1): 1-21.
MALIK, Malieha
2008 'Complex Equality; Muslim Women and the Headscarf'. *Droit et Societé, Revue Internationale de Théorie du Droit et Sociologie Juridique* 68(1): 127–152.
2010 '*R (Begum) v. Governors of Denbigh High School*: Judgment.' Pp. 336-344 in Rosemary Hunter, Clare McGlynn and Erika Rackley (eds.) *Feminist Judgments: From Theory to Practice*. Oxford: Hart Publishing.

MARSHALL, Jill
2008 'Women's Right to Autonomy and Identity in European Human Rights Law: Manifesting One's Religion'. *Res Publica* 14: 177-192.
MEERSCHAUT, Karen and Serge GUTWIRTH
2008 'Legal pluralism and Islam in the scales of the European Court of Human Rights: the limits of categorical balancing'. Pp. 431-465 in Eva Brems (ed.) *Conflicts Between Fundamental Rights*. Antwerp: Intersentia.
MELISSARIS, Emmanuel
2009 *Ubiquitous Law: Legal Theory and the Space for Legal Pluralism*. Bodmin: MPG Books.
MENSKI, Werner
2009 'Flying Kites in a Globalizing Sky and Dodgy Weather Forecast: Accommodating Ethnic Minority Laws in the UK'. *Journal of Multilingual Multicultural Studies and Practices* 2: 26-45 (in Japanese with an English abstract).
MENSKI, Werner and David PEARL
1998 *Muslim Family Law*. London: Sweet and Maxwell.
MOORE, Sally Falk
1973 'Law and Social Change: The Semi-Autonomous Social Field as an Appropriate Subject of Study'. *Law and Society Review* 7(4): 719–746.
MOTHA, Stewart
2007 'Veiled Women and the Affect of Religion in Democracy'. *Journal of Law and Society* 1(34): 139-162.
NASH, Kate
2003 'Cosmopolitan Political Community: Why Does It Feel So Right?' *Constellations* 10(4): 506-518.
REBOUCHÉ, Rachel
2009 'The Substance of Substantive Equality: Gender Equality and Turkey's Headscarf Debate'. *American University International Law Review* 24 (4): 711-737.
REINARCH, Adolf
1983 'The Apriori Foundations of the Civil Law', trans John F. Cosby. *Alethia* 3: 1-142.
SANDBERG, Russell
2011 *Law and Religion*. Cambridge: Cambridge University Press.
SANDBERG, Russell and Amy JACKSON
n.d. *Religion and Legal Pluralism*. Farnham: Ashgate, forthcoming.
SCHUTZ, Alfred
1962 *Collected Papers I: The Problem of Social Reality*. The Hague: Martinus Nijhof.

SHAH, Prakash
2005 *Legal Pluralism in Conflict: Coping with Cultural Diversity in Law*. London: Glasshouse Press.
2009 'Transforming to Accommodate? Reflections on the Shari'a Debate in Britain'. Pp. 73–93 in Ralph Grillo et al. (eds.), *Legal Practice and Cultural Diversity*. London: Ashgate.
SOKOLOWSKI, Robert
2000 *Introduction to Phenomenology*. Cambridge: Cambridge University Press.
SSENYONJO, Manisuli
2008 'Moslem Women, Religion and the Hijab: A Human Rights Perspective'. *South East African Journal of Peace and Human Rights* 14(1): 148–198.
SUMNER, Geoff
2008 'We'll Sometimes Have Strasbourg: Privileged Status of Community Law before the European Court of Human Rights'. *Irish Student Law Review* 16: 127-170.
SWEET, Alec Stone
2009 'Constitutionalism, Legal Pluralism, and International Regimes'. *Indiana Journal of Global Legal Studies* 16(2): 621-645.
TAYLOR, Charles
1985 *Human Agency and Language*. Cambridge: Cambridge University Press.
TODOROV, Tzvetan
2010 *Fear of the Barbarians*. Cambridge: Polity.
UN (UNITED NATIONS)
2010 'Concluding Observations of the Committee on the Elimination of Discrimination Against Women: Turkey.' United Nations: CEDAW/TUR/CO/6.
VAKULENKO, Anastasia
2007 '"Islamic Headscarves" and the European Convention on Human Rights: an Intersectional Perspective'. *Social and Legal Studies* 16: 183-199.
VAN DEN BERGHE, Frederic M.
2010 'The EU and Issues of Human Rights Protection: Same Solutions to More Acute Problems?' *European Law Journal* 16(2): 112-157.
WEILER, Joseph H.H
2010 'Lautsi: Crucifix in the Classroom Redux'. *European Journal of International Law* 21(1): 1-6.

# WHO IS GOVERNING FOOD SYSTEMS? POWER AND LEGAL PLURALISM IN LOBSTER TRACEABILITY

Courtenay E. Parlee and Melanie G. Wiber

## Introduction

Lobster fishing has a long history in Atlantic Canada and lobster has an iconic status in the region, as it is one of the few healthy commercial stocks remaining and is the economic mainstay of the independent, owner-operated inshore fleet.[1] Without lobster, many of the coastal communities impacted by the collapse of the groundfish stock would have collapsed in their turn. While lobster landings have been high, however, this has not translated into secure livelihoods, as marketing lobster remains a challenge. Many consumers view it as a luxury item and in the aftermath of the market shocks in 2009, and despite falling prices, lobster sales have declined. Both federal and provincial regulators[2] as well as regional

[1] The Atlantic Canada inshore fleet is comprised of owner-operated boats of under 50 feet in length. They are quite distinct from the midshore and offshore fleets, which are corporately owned and managed. Most inshore fishermen own multiple licenses and fish some combination of lobster, scallop, herring, groundfish, crab, gaspereau, shad and shrimp. Canadian fisheries "fleet separation" policy requires that boats in the inshore fleet remain independent from corporate (processor) control.

[2] Fisheries and Oceans Canada (DFO) is the federal department responsible for managing marine fisheries. Due to the Canadian division of powers, coastal provinces also have fishery departments.

© Copyright 2011 - Courtenay E. Parlee and Melanie G. Wiber.

fishermen's organizations responded with efforts to improve both market share and price. One option was to pursue some kind of market certification. In September 2010, the regional fishermen's organization in the Scotia-Fundy region of Atlantic Canada convinced several lobstermen to undertake a pilot traceability project. While traceability in the literature is often associated with food safety concerns, lobstermen were interested in traceability for quite different reasons. They hoped to accomplish several linked objectives, including: building confidence in the sustainability of lobster fishing; demonstrating the social and cultural value of the small boat sector and associated labour practices; improving the market share of Canadian lobster in the seafood retail sector; and obtaining a premium price for fishermen. Thus, traceability in the case of the Atlantic Canada lobster fishery was designed to pursue several goals. As will be outlined below, the emphasis on these goals differed depending on the position of participants in the market chain.

Some of the fishermen involved in the pilot traceability project were members of the Coastal Community University Research Alliance (Coastal CURA). This six-year, participatory research project had brought fishermen's organizations from three Canadian provinces and social scientists from three universities together to investigate and improve the role of communities in integrated ocean management (see www.coastalcura.ca)[3]. Several social scientists from the Coastal CURA agreed with fishermen that the traceability project provided an opportunity to assess the way that new regulations in the lobster industry were evolving. We began a qualitative analysis of lobster traceability by interviewing a lobster fisherman who was an early adopter of the traceability program. Using snowball sampling to identify further informants, we followed up with semi-structured interviews with executive directors of both local and national fishermen's organizations; these individuals had advocated for traceability among their membership and had taken a lead in negotiating with government agents and with a supportive NGO to develop the program. We then interviewed past and present employees of the environmental NGO involved in developing the lobster traceability project. We were also invited to attend several meetings where fishermen and lobster buyers discussed the program, as well as a workshop where fishermen, bureaucrats, wholesalers, retailers and staff from the NGO evaluated

[3] We gratefully acknowledge the contribution of several Coastal CURA students in the development of this paper, including D. Curtis, L. Wilson and K. Bigney. We also thank the Coastal CURA and the Canadian Social Sciences and Humanities Research Council for the funding support that enabled us to undertake this research.

the pilot project. Finally, we spoke to informants involved in several MSC certified fisheries, including the northern shrimp, Alaskan salmon and pollack fisheries. We report here on our case study findings.

This lobster traceability project proved a unique opportunity to investigate the assembly of people, organizations and regulatory approaches that are involved in lobster fisheries and marketing, as well as some of the consequences of that assembly. Live lobster, as a component of the fresh seafood industry offers a manageable case study, as there are no processing stages to track between ocean and plate. Nevertheless, even such a relatively simple case study illustrates the many "jurisgenerative institutions" (Anderson 1998) at various scales that are currently involved in governing food systems, and also traces some of the impacts of those multiple institutions on one industry. As a result, this project allows us to address several theoretical questions relating to governance and to legal pluralism.

We are sensitive to Offe's critique of the burgeoning use of the term governance, but here use the term in the sense he outlines, as:

> ...institutionalized, if often "informal" modes of interaction, in which the participants cooperate in a conscious and goal-oriented manner, while not exclusively pursuing their own interests, but also the common concerns of the members of a political community (or a large corporation). These, in turn, cannot be promoted (or at least not exclusively and in an efficient and effective way) through hierarchical sovereign action by the state... (Offe 2009: 553).

As Offe goes on to argue, the concept is attractive precisely because it acknowledges that neither state nor market are sufficient for some kinds of social coordination, but that "behind this voluntaristic façade, actual power relations and dependencies have all the more impact" (Offe 2009: 554). Following Foucault (1991) and Dean (1996), we are interested in the implications of the lobster traceability case study for understanding how governmentality[4] is connected to governance – that is, how technologies of power and of agency can be understood within this larger 'social coordination' context - how does traceability empower

[4] Following Foucault, government, as Dean notes, has been defined as "the conduct of conduct". A related concept is governmentality or "ways of thinking about, calculating and responding to a problem" (Dean 2010: 24).

some actors and perhaps disempower others? How do fishermen become convinced that they must be active participants within such governance projects? What is the (remaining) role of the state given the many other actors and agencies involved?

Recent literature on food governance provided a framework to explore the "tangled hierarchies" that bring state, international and local players together in food regulation. Linking food governance literature to the legal pluralism literature allowed us to think about how new traceability requirements in some jurisdictions generated multiple regulatory reactions in other jurisdictions. We could then examine the complexity and dynamics of the interrelationships that arise from multiple regulatory systems and to trace out their social and political significance (F. von Benda-Beckmann 2002: 65). This 'governance traceability' is something that cannot be tracked well with legal centrist approaches, which presuppose that the only relevant law is state law (sensu Anderson 1998; see also Zips and Weilenmann 2011).

We argue that the lobster traceability project also raises questions about transparency, legitimacy and democracy (see also Offe 2009: 556). The scale of such a project has meant that different agendas can be furthered at the same time, such as ecological sustainability, informed consumer choice, support for the inshore fishery and risk management. The resulting process has distributed power widely as Foucault once argued (Foucault 1991), but also led to power struggles. Finally, we illustrate that one outcome of such projects is legal pluralism in food governance.

## Traceability versus Sustainability Certification

There are some key areas of overlap but also some important differences between sustainability certification (often through eco-labels) and traceability, differences that are often obscured by the explosive growth of various kinds of food certification (Logan et al. 2008:1592; Jacquet and Pauly 2008; Foley n.d.). For purpose of clarification then, sustainability certification can be described as an environmental standard in which compliance to requirements are certified through various assessment methods. The requirements and assessments are typically issued by an independent certification organization (Global Development Research Center 2011). In fisheries, examples include the Marine Stewardship Council (MSC) and the FAO-Based Responsible Fisheries Management certification. From a public policy perspective, the objective of such certification is to inform consumers about the environmental consequences of the production and consumption of a product, in order to influence their purchasing behaviour and diminish negative environmental impacts (Jacquet and Pauly 2007). The objective of food traceability, on the other hand, is to address the growing complexity in a food product 'chain of custody', which is increasingly affected by mass production, global distribution and consumption patterns and that may affect food safety (Coff et al. 2008). A seafood traceability system, for example, requires that a seafood component be traceable from ocean to plate and through all intermediate steps. Because traceability is not always linked to sustainability objectives, and because sustainability certification is not always linked to traceability from ocean to plate (see Goyert et al. 2010; Logan et al. 2008; Jacquet and Pauly 2008), we deal with them here as separate issues.[5]

The MSC seafood label was developed in 1997 through a partnership between Unilever (one of the largest vertically-integrated food conglomerates in the world) and the World Wildlife Fund (Jacquet and Pauly 2007). It is an international private contractual standard that is often sought by producers and celebrated by food retailers and consumers. The credibility of an MSC label rests on adherence to agreed-upon standards (Kaiser and Edwards-Jones 2004). However, the connection between these standards and sustainability has been questioned (Foley 2012, n.d.), and one of the problems relates to traceability. The lobster industry provides an excellent example. As Foley notes, MSC assessment is done on behalf of 'clients', but those clients may not exclusively 'own' or engage with the entire fish stock upon which they rely (Foley 2012: 436-437). A case in point is the lobster industry. Fishermen's organizations in both Canada and the US have applied for separate MSC certification for the lobster fishery; whichever one achieves it first will have a significant market advantage. Those in the Scotia-Fundy region of Canada underwent a third party pre-assessment in 2009-2010. During this pre-assessment, problems were identified in all three of the principal areas assessed by MSC performance indicators, and fishermen were advised that MSC certification would fail (Park 2010: 87-88; MSC Review Committee 2010). Meanwhile, lobster fishermen in the adjacent US state of Maine are still pursuing certification, with the financial assistance of "a private organization" (Goyert et al. 2010: 1104). But as Canadian lobster fishermen know, lobster trace a tangled path on the way from ocean waters to consumer plate (ibid.). Given colder waters and

[5] Recent literature on MSC Certification, for example, identifies these as two separate but linked processes (Foley 2012: 439; Gale and Howard 2011). From the consumer point of view, both need to be in place to make informed choices.

harder shells, lobsters sourced from Canadian waters are often higher quality. They can be and often are marketed under brand names that represent them as having been caught in US waters. Further, many soft shell lobster sourced from US waters are processed in Canadian canneries (Goyert et al. 2010: 1104). As a result, it would be difficult to tell if all lobsters retailed through Walmart[6] were sourced only from US waters.

From the fishermen's perspective, the realities of the seafood industry have created some disenchantment with MSC certification, for several reasons, including: inability of fishermen to address ecological and governance problems assessed under MSC; the high cost of initial assessment and follow-up annual auditing (on both points see Goyert et al. 2010); and the political struggles between separate fishing organizations who fish the same stocks and compete for the advantages of MSC certification (see Foley 2012). Foley has also drawn attention to how the role of the Canadian government in meeting conditions of certification has actually strengthened state mechanisms of control (Foley n.d.). Even fisheries that have received certification have become disenchanted with MSC as is obvious from the salmon and pollack fisheries in Alaska.[7]

As many consumers have become aware, the difficulty of tracking seafood from sea to plate given the realities of wholesale practises has resulted in criticism for the certification approach. For example, there is room for 'counter marketing strategies' whereby exporters and domestic suppliers are able to re-label fish and sell them as eco-friendlier or higher quality versions (Jacquet and Pauly 2008; Logan et al. 2008). One result is a loss of confidence in the environmental regulations and consumer awareness campaigns upon which eco-labels rely (Jacquet and Pauly 2007). This may be one reason why Canadian lobster

[6] Walmart made a highly publicized commitment to sell only MSC certified seafood by the end of 2011, quickly followed by other major retailers. See http://www.msc.org/newsroom/news/kroger-costco-supervalu-and-walmart-include-msc-in-seafood-sustainability-commitments, last accessed February 8, 2012.

[7] Mark Buckley, personal communication May 22, 2012. Processors in the Alaskan salmon fishery have promoted the FAO-Based Responsible Fishing Standards as an alternative to MSC, see http://www.scribd.com/doc/78700313/ASMI-press-release-on-MSC, last accessed May 23, 2012, and http://www.scribd.com/doc/94253370/Alaska-salmon-processors-clarify-MSC-position, last accessed May 23, 2012.

fishermen we spoke to view food traceability systems as an alternative to MSC as we will explain further below.

The objective of food traceability is to address the growing complexity in a food product "chain of custody", which is increasingly affected by mass production, global distribution and consumption patterns (Coff et al. 2008). Martinez and Poole maintain that a secure food traceability system is based on four pillars that include: product identification (such as weight, volume, date of capture); data (including numbers, typologies and data storage requirements); product routing (the production cycle and equipment involved); and traceability tools that ensure data accuracy and data reliability (Martinez and Poole 2004: 350). Not all four of these are present in the lobster case, as the routing aspect remains underdeveloped to date. Despite this, the lobster traceability system as recently introduced in Atlantic Canada meets most regulatory requirements of food traceability as will become evident in this paper.

Food traceability is typically introduced for three reasons, including: risk management, to increase consumer trust and confidence, and to help in the search for efficiency gains (Hall 2010: 827). In this paper, we are concerned with the first two reasons, risk management and consumer choice. Arienzo et al. define risk management as "a device for the attribution for responsibility and reduction of risk" (Arienzo et al. 2008: 34). From this perspective, the primary beneficiary of traceability is thought to be any level of government that has the mandate to prevent and/or punish food safety failures. In this sense, traceability can serve as a 'technology of power' in Foucault's terms. A problem has been identified (food safety), defined as technical (linked to failures of sourcing, handling, processing, storage or distribution), a technical solution is devised (regulation, inspections, fines) and this in turn empowers government actors. We argue that traceability is a technical solution with regulatory and normative effects, and there are two reasons for this. First, the processes involved in the traceability project have created self-governing individuals who fit into new schemes of "order socialities" (see Edwards 2003). Second, this particular kind of assemblage has resulted in individuals agreeing to a range of normalizing measures and practices designed to empower fishermen and optimize their skills and entrepreneurship (see Dean 1996). These points will be illustrated in the following discussion.

Food traceability is also seen as enhancing informed choice for consumers, especially consumers who want to "capture and map the ethical dimensions of values and processes in the food production chain" (Coff et al. 2007: 4). For example, Coff et al. define traceability by reference to the highly public and visible "means of recorded identification" (Coff et al. 2007: 4), so that consumers can make choices based on more information than the market usually provides. This information can refer to labour practices, ecological sustainability, poverty reduction or other values that are normally hidden in price-driven mechanisms of the marketplace. The market visibility of labour practises was explicitly raised by the Executive Director of the Canadian Council of Professional Fish Harvesters[8], for example, when he spoke about the difference between the inshore fishery, with local, kin-based employment and remuneration through catch shares, and the large offshore factory trawlers that often exploit foreign workers[9]. He noted:

> These traceability tags are changing the face of marketing in the fishery. They knit together community - owner operator - and consumer preference. They are key to the decommodification of fish. For most commodities in the marketplace, the labor costs or community impact of how the commodity is produced is invisible. The customer only gets to choose on the basis of price. But these tags make the fishery visible to the buyer. Customers want to know the fishermen. Big corporate boats don't like [the tags] because consumers don't want to see factory trawlers as the source of their food. They want to feel they are supporting coastal communities and sustainable fisheries with their purchase.

This quote illustrates two other benefits for traceability that are cited in the literature. First, whether it is being pursued for risk management or consumer choice, traceability can enable consumers to participate in democratic processes that influence the current food supply. Second, it can provide food producers such as the lobster fishers in Atlantic Canada with the ability to promote the ethical aspects of their production practices and to communicate the ethical values of their products to consumers (Coff et al. 2008: 1). In Dean's terms, this may make traceability a 'technology of agency' in that subjects of the state are convinced that to engage with certain kinds of technology will help them to obtain their own ends, but often with unforeseen consequences that may also empower others (Dean

[8] This non-profit organization was founded in 1995 and promotes the health of the Canadian fishing industry by ensuring that harvesters have the knowledge and skills to meet present and future human resource needs in the fishery (see http://www.fishharvesterspecheurs.ca/about, last accessed May 2012).

[9] For an example of the problematic labor practices sometimes found associated with the international corporate fleets, see Stringer et al. 2011.

1996).

We were curious about these two somewhat contradictory views about traceability (technology of power versus technology of agency) and hoped that an analysis of one traceability project could shed some light on the question of who is empowered by traceability projects and how. The project also illustrates how new governance processes generate situations of legal pluralism, the issue that we next address.

## Legal Orders of Food Traceability

The rise of industrialization, globalization of food production and the increasing number of intermediaries involved in the process of food distribution has resulted in new regulatory standards for food that have begun to have global reach (Arienzo et al. 2008). As early as 1963, global standards for food safety were being introduced through the Codex Alimentarius initiative, a joint effort between the Food and Agriculture Organization (FAO) and the World Health Organization (WHO) (WHO and FAO 2006). While these guidelines emphasized quality issues, they also explicitly referred to ensuring that consumers receive products that were "safe", in that they did not pose any health threat (Regattieri et al. 2007). The Codex Alimentarius standards influenced many jurisdictions to adopt food safety measures, especially following the outbreaks of Bovine spongiform encephalopathy (BSE), commonly known as mad cow disease.

The European Union (EU) for example, began introducing food governance legislation and has expanded these after every subsequent food crises. The EU approach has been mandatory state regulated traceability for many food industries, perhaps as a result of public concerns about the ability of the existing institutions and their processes to manage risk in the food supply (Arienzo et al 2008). In 2002, the EU required that all seafood entering EU markets be traceable, with the legislation to come into effect in 2005 (EU 2002; Schroder 2008; Arienzo et al. 2008). In contrast to the EU mandatory approach, the US has developed a voluntary approach. In 2002, the US Department of Agriculture published a paper wherein they set out the case for voluntary traceability within the food system. Their argument was that government responsibility was to ensure that private sector organizations involved in traceability systems met performance targets for food safety, and that the government would not set out prescriptions, but rather make informed suggestions on how the goal of traceability should be achieved (Regattieri et al. 2007). EU mandatory standards have been criticized for making formally legal foods illegal in countries that have recently joined the EU (Knudsen 2011). Whether voluntary or legislated, standards have also been criticized for excluding producers who are either small-scale or from developing nations and who can be forced out of the market if they are unable to meet the expensive and stringent quality management standards (Hanak et al. 2002; Martinez and Poole 2004; Fulponi 2006). In fact, all producers have felt the impact of these standards, as we discuss further in this case study.

Given the number of Canadian food products that go to international markets, it is not surprising that legislative changes in the EU, and corresponding voluntary changes in the US, had a rapid impact in Canada. The Canadian seafood traceability system is a direct response to these changes, but as Martinez and Poole note, food traceability programs are mixed and contradictory, and this has been the case in Canada as well (Martinez and Poole 2004).

In response to the EU deadline, the federal Fisheries and Oceans Department in Canada first suggested state legislation to require traceability, but argued that this could not be in place before 2010. In preparation for this, a Traceability Task Group was formed in 2008, involving federal, provincial and industry representatives (Fisheries and Oceans Canada 2009). However, our informants from both national fisheries organizations and from the NGO Ecotrust reported that seafood processors quickly mobilized to reject mandatory traceability and pushed instead for the US model of voluntary, private traceability programs. The government then agreed to let the seafood industry in Canada attempt to create a traceability program that would satisfy both EU and US standards. It is clear from our interviews that the result was a power struggle in Canada over which private sector actors would control traceability systems.

In 2009, the independent, owner-operator sector of the Canadian fisheries began to organize in order to have an influence on the shape and nature of any seafood traceability system in Canada, with the intention to highlight the relative sustainability of the fleets that they represented as opposed to the larger, corporate sector fleets. As a result, the Canadian Council of Professional Fish Harvesters (CCPFH), which largely represents owner-operator fleets, approached the Canadian environmental NGO Ecotrust[10] to partner on various traceability pilot

[10] Ecotrust, a non-profit institution founded in 1991, is a conservation organization that promotes what they call a "conservation economy". They link conservation with community development (see http://www.ecotrust.org/ last accessed May 2012).

projects on both the west and east coasts of Canada. According to the program officer who began development of the traceability project for Ecotrust, they at first proposed contractually enforceable traceability agreements that involved all the steps from fishermen to final consumer; this idea was supported by the owner-operator fishermen but was rejected by the processing sector. As a result, Ecotrust instead designed a program called ThisFish that involves voluntary relationships and agreements between fishermen, processors, wholesalers and retailers. In partnership with the CCPFH, Ecotrust began to develop and test prototypes for an internet-based system that relied on numbered tags that would be attached to individual fish and would allow consumers to trace the source of their purchase. In collaboration with fishermen, they developed tags, websites and formats for providing information about the fishing enterprise. In the final version of the program, none of the participants in the market chain (fishermen, wholesalers, processors, or retailers) is required to participate; they may choose to do so voluntarily. Thus, as the ThisFish website[11] explains, the resulting traceability system attempts to serve several agendas. First, it aims to make the supply chain more transparent, especially as relates to labour practices, environmental impact of gear used and benefits to fishing communities. Second, it aims to attract participants and create a viable network of like-minded people who all agree to further sustainable seafood systems. Finally, it aims to build consumer confidence and trust in the quality and sustainability of seafood (Ecotrust 2011)[12].

## The Introduction of the 'ThisFish' Program in Atlantic Canada: the Launch in Southwest Nova Scotia

The lobster traceability project was launched in September of 2010 in Lobster Fishing Areas[13] 34 and 35, with the support of both federal and provincial fisheries regulators. A government funding-agency, the Atlantic Canadian Opportunities Agency (ACOA), provided funds for the lobster project. Thus, Canadian public funding supported the development and spread of private governance systems (see

[11] See http://thisfish.info/ last accessed May 2012.

[12] To find out the species currently traced using ThisFish on the both coasts of Canada visit: http://thisfish.info/fishery/species/ last accessed May 2012.

[13] Lobster fishing is regulated under geographic areas known as Lobster Fishing Areas or LFAs. Regulation is broadly the same across LFAs but there are differences in season openings and closures, and some differences in gear.

Hall 2010). Currently, the only information that Fisheries and Oceans Canada asks the participating fishermen to document is the tag numbers attached to individual lobsters, which are to be recorded in their logbooks[14]. Initially, eight lobster fishermen signed on to the project. More fishermen joined as the program quickly became viewed as a way to promote both the product and the lobster industry as a sustainable fishery. The early participants were heavily involved in developing a working system, particularly with respect to tags that could be efficiently and effectively attached as part of the normal catch operation. Ecotrust also used fishermen's feedback to adapt the ThisFish website so that tag numbers could be uploaded efficiently and effectively.

The final version of the system is very simple. When a participating fisherman opens a lobster trap and finds a market size lobster within, he grades it for the fresh market or the cannery. Fresh market lobster will have an individual tag attached to one claw. These tagged lobsters are then directed to a wholesaler or retailer who may or may not agreed to distribute the tagged lobster to their retail customers. If a tagged lobster ultimately reaches a customer, the tag instructs them on how to enter the ThisFish website and where to type in the number found on the tag. Once they do this, they receive information about the fisherman and the fishing enterprise that landed the lobster. This information is based on a standardized information form which fishermen fill out, including their years of fishing experience, their crew members, and their home port. In addition, fishermen have the choice to upload pictures of themselves, their boats and their harbours and in some cases, video lessons on how to cook and eat a lobster[15]. Fishers use the website not only to upload tag numbers, but also to communicate with consumers and to get a geographical snap shot of where their tags end up via another web-based service called GeoCommons. As of May 2011, of the 1700 lobsters tagged in Lobster Fishing Area (LFA) 34 800 had been traced back to the GeoCommons website, and from places as far away as Japan and Europe.

Both Ecotrust representatives and the fishermen we interviewed spoke of promoting the program among middlemen, but reported that not all middlemen

[14] In the fishing industry, a logbook is an official record required under fisheries regulations in order to document data on catch location and volume. It can be submitted when and as required by fishing authorities.

[15] As one reviewer of this paper noted, the identity construct of these fishermen is often linked to a deep local history, including indigeneity, which has value in the 'alternative market' that Ecotrust endorses.

were interested in tagged lobsters. The support or lack of support among seafood middlemen has turned out to be crucial. One lobster buyer told us that some middlemen have concerns about how such tags might limit the product branding that they use in their marketing. As was mentioned above, the same lobsters can be branded as from Canada (as in 'Bay of Fundy' lobsters), or as from the US (as in 'Maine' lobsters.) Fishermen reported that some middlemen removed tags, dropping them back into the shipping crates, and returning the crates (and tags) to the fishermen. Fishermen interpreted this as a message that those middlemen did not want tagged lobsters delivered to them.

Where tags are left in place, not only consumers, but retailers, chefs in restaurants and anyone else along the market chain are able to go to the ThisFish website, type in the number from the tag and not only see where their lobsters came from, but who caught them and how. Further, where fishermen have included their email contact, these individuals can provide direct feedback to the fishermen about their lobster buying or eating experience. We were told that fishermen have so far received positive feedback from people who contact them directly.

This line of communication also provides consumers with the chance to ask questions. In one such case, a consumer asked about black liquid that drained out of a cooked lobster. While the fisherman could not answer this question, he knew of someone at the Prince Edward Island Provincial Veterinarian Lab who was able to answer it. The fisherman then emailed the consumer to let them know that the black liquid was nothing to worry about. This situation proved a learning opportunity for both the lobster fisher and the consumer. In a second case, the "Ask a Fishermen" page on the ThisFish website provided a venue for customers to ask about product quality and the connection to fishing seasons[16]. For example, in response to a comment by a customer that the dates of fishing season should be designed to produce the best quality for the fish, Capt. Hubert E. Saulnier responded that quality is difficult to predict for reasons having to do with climate change. Further, because there are 40 different LFAs in Atlantic Canada, each with their own opening and closing season, every area is not able to benefit from the cold water months. Another customer inquired as to the reason that she was eating lobster in September that had been caught in June. Capt. Kevin Squires responded in saying that the staggered seasons for LFAs and specialized live lobster holding facilities allow the market to be supplied year round. These are

[16] See http://www.thisfish.info/generic/ask_a_fisherman/ and http://www.thisfish.info/generic/qa/9/ both last accessed May 23, 2012.

both examples of what Leitner and Miller have called “a scale making project” as it allows fishermen and fish consumers to connect across space and time (Leitner and Miller 2007).

Our case study of this lobster traceability project illustrates the marriage between barcode technology, databases and the Internet (Wyman 2003). Following Thompson et al., the lobster traceability program can be seen as an “identity preservation system” in that it allows for the source and nature of the market “batch” to be identified, particularly as tag numbers are entered into fishermen’s log books so that catch location, time and date are recorded (Thompson et al. 2005: 3). Further, it could act as a form of “chain traceability” which traces a batch throughout the entire food chain including fishers, buyers, processors, wholesalers, transporters, retailers and customers (ibid.), although it is not currently operating in this way.

Several issues are raised throughout the description of the lobster traceability project in Atlantic Canada and they include the multiple legal jurisdictions that the traceability project is responsive to, the Canadian governments’ support for private governance and the implications of ‘scale making’ projects. We now turn to exploring and analyzing these in more detail.

## Private Governance

Hall has argued that the global food system is one area where private forms of governance have spread most quickly through the application of “soft law” and market based regulatory instruments such as eco-labels and, we would argue, voluntary food traceability systems (Hall 2010). But the food security story is more complicated than that. EU mandatory standards that require traceability for all seafood imported into the EU have made new regulatory demands on Canadian suppliers. Meanwhile, volunteer standards within the US have allowed multinational corporations such as Walmart and Costco, which currently conduct business in Canada, to restrict their seafood purchases to fishing sectors that carry MSC certification (Information Resource of Maine 2008). These two major trading partners thereby stimulated private governance for Canadian producers. The Canadian government, meanwhile, is supporting private governance by encouraging organizations such as Ecotrust to design and introduce traceability and by providing financial support through ACOA and operational encouragement through federal and provincial fisheries offices. These “tangled hierarchies” increasingly govern “rural areas” (Goodwin 1998: 6) and the lobster fishermen as primary producers. Further, these new forms of "governance-beyond-the-state" (following Swynedouw 2005) create new relationships between the actors involved in the chain of food custody.

Fulponi suggests that in regions such as Canada, Europe and the US, where neo-liberalism is the dominant economic perspective, there are budgetary constraints that limit government capacity to regulate activities such as food safety in a globalized setting (Fulponi 2006: 3). As a result, governments are willing to give private standards such as those introduced by traceability systems, a bigger role in governing food systems. This has led to the development and influence of private firm coalitions and organizations that in turn set environmental policy initiatives previously only achievable by state governments (Jacquet and Pauly 2007). Some have interpreted the resulting governance relationships in the following way:

> …the 'withdrawal of the state' can be deciphered as a technique of government….the reduction in forms of welfare-state intervention therefore lead less to the state losing powers of regulation and control and can instead be construed as a reorganization or restructuring of government techniques, shifting the regulatory competence of the state onto 'responsible' and 'rational' individuals (Lemke, cited in Swynedouw 2005: 1997).

What Lemke is describing is a shift in the welfare state to enable rather than to provide (Edwards 2003: 1). More specifically, neo-liberalism presents a framework whereby several agendas can be furthered at the same time. Technologies of power allow governments to pursue their agenda such as risk management, while technologies of agency allow private networks to pursue their agenda, which in this case includes consumer choice[17].

## The Pursuit of Multiple Agendas

Governments have positioned individuals and collectives such as those involved in the ThisFish project, so that they rather than the government become accountable for ensuring that safe food distribution and responsible (ie. sustainable) consumption takes place. Private organizations have become involved in the

[17] We thank one reviewer who drew our attention to the "entrepreneurial" character of state legal frameworks that enhance markets for certified foods.

voluntary governing of seafood by developing traceability systems. Such techniques and practices for governing populations direct both the thought and actions of individuals. Foucault refers to these "form[s] of activity [that] aim to shape, guide or affect the conduct of some persons or persons" as "technologies of power". They are designed to "observe, monitor, shape and control" the behaviour of individuals in society (Foucault 1991: 2, 3-4).

Technologies of power are constructed though the creation of networks (following Edwards 2003) and knowledge shaping processes (following Bonds 2011). Edwards explains that the government encourages actants to come together into a network of interests that represent a certain "view of the future" (Edwards 2003). Swynedouw refers to these networks as a "regime" (Swynedouw 2005). In this case study, the network is comprised of Ecotrust, the lobster fishers, some middlemen, producers, retailers, consumers and bureaucrats. The view of the future is lobster traceability in support of a sustainable (inshore) fishery and a healthy lobster market. This private governance network is an assemblage that has voluntarily participated in developing solutions (i.e. policy) dealing with the regulation of seafood standards. These networks then become the target of government management and evaluation practices so that they gain "the capacity to learn to choose and choose to learn" (Edwards 2003: 6). The capacity to choose is explained as being both desirable and good because as de Gay explains, "no matter what hand circumstances have dealt a person, he or she remains continuously engaged" (de Gay as cited in Edwards 2003: 6). Fishermen we spoke to had a similar view of engagement, noting that: "you are either part of the problem or part of the solution". In de Gay's view, government continues to exercise power by acting indirectly through techniques that enable private governance institutions and the management of risk (see also Foucault 1991).

Bonds argues that such techniques are part of the knowledge shaping process whereby 'elites' actively work to influence and control what is known about a specific subject in order to achieve their goals (Bonds 2011: 430). For Bonds, the knowledge shaping process involves four distinct exercises of power: first is the suppression of harmful information; second is funding research that is useful to elite goals; third is funding experts who are willing to attack and discredit potentially damaging research and fourth is attempting to influence knowledge administration (Bonds 2011: 431). 'Elites' work to control what counts as knowledge through their participation in the interpretation and implementation of scientific data in management regimes. Such information struggles were described by our informants, particularly as related to regulatory changes that may impact labour arrangements[18], environmental changes that may impact seafood quality and safety such as potential water quality changes around aquaculture sites[19], state approval for "deleterious substances" added to marine waters to control sea lice in salmon aquaculture operations, and federal approaches to habitat protection (especially for commercial species). Given the tangled hierarchies involving the actors in the lobster industry, however, identifying the 'elites' is more difficult than Bonds leads us to expect.

The role of science is interesting in this regard. In the use of science to describe and prescribe for problems in building sustainable fisheries or in food safety, government does not eliminate public conflict so much as they transform it. This is what Nikolas Rose refers to as a 'switch point', when a critique is used to identify a problem for which a new technical solution builds additional technologies of power (Bonds 2011: 442). However, because scientific data does not have pure meaning, it is subject to interpretation and change as to what constitutes a problem and or a solution (Bonds 2011). As a result, environmental science has become a central political arena where the state, corporations, environmentalists and civil society produce and contest particular knowledge sets (Bonds 2011: 422).

Whatever their source, the resulting technical solutions have a normative quality. In other words, the government's choice to 'contract out' former public services such as food safety to private networks is an example of a technology of power that has the potential to suggest new normative standards of behaviour and thus to enhance or deploy actor agency. But as Foucault noted, power is not only negotiated but also is contested (Foucault 1991). Dean showed how new standards of behaviour can emerge as technologies of agency (Dean 1996: 167). Technologies of agency "include the instruments of 'voice' and 'representation' by which claims of user groups can enter into the negotiation over needs" (Yeatman as cited by Dean 1996: 168). This argument is supported by Edwards who states that power technologies can only shape, and not fundamentally determine how actors think and make decisions, as people are independent, free thinking subjects, with the ability to interpret, act, mobilize and be mobilized (Edwards 2003: 6). Thus, technologies in the Foucault sense can be both empowering and

[18] See also Pinkerton and Edwards 2009, who describe the social and economic costs for west coast boat captains and crew who have to lease quota at a very high cost in order to continue fishing.

[19] See also Wiber et al. 2012, who describe fishermen's local knowledge with respect to these impacts.

disempowering. To put this into context, multiple agendas, whether of government, NGOs or lobster fishermen, can be pursued at the same time, by multiple sets of different 'elites'. This is illustrated in the scale making projects that are present in Atlantic Canada and that developed as a result of the lobster traceability project.

## Scale-Making Projects

In governance projects, such as ThisFish, that exist 'beyond the state', Leitner and Miller argue that it is important to pay attention to social practices and three dimensions of scale, including size, level and relationships, in order to understand how agents produce and are affected by particular forms of spatiality (Leitner and Miller 2007). Marsden and Smith for example, draw attention to how scale plays an important role in 'ecological entrepreneurship', where local producers build relationships with local retailers to better meet consumer sustainability demands (Marsden and Smith 2005). While the government of Canada has provided the regulatory room to manage risk through non-state arrangements for seafood traceability, the actors in the resulting quasi-private institutions pursue their own agendas and the results often have similar scale-making consequences.

In Atlantic Canada, we found that several diverse actors, including food retail corporations, environmentalists and lobster fishers, were (re)constructing scalar relations by working in new ways (see Leitner and Miller 2007: 118). The lobster fishermen and Ecotrust have collaborated to create a new private traceability structure that is developing, protecting and promoting a niche market that is visible to consumers around the world. The ThisFish website links producers directly with those consumers wherever those consumers are located, either spontaneously through email, or through more formal channels on the "Ask a Fisherman" website page. This facilitates communication both within and across spaces (provincially, nationally, internationally). The resulting communication flow is also two-way. The fishers are able to provide consumers with the 'dock price' of lobster on their websites and in emails and to make customers aware of some of the realities being faced by fishermen in the Canadian fishing industry. They are able to respond directly to consumer questions and conversely they receive emails from consumers that are grateful for their seafood experience. Fishermen report that these communicative acts have empowering effects given the struggles they experience in their industry.

At the other end of the scale, this niche market visibility is also attractive to local supermarkets that wish to obtain a premium price by offering consumers better-informed choices and images of 'locality' that suggest sustainability and a lower 'environmental footprint'. In a 2011 meeting of all parties to assess the lobster traceability pilot project, representatives from the retail sector reported on one measure of success - seafood products with traceability tags were selling up to three times more volume than untagged products. Fishermen reported another measure of success, in that local supermarkets were asking them to deliver tagged lobster directly, which given a premium price to fishermen, could promote 'ecological entrepreneurship' (Marsden and Smith 2005). Ecological entrepreneurship would rely on relationships and new 'spatially based networks' between Ecotrust, the lobster fishers and retailers. There is interest in setting up and continuing to delineate such new spatial and competitive relations and boundaries while remaining within the conventional food system.

However, these new spatial and competitive relationships have the potential to reroute supply chains in particular spaces (Marsden and Smith 2005: 443). While ecological entrepreneurship may be attractive to lobstermen and to retailers, wholesalers may lose out in any such new arrangements. Through the opportunities for direct email contact via the ThisFish website, some international buyers have contacted individual lobster fishermen looking to purchase the product directly. Lobster fishermen have explained to the international buyers (as they have to local supermarkets) that they are both unwilling and unable to supply them directly so long as this threatens their relationship with their normal buyers who take the bulk of their landings. Local wholesalers, meanwhile, are aware that their share of the market chain could be considerably reduced and their businesses could lose their local economic and social importance if the lobster market changed as a result of these opportunities. This fear explains why some middlemen are returning lobster tags to fishermen. Nevertheless, many middlemen have expressed support for lobster traceability by participating in the project. They too are able to communicate more directly with individual fishermen. For example, a few middlemen have contacted fishermen directly with their concerns when they have noticed that some of the tagged lobsters are 'lower quality'[20]. The fishers can then choose whether in the future they will hold back such lobster for cannery processing and save tags for higher quality lobster for live marketing.

Finally, some lobster fishermen are concerned about their potential disempowerment, as well. Given their position as primary producers, the

[20]Lower quality here is referring to lobsters that have softer shells.

traceability system allows the product to be traced back to them as the first in the long line of many different actors involved in the distribution of the product. Since the increased transparency in the supply chain applies mainly to them, some lobstermen are concerned that they will be held solely accountable for any problems that may or may not be within their power to change. For example, water quality around aquaculture operations has in some cases led to algae blooms linked in turn to shellfish food safety concerns (see Wiber et al. 2012). Some lobster fishermen fear that their product brand (i.e. Bay of Fundy lobster) may be harmed in international markets by such problems, when in fact the area within the Bay affected by aquaculture is relatively small.

Such scale jumping on the part of all actors illustrates the ways in which actors may face limitations in transforming the market chain but also demonstrates that scalar relations may be contested and subject to struggle. Such actors have engaged in "socio-spatial strategies of resistance", which illustrates how scalar relations are never fixed but are perpetually under redesign (Leitner and Miller 2007: 117). While middlemen may be disempowered as a result of such scale-making projects, in a voluntary traceability process, they have the power to remove themselves from the chain of custody. If traceability is legislated and made mandatory by the Canadian government, however, the middlemen may not have that same power. Thus, middlemen must decide whether to support voluntary traceability or to undercut it and risk a mandatory government regulatory system.

For now, it is evident that the implications of traceability for technologies of power and of agency are uneven. In some contexts, actors such as government bureaucrats, Ecotrust, the lobster fishermen and eco-conscious consumers have their agendas furthered by participation. However, other actors, including some middlemen and lobster fishermen, may experience consequences that are disempowering. The rise of private governance institutions not only allows multiple agendas to be pursued at the same time, but enables diverse actors to be differentially involved in setting environmental policy and participating in the governance of food systems.

## Legitimacy, Democracy and Transparency

With the emergence of private governance institutions, the state is no longer the only source of normativity, regulation, rules and laws but part of a world that is now constructed of many 'jurisgenerative institutions', including voluntary organizations such as Ecotrust and corporations such as Walmart and Costco

(Anderson 1998: 4). This new reality and form of governance exposes the new rationality for governing that combines new technologies, instruments and strategies for cooperative rule making and regulatory enforcement. Swynedouw suggests that these also demand new standards for political democracy (Swynedouw 2005).

Goodwin, Swynedouw and Offe all raise concerns about legitimacy when partnerships between state, civil society and the market involve "informal yet relatively stable conditions (or partnerships) composed of elites drawn from the public and private sectors" (Goodwin 1998: 9; see also: Swynedouw 2005; Offe 2009). This "blurring of boundaries" between and within the private and public sectors raises questions about the ways that governmental and non-governmental organizations work together and the ways that political power is now being distributed (Goodwin 1998: 5). In some instances, these actors might share power equally, mesh well and continue to govern under relatively stable coalitions. Swynedouw suggests that this relies on the horizontal nature of 'regimes', their networked arrangements and the interactive relations that develop between actors who seemingly share a significant degree of trust even though there may be internal conflict or opposing agendas (Swynedouw 2005: 1995).

However, the blurring of boundaries between private and public sectors can quickly jeopardize trust, legitimacy and transparency. For instance, if serious food safety issues were to arise, the parties involved in the chain of custody can escape responsibility by blaming the others involved. As a result, it may be very difficult when safety problems arise to hold anyone accountable. Structural jurisdictional conflict can also arise from the 'blame game' if responsibility is assigned to another party who denies the claim (see Parlee 2011: 123). The other concern that has already been discussed is the potential for the first person in the chain of custody which is the fish harvester, to be held responsible simply because they are the primary producer and the easiest to track. In this case, the legitimacy and transparency of projects that exist 'beyond the state' may be compromised.

The potential for this to occur exists because currently in these new shared governance arrangements, there are no codified rules and regulations that define participation and exact domains of power and responsibility have not been identified (Swynedouw 2005: 1999). Goodwin maintains that these complex emergent systems "lack the 'simple' legitimacy of accountability and elected democracies" (Goodwin 1998: 8). When there is a lack of legitimacy in structures or 'regimes' that are centered on food governance, power holders will most likely be ineffective in the long run, giving rise to a "democratic deficit of governance beyond the state" (Swynedouw 2005: 1993). Additionally, tensions and difficulties over power and values will inevitably exist between partner institutions (Bastien-Daigle et al. 2008: 121); governance failure may be the end result (Goodwin 1998: 9). Existing seafood traceability may promote neither food safety nor good consumer confidence. Because no single actor has the knowledge or capacity to tackle these problems effectively (Goodwin 1998), we argue that legal pluralism is made inevitable. The lobster traceability system generates and is subject to multiple regulatory systems that will not coexist without difficulty.

## Conclusion

Through the assemblage of seafood governance viewed through this case study, we can draw a few preliminary conclusions. First, in the current space for seafood governance in Canada, the public promotion of private governance (Hall 2010) has created a contingent, somewhat fragile governance system that could go in either a public or private direction, depending on how the power struggles play out in the near future. What is clear is that both corporations such as Walmart and Costo, and NGOs such as Ecotrust, are now more powerful than many governments in terms of setting international seafood awareness agendas (Jacquet and Pauly 2007). They set corporate codes of conduct, soft law and market based regulatory instruments such as eco-labels. With the rise of these new governance arrangements, governance failure is a real possibility as traceability may not be successful in promoting food safety, ecological sustainability, or consumer trust. The shift in power from state to the private institutions of the marketplace therefore raises serious concerns about democratic accountability and legitimacy. Second, if we consider more deeply Foucault's argument about governance and technologies of power - the voluntary traceability system that currently exists in Canada empowers fishermen to jump across scales and reach consumers from the local and to the global level with their message of a sustainable fishery, while other actors in the chain of custody may be disempowered by the system.

As a technology of power, the lobster traceability project in Canada is still in its infancy. So far, the Canadian government has played a very low-key role in this traceability project and we have heard very little about traceability to track problems and assess risk in seafood. On the other hand, some fishermen feel that where tag numbers are recorded in their logbooks, government will be able to devolve the responsibility for environmental risks over which fishermen have no control onto fishermen. With such a complex project and with so many players involved, the opportunity to break the chain of custody by refusing to participate means that power is distributed in different ways throughout the players - even if it is only the power to say 'no'. As was illustrated by the actions of some middleman, there is resistance to the project, perhaps for reasons of branding.

Also, there are spatial and scalar dimensions of the program that have a significant impact on all of the actors involved in the chain of custody. For example, technologies[21] allow the fishers to bridge geographical distances and connect to consumers in new ways. Consumers who are also aided by technology have new ways to visualize and interact with the space of fishing. Technology also connects fishermen's knowledge networks to consumers as in the "Ask a Fisherman" questions. These networks may not be empowering for all players as was illustrated in the case of the local buyers or middlemen.

Finally, legal pluralism is enhanced and continues to grow as a result of the "tangled hierarchies" (Goodwin 1998) that are woven together in food governance. We conclude that legal pluralism is an important constituent in global food security and food governance, and that this characteristic of our emerging food governance institutions requires more careful study.

## References

ANDERSON, Gavin W.

1998 'Corporations, democracy and the implied freedom of political communication: Towards a pluralistic analysis of constitutional law.' *Melbourne University Law Review* 22(1): 1-23.

ARIENZO, Alessandro, Christian COFF, and David BARLING

2008 'The European Union and the Regulation of Food Traceability: From Risk Management to Informed Choice?' Pp. 23-42 in Christian Coff, David Barling, Michiel Korthals and Thorkild Nielson (Eds.), *Ethical Traceability and Communicating Food.* New York, NY: Springer Publishing.

[21] It would be interesting to pursue the impact of new technologies on primary producers through Science and Technology Studies. Escobar, for example, has suggested that cyberspace is becoming an important resource for subject-subject interaction, creating networked cultures and fostering new routes for the circulation of ideas (Escobar 2005; see also Hess 2007).

BASTIEN-DAIGLE, Sophie, Jean-Paul VANDERLINDEN and Omer CHOUINARD

2008 'Learning the ropes: Lessons in integrated management of coastal resources in Canada's Maritime Provinces.' *Ocean & Coastal Management* 51(2): 96-125.

BENDA-BECKMANN, Franz von

2002 'Who's Afraid of Legal Pluralism?' *Journal of Legal Pluralism and Unofficial Law* 47: 37-82.

BONDS, Eric

2011 'The Knowledge-Shaping Process: Elite Mobilization and Environmental Policy.' *Critical Sociology* 37: 29-446.

COFF, Christian, David BARLING, Michiel KORTHALS, and Thorkild NEILSON

2008 'Ethical Traceability and Communicating Food.' Pp. 1-18 in Christian Coff, David Barling, Michiel Korthals and Thorkild Nielson (Eds.), *Ethical Traceability and Communicating Food.* New York, NY: Springer Publishing.

COFF, Christian, Alessandro ARIENZO, David BARLING, Volkert BEEKMAN, Mai BJERG, Marco CASTANGA, Fabio CIARAMELLI, Thora EINARSDOTTIR, Manolis KABOURAKIS, Niels Heine KRISTENSEN, Michiel KORTHALS, Tim LANG, Guido NICOLOSI, Thorkild NIELSON, Dimitris PAPADOPOULOS, Liesbeth SCHIPPER, Rosalind SHARPE and Agapi VASSILIOU

2007 'Ethical Traceability.' Retrieved August 22, 2011 from: http://chrcoff.dk/Rapporter/Ethicaltraceability.pdf, last accessed May 2012.

DEAN, Mitchell

1996 'Putting the technological into government.' *History of the Human Sciences* 9: 47-68.

2010 *Governmentality. Power and Rule in Modern Society,* 2nd Edition. London and Thousand Oaks: Sage Publications.

ECOTRUST

2011 'ThisFish and Our Philosophy.' Retrieved August 10th, 2011 from: http://thisfish.info/about/philosophy/, last accessed May 2012.

EDWARDS, Richard

2003 'Ordering Subjects: Actor-Networks and Intellectual Technologies in Lifelong Learning.' *Studies in the Education of Adults* 35(1): 1-14.

ESCOBAR, Arturo

2005 'Other worlds are (already) possible: Cyber-internationalism and post-capitalist cultures.' Revista TEXTOS de la CiberSociedad 5. Available at http://www.cibersociedad.net, last accessed May 2012.

EUROPEAN UNION

2002 Regulation (EC) 178/2002 Of the European Parliament and of the Council. Chapter 2: General Food Law. Retrieved August 20th, 2011 from: http://eur-lex.europa.eu/LexUriServ/LexUriServ.do?uri=CONSLEG:2002R0178:20080325:EN:PDF

FISHERIES AND OCEANS CANADA

2009 'Backgrounder - Canada's Response To New EU Traceability Requirements.' Retrieved 2 October, 2011 from: http://www.dfo-mpo.gc.ca/fm-gp/peches-fisheries/fish-ren-peche/sff-cpd/traceability-back-tracabilite-eng.htm, last accessed May 2012.

FOLEY, Paul

2012 'The Political Economy of Marine Stewardship Council Certification: Processors and Access in Newfoundland and Labrador's Inshore Shrimp Industry.' *Journal of Agrarian Change* 12(2, 3): 436-457.

n.d. 'National Government Responses to Marine Stewardship Council (MSC) Fisheries Certification: Insights from Atlantic Canada.' To appear in *New Political Economy*. (In press)

FOUCAULT, Michel

1991 'Governmentality.' Pp. 87-104 in Graham Burchell, Colin Gordon and Peter Miller (Eds.), *The Foucault Effect. Studies in Governmentality*. Chicago: The University of Chicago Press.

FULPONI, Linda

2006 'Private voluntary standards in the food system: the perspectives of major food retailers in OECD countries.' *Food Policy* 31: 1-13.

GALE, Fred and Marcus HOWARD

2011 *Global Commodity Governance: State Responses to Sustainable Forest and Fisheries Certification*. New York: Palgrave Macmillan.

GLOBAL DEVELOPMENT RESEARCH CENTER

2011 *Sustainability Concepts: Eco-Labelling*. Retrieved from: http://www.gdrc.org/sustdev/concepts/05-e-label.html, last accessed 7 November, 2011.

GOODWIN, Mark

1998 'The governance of rural areas: some emerging research issues and agendas.' *Journal of Rural Studies* 14(1): 5-12.

GOYERT, Wendy, Raphael SAGARIN and John ANNALA

2010 'The promise and pitfalls of Marine Stewardship Council certification: Maine lobster as a case study.' *Marine Policy* 34: 1103-1109.

HALL, Derek
2010 'Food with a visible face: traceability and the public promotion of private governance in the Japanese food system.' *Geoforum* 41: 826-835.
HANAK, E., E. BOUTRIF, P. FABRE and M. PINEIRO
2002 'Food safety management in developing countries.' *Proceedings of the International Workshop, CIRAD-FAO*, 11-13 December 2000. Montpelier, France.
HESS, David J.
2007 'Crosscurrent: Social movements and the anthropology of science and technology.' *American Anthropologist* 109(3): 463-472.
INFORMATION RESOURCE OF MAINE
2008 'Governor Creates Working Group to Pursue Sustainable Fishery Certification for Lobster Industry.' Retrieved from: http://www.maine.gov/tools/whatsnew/index.php?topic=Gov+News&id=51550&v=Article-2006, last accessed May 2012.
JACQUET, Jennifer L. and Daniel PAULY
2007 'The rise of seafood awareness campaigns in an era of collapsing fisheries.' *Marine Policy* 31: 308-313.
2008 'Trade secrets: Renaming and mislabelling of seafood.' *Marine Policy* 32: 309-318.
KAISER, Michel J. and Gareth EDWARD-JONES
2004 'The role of ecolabeling in fisheries management and conservation.' *Conservation Biology* 20(2): 392-398.
KNUDSEN, Ida Harboe
2011 'The insiders and the outsiders: standardization and 'failed' person-making in a Lithuanian marketplace.' *Journal of Legal Pluralism* 61: 72-93.
LEITNER, Helga and Byron MILLER
2007 'Scale and the limitations of ontological debate: a commentary on Marston, Jones and Woodward.' *Transactions of the Institute of British Geographers* NS 32: 116-125.
LOGAN, Cheryle A., S. Elizabeth ALTER, Alison J. HAUPT and Katherine TOMALTY
2008 'An impediment to consumer choice: Overfished species are sold as Pacific red snapper.' *Biological Conservation 141: 1591-1599.*
MARSDEN, T. and E. SMITH
2005 'Ecological Entrepreneurship: Sustainable Development in Local Communities Through Quality Food Production and Local Branding.' *Geoforum* 36: 440-451.

MARTINEZ, M. G. and Nigel POOLE
2004 'The development of private fresh produce safety standards: implications for developing Mediterranean exporting countries.' *Food Policy* 29: 229-255.
MSC (MARINE STEWARDSHIP COUNCIL) REVIEW COMMITTEE
2010 'Minutes of the MSC Review Committee Meeting, Scotia Fundy Region.' Halifax, Nova Scotia. September 9, 2010. Copy on file with authors.
OFFE, Claus
2009 'Governance: An "empty signifier"?' *Constellations* 16(4): 550-562.
PARK, Amanda
2010 'Pre-assessment Report for American Lobster (Homarus americanus) Trap Fishery. Conducted in Lobster Fishing Areas 27-36.' Moody Marine Ltd. Ref: 82516. Dartmouth, Nova Scotia.
PARLEE, Courtenay E.
2011 Alternative Dispute Resolution: Can it Advance the Stated Policies of Integrated Coastal Zone Management in Canadian Fisheries and Oceans? Interdisciplinary Studies Thesis, Master of Philosophy, University of New Brunswick.
PINKERTON, Evelyn and Danielle EDWARDS
2009 'The elephant in the room: the hidden costs of leasing individual transferable fishing quotas.' Marine Policy 33: 707-713.
REGATTIERI, Alberto, M. GAMERIA and R. MANZINI
2007 'Traceability of Food Products: General Framework and Experimental Evidence.' *Journal of Food Engineering* 81: 347-356.
SCHRODER, Ute
2008 'Challenges in the traceability of seafood.' *Journal for Consumer Protection and Food Safety (J. Verbr. Lebensm.)* 3: 45-48.
STRINGER, Christina, Glen SIMMONS and Daren COULSTON
2011 'Not in New Zealand's waters, surely? Labour and human rights abuses aboard foreign fishing vessels.' New Zealand Asia Institute Working Paper 11-01. University of Aukland.
SWYNEDOUW, Erik
2005 'Governance innovation and the citizen: the Janus face of governance-beyond-the-state.' *Urban Studies* 42: 1991-2006.
THOMPSON, M., Gil SYLVIA and Michael T. MORRISSEY
2005 'Seafood traceability in the United States: Current trends, system design, and potential applications.' *Comprehensive Reviews in Food Science and Safety* 1: 1-7.

WHO (WORLD HEALTH ORGANIZATION) and FAO (FOOD AND AGRICULTURE ORGANIZATION)
2006 Understanding the Codex Alimentarius (3rd Ed.) Retrieved from: ftp://ftp.fao.org/codex/Publications/understanding/Understanding_EN.pdf , last accessed October 4th, 2011.

WIBER, Melanie, Lisette WILSON and Sheena YOUNG
2012 'Impact of Aquaculture on Commercial Fisheries: Fishermen's Local Ecological Knowledge.' *Human Ecology* 40(1): 29-40.

WYMAN, Jeb
2003 'Where'd you get that fish?' *SPC Fisheries Newsletter* 107: 17-19.

ZIPS, Werner and Markus WEILENMANN
2011 'Introduction: Governance and Legal Pluralism - An emerging symbiotic relationship?' Pp. 1-34 in Werner Zips and Markus Weilenmann (eds.), *The Governance of Legal Pluralism. Empirical Studies from Africa and Beyond*. LIT Verlag.

# LEGAL PLURALISM AND THE GOVERNABILITY OF FISHERIES AND COASTAL SYSTEMS[1]

Svein Jentoft

## 1. Introduction

This article discusses how interactive governance and legal pluralism may mutually benefit each other, particularly in highlighting factors that help inhibit and enhance the governability of fisheries and coastal systems. Governability is here understood as "the overall capacity for governance of any societal entity or system" (Kooiman 2008: 173). Governance, on the other hand, is basically seen as an interactive and collaborative process involving government, markets and civil society, the latter also in a proactive role.

Zips and Weilenmann observe that "governance and legal pluralism belong to separate academic idioms" (Zips and Weilenmann 2011: 7) A reason for this is perhaps that, whereas governance theory has evolved from a government (largely state)[2] centric perspective and the idea of government failure, the legal pluralism

---

[1] This article was first presented at the Jubilee Conference Jubilee Congress of the Commission of Legal Pluralism, Cape Town, South Africa, in September 8-11, 2011. A revised and much elaborated version was later presented at the Conference on Legal Pluralism in Natural Resource Management, Amrita University, Coimbatore, India, in April 29-30, 2012. It has benefited from constructive comments from Maarten Bavinck, Ratana Chuenpagdee and Knut H. Mikalsen, and two anonymous reviewers.

[2] Government is here seen as the institution that administers public policy, and exercises executive, political and sovereign power through regulatory orders within a state. The concepts of government and state will, in this paper, be used interchangeably if nothing else is specified.

perspective has largely emerged "from below", i.e. from the level of the local community. Still, at closer inspection there is considerable common ground between the two analytical perspectives, most prominently in their similar insistence on the need to look beyond state for governance mechanisms and actions. The move "from government to governance," and the involvement of non-government stakeholders in governance, as noted by Heere, leads to a more "heterogeneous state" (Heere 2004). It also results in a more complex and "hybrid" legal system (Santos 2006). The fallacy of regarding the state as the only governor is juxtaposed by the argument that "the longstanding vision of uniform and monopolistic law that governs a community is obsolete" (Tamanaha 2008: 409). This is an opinion that most scholars working in the field of interactive governance would support.

With the concept of interactive governance, Kooiman (2003; see also Kooiman et al. 2005) stresses the complexity, diversity, dynamics, and scale of social and ecological systems. Legal pluralism is obviously one of several causes and outcomes of these traits. A study of multiple normative orders, legal pluralism asks questions about what norms and rules exist in particular situations, how they connect and add up, what social values underpin them, and what mechanisms are working to reconcile legal differences that may exist at temporal and spatial scales (cf. Griffiths 1986; Pimentel 2010). A particular concern is the mutual influence of state and local law and the degree to which one has hegemony over the other (Guillet 1998; Tamanaha 2008). Similarly, interactive governance theory is concerned with ways to recognize and reconcile inconsistencies and conflicts between different governance norms and principles, and to identify potential for enhancing governability where this is essential for solving important ecological and societal problems, such as overfishing and marine ecosystem degradation (Kooiman and Jentoft 2009). Legal pluralism would here be seen to involve a potential hindrance but also an opportunity, which may provide governors with a toolbox to govern better. For this reason, interactive governance would be particularly interested in governing institutions that are hybrid, flexible and adaptive (Kickert 2001).

In what follows, I start out by comparing the two perspectives; how do they relate to each other, what overlaps exist, how can they be of mutual benefit? The subsequent sections present the essential features of interactive governance, stressing the need to distinguish between interactive governance as an empirical phenomenon, a normative theory, and an analytical perspective. Interactive governance as an analytical perspective is emphasized in section four, which gives an introduction into its particular conceptual framework, and suggests how it may be applied in the context of legal pluralism.

## 2. Comparing perspectives

Analytical perspectives such as interactive governance and legal pluralism are ways of searching and seeing. They are places to start from and maps to navigate by. They make things stand out, they sharpen our vision, and they help us see the trees for the forest. Franz von Benda-Beckmann makes this case when he states that "thinking in terms of legal pluralism can help in providing better insight into the complexities around law and rights" (F. von Benda-Beckmann 2001: 54) The same thing can be said about interactive governance. Still, analytical perspectives are also "prejudgments", as Gadamer coined it; they come with a lens that highlights some issues while leaving others out of focus. Needless to say, this is true of both legal pluralism and interactive governance. Therefore, it is important to be aware of the bias that comes with a particular perspective (cf. Gadamer 2003: 269).

Notably, not only do analytical perspectives make us look at things in a certain way; they also compel us to see one thing at a time. This can be illustrated with the famous image of the young and the old woman in one and the same sketch; we are not capable of seeing both women simultaneously. Even so, what makes this image particularly interesting is the fact that we know that it is possible to identify both of them if we switch between perspectives. Without that knowledge, once we have identified one of the women, we will be inclined to stop looking for the other, and we will have missed something very essential. This is what academic disciplines tend to do and why cross-disciplinarity is such a rare occurrence. The specificity and boundaries that comes with disciplines induces us to stay put within one perspective and make us believe that we have seen it all. Clearly, in fisheries and coastal governance, a limitation of governability is hidden here. It is an area of research that requires the perspectives of several disciplines; yet the extent of cross-fertilization between disciplines is remarkably low (Buanes and Jentoft 2009). This seems to be true for the crossing between governance theory and legal pluralism as well. Bavinck's work on fisheries and coastal management in South India is an exception here (Bavinck 2001, 2005). However, each perspective lacks a specific disciplinary identity, but draw on insights and methodologies from several academic disciplines such as anthropology, sociology, law and political science (F. von Benda-Beckmann 2002). In that way interactive governance and legal pluralism are both transdisciplinary.

Together, interactive governance and legal pluralism present a richer picture and a more nuanced set of policy options for fisheries governance. As far as interactive governance is concerned, it is essential to recognize the fact that multiple normative orders, be they formal or informal, exist in the real world. Consequently, governors must learn to deal with norms and principles that differ and are sometimes in conflict. For legal pluralism, a governance perspective may help to bridge theory and research with policy recommendations and implications. Interactive governance may help to answer the question of what it would take to bring the insights of legal pluralism into the governance process in a way that has real consequences for decision-making and outcomes.

Both perspectives share the observation that the state is not, and in this day and age cannot possibly be, the only governor; that one should not underestimate the fact that markets and civil society are also governing (and legal) systems in their own right with a collective capacity for societal governance (Donaue and Zechhauser 2011; Kooiman 2003; Offe 2009). They are not passive recipients of rules and regulations but are often involved in shaping them. Just think of a business corporation, an interest organization or a religious institution (Berman 2007; Blacket 2001). Not only are they active in influencing the rules that the state in the next instance is imposing on them, people who work within such systems are also themselves subjugated to rules that have been internally generated. They are indeed plural legal systems in themselves. Thus, legal pluralism aligns well with interactive governance thinking. Legislation is, after all, an act of governance, which results from a course of action that involves state as well as non-state actors.

Governments cannot expect citizen support if the law contradicts perceptions of fairness prevalent within society as a whole. How popular perceptions of justice originate and become the law of the community or the land is therefore an interesting research issue within both legal pluralism and interactive governance. One should not expect such a process to be smooth. Why are they in some instances different from community to community and from community to state? And how do they score relative to each other with regard to good governance indicators such as effectiveness, transparency and accountability? These are all relevant research questions whether one commences in interactive governance theory or in legal pluralism.

Interactive governance is the younger perspective of the two. However, it is a broader perspective, at least when we think of legal pluralism as a governance perspective, which it also is. This does not imply that interactive governance has nothing to gain from legal pluralism or that the need for learning only goes in one direction; quite the contrary. It goes without saying that interactive governance theory has to assume a sharp focus on legal orders, that they are essential to understanding the complexity of governance challenges, and that they may help augment governability, for instance as far as poverty alleviation is concerned (Meinzen-Dick 2009; Jentoft and Eide 2011). Think here of the role of tenure and resource rights and the role they play in securing people's livelihoods. It is important not to be oblivious to the possibility that legal pluralism may complicate governability in some instances, as when rival stakeholders claim competing rights by referring to different legal norms (Meinzen-Dick and Pradhan 2002). The need to recognize legal pluralism in particular social and ecological contexts as conditions for governability is consistent with the general argument that both perspectives are advancing. This overlap stems from the fact that the two analytical perspectives often apply to similar research settings. As far as fisheries and coasts are concerned, one cannot assess their governability without focusing on the role of law, be it statutory or customary and how they are linked. Omitting legal pluralism from empirical investigation of fisheries governance would clearly be a mistake. The same is true for governors, who need to be equally sensitized to this phenomenon as those who do research. Once the existence of legal pluralism has been discerned, it must be taken into account when governing institutions are designed. As Kraan argues with reference to small-scale fisheries governance in the case of Ghana, "creating institutions in a top-down way to improve natural resource management is doomed to fail if these institutions are not embedded in local dynamics with plural normative orders" (Kraan 2009: 293).

## 3. Explaining interactive governance

Similar to legal pluralism (cf. Rouland 1994; Woodman 1999), governance comes with several definitions. Fundamental is the perception of governance as a conscious, collaborative, deliberative and goal-oriented steering process involving both public and private actors, often organized in a formal partnership arrangement (cf. for definitions see, for example, Ansell and Gash 2007; Stoker 1998; Offe 2009). Kooiman's idea of "interactive governance" is:

> the whole of public as well as private interaction taken to solve

> societal problems and create societal opportunities. It includes the formulation and application of principles guiding those interactions and care for institutions that enable them (Kooiman 2003: 4).

The prominence of interaction in Kooiman's definition highlights communication, negotiation, and exchange. It also implies a focus on process as well as institutional design beyond the realm of the state. This is also how legal pluralism, as expressed by Zips and Weilenmann, sees it:

> While it may be overstating the case to claim that governance and legal pluralism are two sides of the coin, the very fact of a particular constellation of legal pluralism brings about pressure to employ a set or network of institutions, actors and practices different from (state) government (Zips and Weilenmann 2011: 7-8)

From both perspectives, it is essential to discern what the rules are, and where, when and how they apply in real settings and institutions, and who gains or loses because of them. It is also equally as important to assess how institutions, within which rules play an essential part, come about, and how they shape (restrict or enable) social interaction and collective action (Ostrom 1993). The dynamic aspects of rules are as relevant as their static dimensions, and there is no implicit assumption neither within interactive governance nor legal pluralism that arrangements, rules, procedures and outcomes are necessarily socially just (Kooiman 2003; F. von Benda-Beckmann 2001; Pimentel 2010). Rather, the justice implications of both are essential research issues.

As a partnership, governance typically involves sharing power, but not necessarily in an equal or equitable manner. How power is actually distributed may determine whether a social and ecological system is governable or not (Jentoft 2007b). Some management functions may be delegated to stakeholder organizations through a co-management arrangement, such as with fisher associations or multi-stakeholder organizations (Wilson et al. 2003). In other instances, stakeholder organizations play a more reactive and advisory role, as with the Regional Management Councils in the case of European Union fisheries (Long 2010; Linke et al. 2011). The balance between 'state-centred' and 'society-centred' governance may vary and, as Pierre and Peters argue, it therefore makes more sense to think of the two as forming a continuum rather than a dichotomy (Pierre and Peters 2000).

Moving from government to more capable governance (Rhodes 1996; Kooiman 2003) by including stakeholders in societal steering is essentially thought of as a means of enhancing governability; it is expected to provide more legitimate and effective governing by forming a more committed and responsible stakeholder community and a broader knowledge base. In fisheries and coastal management, for instance, it is assumed to induce more compliance to harvest regulations (cf. Jagers et al. 2012).

Interactive governance theory does not think of governance as a necessarily formal mechanism – which is consistent with what legal pluralism argues when emphasizing the importance of both state and non-state law ('living law'). In the same vein as legal pluralism, governance can be unofficial and tacit. Neither must governance be "good" (as defined by the World Bank - see Kjær 2004). Despite the common assumption, there is no guarantee that a move from government to governance will enhance governability. In fact, the outcome might be the opposite. As governance in the co- and self-governing modes blurs the distinction between the subject (governor) and object (those that governing target, governance risks being captured by powerful stakeholders who take the opportunity "to usurp genuinely public tasks" or to engage in "outright corrupt practices" (Offe 2009: 553). Therefore, we must investigate the conditions under which governability increases or falters. Many of those conditions are likely to be highly contextual, suggesting that there is no single governance formula for all situations. This is also the idea behind the concept of "adaptive governance" (Folke et al. 2005), i.e. a less uniform and standardised form of governance, although the aim is one that is more tailored to particular circumstances and more sensitive and reactive to change.

## 4. Empirical and normative aspects of interactive governance

As can be said about legal pluralism, we need to distinguish between interactive governance as: a) an empirical phenomenon, b) a normative theory, and c) an analytical perspective (cf. Pierre and Peters 2000: 24). In the first instance (a), the issue is whether interactive governance as defined here is actually occurring, whether the blurring of traditional boundaries between government and the private sector is really happening; where, when, and how. Is it really true that the traditional role of the state is changing from a governing state to "an enabling state" (Pierre and Peters 2000: 12)? Interactive governance is not necessarily a recent phenomenon. Neither does it have to be the true and only representation of how societal sectors are steered. This is ultimately an empirical question. A comparative study of fisheries governance systems in Europe showed a lot of variation among countries with regard to government-industry interaction (Hoof 2005; Mikalsen and Jentoft 2008). In some countries, fisheries governance is indeed structured according to an interactive model, where user-organizations have an active role in regulatory decision-making and where considerable governance functions are delegated to the sector. This is done in harmony with a legislative framework which defines the mandates, rights and responsibilities that user-organizations have in the governance system. In Spain, for instance, this occurs where regions are granted considerable autonomy, and where local fisher organizations, the *cofradias*, are part of the overall formal governance system. In other countries, as in Scandinavia, consultative arrangements between government and industry are common. The role of Producer Organizations in the fisheries of many European countries is another case in point.

In the second instance (b), as a normative theory, interactive governance argues that the move from government to governance is a progressive one; governing should indeed become (even) more interactive and participatory than it currently is. In fisheries, many argue that the current governance system led by government is too top-down in many cases, and that is a reason why it so often fails (Gray 2005). This is because central government does not have the capacity and the contextual knowledge it needs to govern effectively. It must therefore involve stakeholders in decision-making and in power-sharing. Several arguments are put forward in support of such a shift.

First, as already indicated, the move from government to (interactive) governance has potential functional merits. According to Jessop "... the state gives up part of its capacity for top-down authoritative decision making in exchange for influence over economic agents and more effective overall economic performance" (Jessop 1998: 36), in other words a governability achievement. It may also make governance more effective as it broadens the information base and makes governors more sensitive to the specificities of local contexts. A more interactive and cooperative form of governance should make governing systems able to employ a broader set of tools, and make governors capable of dealing with both macro and micro issues. The same argument would apply to legal processes. This is also why in most instances government is a multi-scale legislative system.

Then there is the issue of legitimacy and trust, which is a prerequisite for governability and hence the effectiveness of governing systems. There are, of course, many ways to make people abide by rules, repression being one (Held 1987). Governing would, however, be less costly if people were to follow rules voluntarily. This is more likely to happen if people are allowed to see why rules sometimes are necessary. Opening governing systems to broader participation would thus facilitate the transparency and experiential learning that would enable people to do that. Moreover, participation is, as Sen argues, also about social justice (Sen 2009). People who have stakes in the outcome have a right to be recognized, and direct involvement of stakeholders in the process is a way to do so. The causal chain is therefore that justice is good for legitimacy, which fosters compliance and ultimately governability.

Finally, it could be argued that interactive governance has intrinsic value in so far as it institutes a more democratic form of governance. This is true regardless of whether interactive governance is living up to all its promises. As with democracy, interactive governance comes with the risk of abuse. It may, as already mentioned, be corrupted by power (Jentoft 2007b). However, the remedy is hardly to abandon democracy, but to make it work better. Accommodating for legal pluralism may be one of the remedies (Jentoft et al. 2009). This means ensuring that legal norms and orders that are "out there" are represented "in here" when decisions pertaining to, for instance, fisheries and coastal management are deliberated and decided on. If legal norms are too tacit to be expressed and integrated directly, they can be represented indirectly by involving those who know about them. Co-management would only provide the beginning of the answer of how to do this. The solution must also be found in the details of the organizational set-up (see Pinkerton 2003); for instance who gets to become represented and how, and therefore whose normative orders are recognized. If the diversity of legal norms is to be taken into consideration, representation must be structured to ensure that the legal pluralism that exist and are relevant for decision-making in particular instances are at the table. It is also therefore reasonable to assume that the legitimacy of co-management would largely depend on its contextualization and its ability to learn and adapt (Armitage et al. 2008). For this, co-management must also pay as much attention to communicative processes as to institutional and legal design.

It would be naïve to assume that more interactive governance is always better, and that blurring the boundaries between government, civil society and markets is necessarily a good thing. Each system has distinct roles, functions and capacities. There is something that only each of them can do. For instance, the state cannot (and should not) replace what a family does, or a business enterprise cannot perform the roles of the former two. At the same time, there are also things that non-state governors cannot do. For example, we need a government when customary law breaks down or fails to deliver on crucial issues. Still, these boundaries are not written in stone; things are constantly moving on the borders between these governing systems. How we look at these boundary issues largely depends on where we start – from a situation where government is largely absent or from a situation where it is omnipresent. Interactive governance theorists commence primarily from the latter situation, where the hierarchical, command and control governing approach of the state is perceived to have inherent governability limitations that interactive governance may compensate for. Interactive governance shares with other governance schools the search for new alternatives to the functioning of the state and its changing borders with other societal systems, such as those of the market and civil society. There is, for instance, the case of Public Management (Eliassen and Kooiman 1987). Later the so-called New Public Management (Christensen and Lægreid 2002; Pollitt and Bouckaert 2011) became a dominant idea, and most recently the concept of Public Governance has emerged (Osborne 2010). Each of these governance schools has its own particular emphases on the normative and empirical features of public and private functions and their boundary traffic. For instance, New Public Management is predominantly concerned with movement along the state-market axis, and is normatively arguing for outsourcing of public functions, such as privatization. It is a champion of "a unilateral infusion of corporate-sector values and objectives into the public sector and public-service production and delivery" (Peters and Pierre 1998: 234).

Legal pluralism theorists, on the other hand, often start from the observation that colonial powers have super-imposed their own legal systems on situations already governed by indigenous, informal, or unofficial law, as in the case of India, Indonesia and in countries of Africa (Hooker 1975; Merry 1988). Many empirical studies of legal pluralism have therefore emerged in those countries. One can easily imagine situations and spheres of life where society needs to be protected against government intervention (and governments from markets, which is the criticism often being raised against New Public Management, and vice versa, which is central to neo-liberal economics). In fisheries, it has been argued that communities in many instances are better left alone to handle their collective choice issues (Anderson 1987; Pinkerton 1987). Communities do not necessarily operate in a legal vacuum or anarchy even if the government is absent. Instead, they work according to rules that they have developed and are able to enforce themselves – thereby contributing to legal pluralism and governability. Bavinck's study of the 'Panchayat' system in South India is a case in point (Bavinck 2001).

Thus, government interference is not necessarily enhancing governability but may well lead to the contrary like when reducing the capacity of local people to manage their fishery by their own initiatives, values and norms, because government techniques tend to deskill locals (Wiber and Milley 2007). Therefore interactive governance raises "the question of the relation between state intervention and societal autonomy" (Offe 2009: 555), and the essentials of creating a truly mutually constructive governing interaction.

In the third instance (c), given that in reality governance is less hierarchical, more interactive and institutionally hybrid than we often tend to believe, and that a move towards more interaction should be supported for reasons given above, we need a conceptual framework by which we can analyse interactive governance both as a reality and as a potential governability enhancement. It is perhaps primarily as an analytical perspective that interactive governance theory may have something to offer legal pluralism. What this entails conceptually is summarized below.

## 5. Applying interactive governance theory to legal pluralism

Interactive governance is developed into a comprehensive conceptual framework by Kooiman (2003) and later applied by Kooiman et al. (2005) for fisheries. The framework is richer than what is possible to depict and explain in a short article like this; the following thus concentrates on aspects that are most relevant from a legal pluralism perspective.

a) *Governance systems*. Interactive governance operates with a two system model: a system-to-be-governed and a governing system, between which there is interaction that may take various "modes" (Figure 1). In fisheries, the system-to-be-governed is partly natural and partly social - comprising ecosystems, natural resources in those ecosystems, as well as various different categories of resource users and their institutions. The governing system, on the other hand, consists of institutions and steering mechanisms, among which legal rules play a prominent part. Interactive governance emphasizes that there are limitations as to how governable these systems are, and that it is essential to understand these limits, where they sit, and how they can possibly be overcome (Jentoft 2007a). Are they, as Mayntz mentions, due to "an implementation problem" or a "knowledge problem within the governing system" or a "motivation problem" at the receiving end of the governing interventions (Mayntz 1994: 13), i.e. within the system-to-be-governed? The governing system does not always possess the capacity to govern or lacks the inclination to do so because the system-to-be- governed is likely too complex, already self-governable or because those who inhabit it reject external (state) intervention (Bavinck 1998; Mahon 2008).

According to interactive governance theory, these limits are, as figure 1 illustrates, related to four key properties that are common to both systems. They tend to be characterized by (i) *diversity*, and thus, there is no single formula for addressing governability; and any measure would need to be tailored to context. The normative order is obviously also part of that specific context, and any governability analysis would naturally need to detect and describe whatever normative orders exist and how individuals need to adapt to them. Legal pluralism does after all stem from sociological pluralism (Rouland 1994). This pluralism may cause problems for people who must learn to live with it. For instance, a fisher who has to move out of and into legal systems that apply to the different communities and fishing grounds as he migrates with the fish has an information problem. How is he supposed to know about them? What if he breaks rules unknowingly?

(ii) *Complexity* refers to the way system components are linked, such as in trophic chains or social networks. Complexities may of course also be of a legal nature. Not only are activities such as fishing, aquaculture, transport, tourism etc. competing for space and resources in the coastal zone; they are also subject to separate legal measures that are often poorly harmonized, in direct conflict, and thus turning coastal zone management into more of a legal battleground than it needs to be (cf. for example Cicin-Sain and Knecht 1998; Buanes and Jentoft 2005; Sanchirico et al. 2010; Wiber and Recchia 2010). The governability of coastal zones will clearly gain from cross-sector legal coordination and harmonization. This is also what Integrated Coastal Zone Management and Marine Spatial Planning attempt to do (cf. for example Cicin-Sain and Knecht 1998; Douvere and Ehler 2009)

(iii) *Dynamics*. In the world of fisheries, targets of governance are constantly moving. Similarly the legislation that underpins governance is not stable, as noted generally by K. von Benda-Beckmann (2001: 20): "There is no legal system that does not change at all." Thus dynamics is a key governability aspect both as a problem and a solution. The governability problem is heightened by the fact that the system-to-be-governed and the governing system are changing at a different pace and the governing system tends to lag behind. Fisheries resources may therefore be depleted before legislative authorities are able to respond. This can be exemplified by the so-called "roving bandits" problem – those fleets that move around the world fishing out unregulated fish stocks and are gone the moment national governments are ready to intervene (Berkes et al. 2006). The need for adaptive governance as a governability enhancement measure is therefore pretty obvious but perhaps not fully attainable for the simple reason that law is not meant to be unstable or flexible, and that legal reform is cumbersome and takes time.

Finally, there is the issue of (iv) *scale*. The governability challenge is not only that legal systems are diverse, inherently complex and often unstable, but also that they exist at different levels, as with state and community law which may or may not be in conflict (Tamanaha 2008). How are fishing people to respond if local rules are in conflict with national legislation (Gezelius 2002)? This is a problem for both the governing system and the system-to-be-governed. For the governing system it is likely to generate low compliance and high transaction costs. For the fisher it represents a dilemma. Whether he chooses to abide by local or state law, he will be a law-breaker. This issue is addressed in the fisheries management literature as well as in the legal pluralism literature. When Vanderlinden talks about the individual as the "converging point" of legal pluralism, he seems to be thinking about this dilemma (Vanderlinden 1989: 151). Similarly, when Ambler (2001: 41) raises the question whether "it is possible to balance the intended universalism of statutory law with the particularism of customary law," he is alluding to the same.

b) *Governance orders*. Interactive governance also distinguishes three "orders" of governance, between which there are linkages and interactions. i) The first order is about the decision-making that occurs routinely on a day-to-day basis. There are rules and guidelines for the procedures regarding how these actions should occur, but they are also supposed to be consistent with norms and principles at a higher order. In fisheries, for instance, these are harvesting and processing rules related to where, how, when, and how much to fish and how to secure a good quality product. Since such rules are predominantly about technical matters which require a lot of specialized expertise, they lend themselves for delegation to administrators and practitioners who, once the basic principles and institutional framework are established, have the normative foundation and guidelines they need for implementing their functions.

ii) The second order concerns institutions. Institutions are about norms and rules that are inscribed in their role composition (Scott 2001). Hence they are legal systems in their own right. In his above quoted definition of interactive governance, Kooiman talks about caring for those institutions that enable "the formulation and application of principles guiding those interactions" (Kooiman 2003: 4). Notably, interactive governance emphasises not only the problem-solving capacity of institutions but also their "opportunity creation". They facilitate, they make things possible, they empower.

Governance systems are typically complex networks of institutions, often in the shape of formal organizations with their own distinct boundaries, structures, cultures and mandates. Both within the governing system as well as in the system-to-be-governed, there is a diversity and fluidity of organizations. The fisheries industry is no exception to this rule. Understanding governability in this sector will therefore require in-depth analysis of these multi-scale organizational networks (Fanning et al. 2007). As a whole these institutional networks embody a legal pluralism, which often confronts members with conflicting values, norms, directives and mandates, thus easily leading to role conflict and normative confusion. In other words, understanding how legal pluralism works within institutional networks and organizational designs is essential for revealing the limitations and opportunities of governability.

iii) The third order ("meta order") governance is about the governing of governance, i.e. those values, images and principles that underpin governance at lower orders and which are essential for understanding what directions governance takes; which goals are prioritized, why certain tools are preferred to others, what criteria constitute good governance and why. Interactive governance argues that these questions are not outside or prior to governance, but central to it. They should therefore be subject to a similar interactive process as that which occurs at lower orders. From a normative perspective, they should be brought out in the open, deliberated and decided upon rather than playing a shadow role (Kooiman and Jentoft 2009).

Constructive communication requires that stakeholders know which position people come from when they argue about concerns that are important in the process and why certain things are left out. Schattschneider's perception of organization as the "mobilization of bias", i.e. that it is inherent to organizations that some issues and concerns are included and some are excluded (Schattschneider 1960), also applies to governance institutions, including those whose responsibility it is to uphold the law. It is essential for any governability assessment to investigate how and why certain values, images and principles are codified as law while others are not, which would inevitably involve the analysis of power and culture. It is, as Bavinck (2005) argues, important to recognize that not all conflicts among stakeholder groups are about interests. They are often about disparate ethics, values, and worldviews, and how to best include these issues in terms of constitutional and operational rules that governors negotiate. How stakeholders argue when they negotiate these rules would therefore be of special interest. Do they for instance invoke state or customary law, or perhaps universal governance principles? In fisheries and coastal governance there is an increasing influence of principles that are negotiated at a global level. The Food and Agriculture Organization of the United Nations' Code of Conduct for Responsible Fisheries (FAO 1995) is meant to inspire and inform governing institutions on how to promote more ecologically and socially sustainable and just fishing practices.

There is also a trend where fishing rights are perceived not just as a management tool but also as a human rights issue, given the way fishing rights interfere in social relations and people's ability and opportunity to sustain their livelihoods (Allison et al. 2012). This also raises the issue of universal versus local perceptions of justice, and how human rights are recognized principles within customary law. From an interactive governance perspective, meta-order governance of local, indigenous law requires a similar critical assessment as that instituted by the state. As K. von Benda-Beckmann maintains:

> Taking legal pluralism seriously, taking local law seriously, is not the same as endorsing every rule, or even any rule at all... To take it seriously means to acknowledge that it is there, that it affects people's behaviour, and that it also affects the way legislation is implemented. (K. von Benda-Beckmann 2001: 40)

Still, contrary to the role of the analyst, it is the role of governors to make value judgements, i.e. either to endorse or reject such rules. But when they do so, interactive governance argues that they need to be explicit with regard to why they choose one over the other, i.e. what meta-governance criteria they are using.

c) *Shifting perspectives.* The system-to-be-governed can also be seen as a governing system in itself. Think for instance of a marine protected area (MPA). Those who inhabit the area to be protected may already have their own governing system of roles, rules, and routines when the government decides to establish an MPA (Jentoft et al. 2007). In this case, we see one governing (legal) system being imposed on another governing system (cf. Pospisil 1971: 125 who talks "about different legal levels that are superimposed one upon the other"). It is also well established through ethnographic research that fisheries communities may have their own governing capacity, and therefore be in no urgent need of exocratic governance, i.e. governing by some external authority like the state. Instead they have the capacity to operate according to principles, norms and rules that are self-generated, often spontaneously, but not always informally. Again, Bavinck's study of the Panchayat system in South India is a case in point (Bavinck 2001). Social researchers should look at indigenous legal systems critically; they may be far from perfect, neither from a functional nor a justice perspective, as K. von Benda-Beckmann suggests above. Indeed, they may suffer from some of the same deficiencies as state law, including the inability to be sufficiently adaptive to changing circumstances.

The governing system, as that of the state, is not only imposing the law on the system-to-be-governed, be it a community or an industry; it also works according to the rule of law itself, and must be assessed as a system-to-be- governed. An issue here is the classic question of "who governs the governors?" Who are those people? How did they come to occupy their positions? What are the norms and rules that they follow, and how are they instituted in the first place? The same applies to governing interactions (cf. Figure 1), i.e. the ways in which the governing system and the system-to-be-governed communicate with each other. Interactive governance argues that in many instances, the "co"- mode (like in co-management) is a well-suited mechanism for assisting such communication, but co-management arrangements are also legal systems; they work according to rules that determine how stakeholders should be represented and how decision-making shall take place. For co-management, we need to examine what the legal norms are and how consistent and flexible they are. It may well be true that local law is "ad hoc pragmatic and free to achieve quick and inexpensive resolutions," as Guillet (1998: 65-66) describes for the evolution of water property rights in north-western Spain, but we may be better served if we make this a proposition a matter of empirical research when applied in other settings.

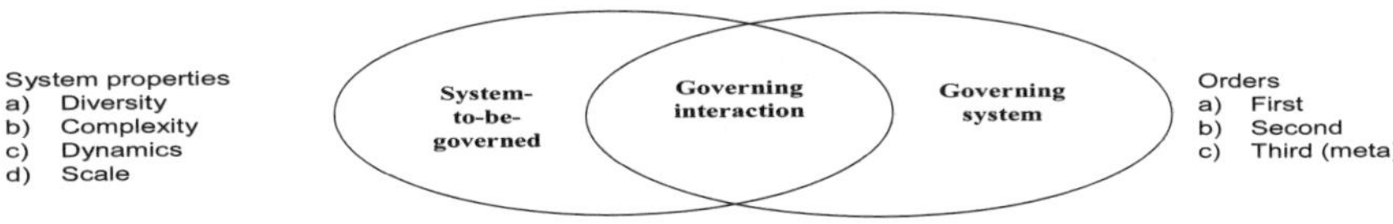


Figure 1. Interactive governance systems model

# 6. Conclusion

When exploring the limits of governability of fisheries and coastal systems, which is needed in order to understand why governance mechanisms often fail and what can be done to prevent it, legal pluralism is an issue that stands out. Is legal pluralism part of the problem or the solution - or both? Interactive governance provides a conceptual framework for such an analysis. It is notably not the only way to investigate governance and legal pluralism, but this is one worth exploring. Specifically, the task would be to search for the diversity, complexity, dynamics and scale of normative orders in their particular contexts, trying to understand how these properties of the governing system, the system-to-be-governed and the governing interactions limit or enhance governability.

Assessing legal pluralism for the sake of understanding (analytical) and enhancing (normative) governability would involve the investigation of the normative orders that are operative in these systems, as well as their linkages and the interactions surrounding them. This calls for comprehensive assessment. Interactive governance offers an array of hypotheses and concepts that are detailed, tested in the literature, and ready to be applied in new settings, including those where legal pluralism plays a role. But the reverse is also true. The legal pluralism discourse has much to offer interactive governance in helping to phrase sharp research questions of relevance to governability.

## References

ALLISON, Edward, H., Blake D. RATNER , Björn ÅSGÅRD, Rolf WILLMAN, Robert POMEROY and John KURIEN

2012 'Rights-based Fisheries Governance: From Fishing Rights to Human Rights.' *Fish and Fisheries* 13: 14-29.

AMBLER, John

2001 'Customary Law and Natural Resource Management: Implications for Integrating State and Local Law in Asia.' *Tai Culture. International Review of Tai Cultural Studies* VI (1&2): 41-62.

ANDERSON, Jr. Eugene N.

1987 'A Malaysian Tragedy of the Commons.' Pp. 327-343 in Bonnie J. McCay and James M. Acheson (eds.), *The Question of the Commons. The Culture and Ecology of Communal Resources*. Tucson: University of Arizona Press.

ANSELL, Chris and Allison GASH

2007 Collaborative Governance in Theory and Practice. *Journal of Public Administration Research and Theory* 18: 543-571.

ARMITAGE, Derek, Fikret BERKES and Nancy DOUBLEDAY

2008 *Adaptive Co-Management: Collaboration, Learning, and Multi-Level Governance*. Vancouver: University of British Columbia Press.

BAVINCK, Maarten

1998 "A Matter of Maintaining Peace." State Accommodation to Subordinate Legal Systems: The Case of Fisheries along the Coromandel Coast of Tamil Nadu, India. *Journal of Legal Pluralism and Unofficial Law* 40: 1451-171.

2001 *Marine Resource Management. Conflict and Regulation in the Fisheries of the Coromandel Coast*. New Dehli: Sage Publications.

2005 'Understanding Fisheries Conflict in the South – A Legal Pluralist Perspective.' *Society & Natural Resources* 18: 805-820.

BENDA-BECKMANN, Franz von

2001 'Legal Pluralism and Social Justice in Economic and Political Development.' *IDS Bulletin* 32/1: 46-56.

2002 'Who's Afraid of Legal Pluralism?' *Journal Legal Pluralism and Unofficial Law* 47: 1-44.

BENDA-BECKMANN, Keebet von

2001 'Legal Pluralism.' *Tai Culture. International Review of Tai Cultural Studies* VI/1&2: 18-40.

BERKES, F., T. P. HUGHES, R. S. STENECK, J. A. WILSON, D. R. BELLWOOD, B. CRONA, C. FOLKE, L. H. GUNDERSON, H. M. LESLIE, J. NORBERG, M. NYSTRÖM, P. OLSSON, H. ÖSTERBLOM. M. SCHEFFER and B. WORM
2006 'Globalization, Roving Bandits, and Marine Resources.' *Science* 311: 1557-1558.
BERMAN, Paul S.
2007 Global Legal Pluralism. *Southern California Review* 80: 1155.
BLACKET, Adelle
2001 'Global Governance, Legal Pluralism and the Decentered State. A Labour Law Critique of Codes of Corporate Conduct.' *Indiana Journal of Global Legal Studies* 8/2: 401-447.
BUANES, Arild and Svein JENTOFT
2005 'Challenges and Myths in Norwegian Coastal Zone Management.' *Coastal Management* 33/2: 153-167.
2009 'Building Bridges, Institutional Perspectives on Inter-disciplinarity.' *FUTURES* 41/5: 446-454.
CHRISTENSEN, Tom and Per LÆGREID
2002 *New Public Management: The Transformation of Ideas and Practice.* Aldershot: Ashgate Publishing.
CICIN-SAIN, Biliana and Robert W. KNECHT
1998 *Integrated Coastal and Ocean Management: Concepts and Practices.* Washington DC: Island Press.
DONAHUE, John D. and Richard J. ZECKHAUSER
2011 *Collaborative Governance: Private Roles for Public Goals in Turbulent Times*. Princeton and Oxford: Princeton University Press.
DOUVERE, Fanny and Charles N. EHLER
2009 'New perspective on sea use management: initial findings from European experience with marine spatial planning.' *Journal of Environmental Management* 90(1): 77-88.
ELIASSEN Kjell A and Jan KOOIMAN (eds.)
1987 *Managing public organizations: Lessons from Contemporary European Experience*. London: Sage.
FANNING, Lucia, Robin MAHON, Patrick MCCONNEY, Jorge ANGULO, Felicity BURROWS, Bisessar CHAKALALL, Diego GIL, Milton HAUGHTON, Sherry HEILEMAN, Sergio MARTINEZ, L'ouverture OSTINE, Adrian OVIEDO, Scott PARSONS, Terrence PHILLIPS, Claudia SANTIZO ARROYA, Bertha SIMMONS and Cesar TORO
2007 'A large marine ecosystem governance framework. *Marine Policy* 31:

434–443.

FAO

1995 The Code of Conduct for Responsible Fisheries. Rome: United Nation's Food and Agriculture Organization.

FOLKE, Carl, Thomas HAHN, Per OLSSON, and Jon NORBERG

2005 'Adaptive Governance of Social-ecological Systems.' *Annual Review of Environment and Resources* 30: 441-473.

GADAMER, Hans-Georg

2003 *Truth and Method.* New York. The Continuum International Publishing Group.

GEZELIUS, Stig S.

2002 'Do norms count? state regulation and compliance in a Norwegian fishing community.' *Acta Sociologica* 45(4): 305-14.

GRAY, Tim (ed.)

2005 *Participation in Fisheries Governance.* Dordrecht: Kluwer.

GRIFFITHS, John

1986 'What is Legal Pluralism?' *Journal of Legal Pluralism* 24: 1-55.

GUILLET, David

1998 'Rethinking Legal Pluralism: Local Law and State Law in the Evolution of Water Property Rights in Northwestern Spain.' *Comparative Studies in Society and History* 40: 42-70.

HEERE, Wybo P.

2004 *From Government to Governance, The Growing Impact of Non-State Actors on the International and European Legal System.* The Hague: T.M.C. Asser Press.

HELD, David

1987 *Models of Democracy.* Cambridge: Polity Press.

HOOF, Luc van (ed.)

2005 *Sharing Responsibilities in Fisheries Management Vol. 1 and 2.* Report from the EU project: Sharing Responsibilities in European Fisheries Management (Q5RS-2001-01998). Agricultural Economics Institute (LEI). The Hague.

HOOKER, M. Barry

1975 *Legal Pluralism: An Introduction to Colonial and Neo-Colonial Laws.* Oxford: Clarendon Press.

JAGERS, Sverker, Daniel BERLIN and Svein JENTOFT

2012 'Why Comply? Attitudes among Swedish Fishers towards Harvesting Regulations.' *Marine Policy* 36: 969-976.

JENTOFT, Svein

2007a 'Limits of Governability? Institutional Implications for Fisheries and Coastal Governance.' *Marine Policy* 31: 360-370.

2007b 'In the Power of Power: The Understated Aspect of Fisheries and Coastal Management.' *Human Organization* 66/4: 426-437.

JENTOFT, Svein, Thijs van SON and Maiken BJØRKAN

2007 'Marine Protected Areas: A Governance System Analysis.' *Human Ecology* 35: 611-622.

JENTOFT, Svein, Maarten BAVINCK, Derek JOHNSON, and Thomson KALEEKAL

2009 'Co-management and Legal Pluralism: How an Analytical Problem Becomes an Institutional one.' *Human Organization* 68/1: 27-38.

JENTOFT, Svein and Arne EIDE (eds.)

2011 *Poverty Mosaics: Realities and Prospects in Small-Scale Fisheries.* Dordrecht: Springer-Verlag.

JESSOP, Bob

1998 'The Rise of Governance and the Risk of Failure: The Case of Economic Development.' *International Social Science Journal* 155: 29-45.

KICKERT, Walter J.M.

2001 'Public Management of Hybrid Organizations: Governance of Quasi-Autonomous Executive Agencies.' *International Public Management Journal* 4: 135-50.

KJÆR, Anne Mette

2004 *Governance*. Cambridge: Polity Press.

KOOIMAN, Jan

2003 *Governing as Governance.* London: Sage Publications.

2008 'Exploring the Concept of Governability.' *Journal of Comparative Policy Analysis* 10/2: 171-190.

KOOIMAN, Jan, Maarten BAVINCK, Svein JENTOFT and Roger PULLIN (eds.)

2005 *Fish for Life. Interactive Governance for Fisheries.* Amsterdam: Amsterdam University Press.

KOOIMAN, Jan and Svein JENTOFT

2009 'Meta-governance: Values, Norms and Principles, and the Making of Hard Choices.' *Public Administration* 87/4: 818-836.

KRAAN, Marloes

2009 *Creating space for fishermen's livelihoods. Anlo-Ewe beach seine fishermen's negotiations for livelihood space within multiple governance structures in Ghana*. Amsterdam: Amsterdam University, PhD. Thesis

LINKE, Sebastian. Marion DREYER, and Piet SELLKE,
2011 'The Regional Advisory Councils: What is their potential to incorporate stakeholder knowledge into fisheries governance?' *AMBIO* 40/2: 133-43.

LONG, Ronán
2010 'The Role of Regional Advisory Councils in the European Common Fisheries Policy: Legal Constraints and Future Options.' *International Journal of Marine and Coastal Law* 25: 289-346.

MAHON, Robin
2008 'Assessing Governability of Fisheries Using the Interactive Governance Approach: Preliminary Examples from the Caribbean.' *The Journal of Transdisciplinary Environmental Studies* 7(1) http://www.journal-tes.dk/.

MAYNTZ, Renate
1994 'Governing Failures and the Problem of Governability: Some Comments on a Theoretical Paradigm. Pp. 9-20 in Jan Kooiman (ed.), *Modern Governance: New Government –Society Interactions*. London: Sage Publications Ltd.

MEINZEN-DICK, Ruth S.
2009 Property Rights for Poverty Reduction? DESA Working Paper No. 91. New York: United Nations Department of Economic and Social Affairs (http://www.un.org/esa/desa/papers/2009/wp91_2009.pdf).

MEINZEN-DICK, Ruth S. and Rajendra PRADHAN
2002 *Legal Pluralism and Dynamic Property Rights*. CAPRI Working paper No. 22. International Food Policy Research Institute. Washington D.C.

MERRY, Sally E
1988 'Legal Pluralism' *Law & Society Review* 22/5: 869-898.

MIKALSEN, Knut H. and Svein JENTOFT
2008 'Participatory Practices in Fisheries across Europe: Making Stakeholders more Responsible.' *Marine Policy* 32: 169-177.

OFFE, Claus
2009 'Governance: An "Empty Signifier"? *Constellations* 16/4: 550-562.

OSBORNE, Stephen P. (ed.)
2010 *The New Public Governance? Emerging Perspectives on the Theory and Practice of Public Governance,* London: Routledge

OSTROM, Elinor
1993 *Governing the Commons. The Evolution of Institutions for Collective Action.* Cambridge: Cambridge University Press.

PETERS B. Guy and Jon PIERRE
1998 'Governance without Government? Rethinking Public Administration.' *Journal of Public Administration, Research and Theory* 8/2: 223-243.

PIERRE, Jon and B. Guy PETERS
2000 *Governance, Politics and the State*. London: Palgrave Macmillan.
PIMENTEL, David T.
2010 'Legal Pluralism and the Rule of Law. Can Indigenous Justice Survive?' *Harvard International Review*. August 1. (http://hir.harvard.edu/law-of-the-land/can-indigenous-justice-survive). Last accessed Dec. 2011.
PINKERTON, Evelyn
1987 'Intercepting the State: Dramatic Processes in the Assertion of Local Co-Management Rights.' Pp. 327-343 in Bonnie J. McCay and James M. Acheson (eds.), *The Question of the Commons; The Culture and Ecology of Communal Resources*. Tucson: University of Arizona Press.
2003 'Towards specificity in complexity.' Pp. 61-78 in Douglas C. Wilson, Jesper Raakjær Nielsen, and Poul Degnbol (eds.), *The Fisheries Co-Management Experience*. Dordrect: Kluwer Academic Press.
POLLITT, Christopher and Geert BOUCKAERT
2011 Public Management Reform. A Comparative Analysis. New Public Management, Governance, and the Neo-Weberian State. Oxford: Oxford University Press.
POSPISIL, Leopold
1971 *Anthropology of Law: A Comparative Theory*. New Haven: HRAF Press.
RHODES, R.A.
1996 The New Governance: Governing without Government. *Political Studies* XLIV: 652-667.
ROULAND, Norbert
1994 *Legal Anthropology*. London: The Athlone Press.
SANCHIRICO, James, N. Josh EAGLE, Steve PALUMBI and Barton H. THOMPSON, Jr.
2010 'Comprehensive Planning, Dominant Use-Zones, and User Rights: A New Era in Ocean Governance.' *Bulletin of Marine Science* 86/2: 249-259.
SANTOS, Boaventura de Sousa
2006 'The Heterogenous State and Legal Pluralism in Mozambique.' *Law & Society Review* 40/1: 39-75.
SCHATTSCHNEIDER, Elmer E.
1960 *The Semi-Sovereign People: A Realist's View of Democracy in America*. Chicago: Holt, Rinehart and Winston.
SCOTT, W. Richard
2001 *Institutions and Organizations*: London: Sage Publications.
SEN, Amartya
2009 *The Idea of Justice*. London: Penguin.

STOKER, Gerry
1998 Governance as Theory: Five Propositions. *International Social Science Journal* 50: 17-28.
TAMANAHA, Brian Z.
2008 'Understanding Legal Pluralism; Past to Present, Local to Global.' *Sydney Law Review* 30: 375-411.
VANDERLINDEN, Jacques
1989 'Return of Legal Pluralism; Twenty Years After.' *Journal of Legal Pluralism* 28: 149-157.
WIBER, Melanie and Chris MILLEY
2007 'After Marshall: Implemention of Aboriginal Fishing Rights in Atlantic Canada." *Journal of Legal Pluralism* 55: 163-186.
WIBER, Melanie G. and Maria RECCHIA
2010 'Legal Pluralism and Integrated Management in Saint John Harbour, Canada.' *Maritime Studies* 9: 81-101.
WILSON, Douglas Clyde, Jesper RAAKJÆR NIELSEN and Poul DEGNBOL (eds.)
2003 *The Fisheries Co-management Experience: Accomplishments, Challenges and Prospects.* Dordrecht: Kluwer Academic Publishers.
WOODMAN, Gordon R.
1999 'The Idea of Legal Pluralism.' Pp. 3- 20 in Baudouin Dupret, Mauritz Berger and Kaila al-Zwani (eds.), *Legal Pluralism in the Arab World*. The Hague; Kluwer Law International.
ZIPS, Werner and Markus WEILENMANN
2011 'Introduction: Governance and Legal Pluralism - and Emerging Symbiotic Relationship.' Pp. 7-34 in W. Zips and M Weilenmann (eds.), *The Governance of Legal Pluralism. Empirical Studies from Africa and Beyond.* Wien: LIT Verlag GmbG & CoKG.

# PURSUING LEGAL PLURALISM: THE POWER OF PARADIGMS IN A GLOBAL WORLD

Anne Griffiths

## Introduction

The Jubilee Congress of the Commission on Legal Pluralism, that took place at the University of Cape Town in September 2011, celebrated thirty years of the Commission's role in promoting an understanding of, and commitment to, the study of legal pluralism worldwide. During its existence its members have engaged in many debates over the subject of what constitutes legal pluralism and how it is to be perceived. From its very inception, at the First symposium of the Commission on Folk Law and Legal Pluralism in Bellagio, Italy, in 1981 there was heated discussion about what to call law other than state law and how to identify its characteristics.[1] Such debates continue today, and my paper seeks to highlight some arenas in which contestations over law and legal pluralism have particular salience. Thus my paper will not provide an historical account of the development of legal pluralism that is addressed elsewhere.[2] Nor will it provide

[1] Terms such as local, folk, customary, informal, people's law and indigenous law were all proposed, but the point was made that there is no characterization that consistently follows any supposed distinction between state and folk law. For details of this discussion refer to Allott and Woodman (1985: 13-20).

[2] For discussion of some key texts see Vanderlinden (1970, 1989); J. Griffiths (1986); Merry (1988); F. von Benda-Beckmann (1998); Woodman (1998); Tamanaha (1993) and A. Griffiths (2002).

© Copyright 2011 - Anne Griffiths.

comprehensive coverage of what legal pluralism entails.[3] Instead, it seeks to highlight a number of domains in which the highly mobile and contingent nature of law is revealed, through the ways in which law is spatialized, representing multi-faceted dimensions of legal pluralism that are constantly in the making. Such a vision is at odds with the more traditional views of legal pluralism that are framed in terms of a state centred paradigm.

In recent years the power of law in all its dimensions has come under scrutiny in attempts to comprehend the forms that it adopts in processes of globalization. The growing recognition of the importance of transnational forms of law and ordering, derived from diverse sources (F. von Benda-Beckmann et al. 2009a, 2009b; Hellum et al. 2010),[4] has focused attention on the plurality of law and promoted a new, or renewed interest in legal pluralism in an age where law and legal institutions cross local, regional and national boundaries. This interest is one in which the 'local' is embedded in and shaped by regional, national and international networks of power and information that have increasingly engaged with discourses on international human rights. As a concept, legal pluralism has generated great controversy over the years[5], as different actors have used it for different purposes in attempts to promote their diverse interests.[6] It has been invoked to uphold notions of authority and legitimacy, to favour or promote one set of legal claims over another, or to validate and acknowledge the existence of alternative or co-existing forms of legal ordering within a particular domain.

---

[3] For examples of what the field may encompass see Greenhouse (1998); Rouland (1994); Tie (1999); K. von Benda-Beckmann (2001); Roberts (2005); Michaels (2005); Berman (2007); A. Griffiths (2009a); Tamanaha (2008) and Twining (2009-2010).

[4] Such sources include the World Bank, the European Convention on Human Rights, the World Trade Organisation, the World Health Organisation, the International Monetary Fund, the African Union as well as religious movements.

[5] For discussion of these debates see A. Griffiths (2002, 2009a).

[6] Such interests have been represented and debated in terms of the weak and strong legal models that have historically dominated discussions on pluralism, representing "the product of differing historical, economic and political factors that have conjoined to create different sites for study over time and space" (A. Griffiths 2002: 289).

Such pursuits raise questions about who has the power to make or remake law in all its various manifestations and for whose benefit. For how law is perceived depends upon the models or paradigms that are applied to its recognition that may vary according to the differing methodological and epistemological approaches that underpin them. These play a crucial role in formulating matters of jurisdiction, creating and ascribing authority and legitimacy that have an impact upon the success or failure of claims that people and institutions pursue. At whatever level they occur, the fate of these claims depends upon the extent to which they concur or are congruent with dominant legal models that are being applied. For if they fail to meet the standards that these models promote, these claims will be ignored or excluded from the arena in which they seek to operate. In the past, with the rise of the nation-state a particular paradigm of law became predominant, one in which state law acquired jurisdiction and took precedence over other forms of ordering within a territorially, bounded, geographic space.[7]

Always subject to contestation, this state law model requires reformulation in the light of what Sassen has termed "the epochal transformation we call globalization" (Sassen 2008: 2), reflected today in the trans-nationalisation of personal, economic, communicative and religious relations that give rise to conditions of legal flux. Such processes, in which local, national and international regulatory domains are enmeshed, reconfigure law both within the nation-state and beyond its boundaries. While law has always been mobile and globalization of law is not a new phenomenon (F. von Benda-Beckmann et al. 2005), there is intensification and increasing density in the flows and patterns of interactions and inter-connectedness between states and societies that constitute the modern world community. These incorporate global and regional networks of activity, institutions, and regimes of governance, as well as transnational social movements and other kinds of transnational association. The actors engaged in these concerns not only include national states acting as sovereign law makers or in concert with other states in the construction of international law, but also national or transnational nongovernmental organizations, 'law merchants,'[8] epistemic

[7] This model of law is often referred to as a positivist or legal centralist paradigm. For more detail on its characteristics see A. Griffiths (1997: 29-38).

[8] These are lawyers who travel the world, usually on behalf of governments, development organizations or multinational law firms, to introduce their law to countries that are in the process of legal reform; see Dezalay and Garth (1996). For the implications that such activities have for the development of transnational

communities,[9] self-regulatory networks, traditional and religious authorities and local communities.

Their activities range widely; from negotiating border disputes, entry to the EU, sponsoring aid for development, to participants in anti globalization protests, activists promoting the interests and human rights of indigenous or ethnic minorities, experts creating blueprints for governance of industries such as fisheries, as well as the work of religious and traditional leaders dealing with disputes among their followers, or local actors engaged in regulating pursuits within their neighbourhoods. What is clear is that all the claims being invoked involve space – physical, territorial, imagined, symbolic - and that the spaces they inhabit are multi layered. Pursuing legal pluralism in these contexts raises questions of scale and projection concerning the range and scope of the investigation, that are in turn dependent upon the standpoint from which legal pluralism is being addressed. For what you look for defines what you see.[10] Thus, any analysis of legal pluralism requires to be explicit about a) who the actors are; b) the purposes for which legal pluralism is being invoked; and c) the sources and methodological approaches that inform the legal inquiry that is at stake.[11]

---

justice see Dezalay and Garth (2012).

[9] See Wiber (2005), who uses this term to refer to a network of persons spread across the globe who share and promote a particular form of knowledge. See also Haas (1992); Maher (2002).

[10] The work of Drummond (2006) discussed later in this paper challenges, for example, the grand narratives of comparative law by exploring perceptions of locality and community that are discursively and historically constructed through a study of marriage practices in Gitano communities. What she renders visible would be rendered invisible under a conventional paradigm of comparative law.

[11] For as the 2009 report of the International Council for Human Rights Policy makes clear, given the complex constellation of factors that are at work, there can be no single paradigm of law that is applicable to the regulation of human rights, as there are no straight forward prescriptions that can be employed on a universal basis (ICHRP 2009). For a discussion of human rights that rejects a holistic or universalist stance in favour of a perception of culture that reflects a "sociological fiction, a shorthand referring to the disordered social field of connected practices and beliefs which are produced out of social action", see Cowan et al. (2001:14). See also Goodale who observes that given the diversity and multiple meanings of human rights it is important to pay attention "to different discursive spaces in

## Repositioning Governance: Multi Spatial Contextualizations of Law

One consequence of the processes outlined above is a recharacterization of international law that has arisen through the rise of global problems and the emergence of non-state actors.[12] As a result international law can no longer "simply coordinate state interests, but rather must facilitate state and non-state cooperation in such areas as humanitarian intervention, promotion of democracy and the rule of law, and transnational accountability" (Koh 2002: 328). Thus international law becomes a form of transnational law that is a subject in its own right as "in time the domestic and the international will become so integrated that we will no longer know whether to characterize certain concepts as quintessentially local or global in nature" (Koh 2002: 328). This is because in contexts where patterns of global legal interactions erode the boundaries between domestic and international law, foreign and domestic legal systems and practices, as well as internal and external juridical authorities (F. von Benda-Beckmann et al. 2005: 2009a; 2009b; Hellum et al. 2010), the idea of a single site of sovereignty embodied in the nation-state cannot be sustained, although states seek to lay claim to this power not only at a rhetorical or ideological level, but also in practice.[13]

### *Multi-Sited Ethnography*

Acknowledging these intersections requires exploring chains of interaction

which transnational human rights networks are constituted" (Goodale 2007: 24).

[12] This has repercussion where professionals, for example, draw selectively on the laws of multiple jurisdictions to create transnational legal constructs to meet their business clients' needs in ways that may subvert national regulations designed to thwart the public interests (McBarnet 2002). It raises questions about the ethics and viability of corporate social responsibility (McBarnet et al. 2007). It also has implications for the delivery of aid through international development agencies and NGOs that acquire 'quasi-state status', and that may undermine the prevailing legal and political orders in recipient countries (Weilenmann 2009).

[13] For an examples of the way in which a state may claim the opposite, and disclaim sovereignty to excuse itself from its failure to carry out its obligations to its citizens see Randeria (2003) on the 'cunning' state of India and its claims to powerlessness in the case of conditions imposed on development aid by the World Bank.

connecting transnational and local actors in multi-sited arenas. Such an approach is in keeping with anthropological and social scientific perspectives on law that engage with ethnography and have expanded its scope to become 'multi-sited' (Marcus 1995) or deterritorialized (Gupta and Ferguson 1992; Lefebvre 1991; Appadurai 1996, 2003; Merry 2006). This has opened up new horizons for study (A. Griffiths 2009b). The kind of multi-sited research that is called for today involves a broad landscape, one that encompasses not only diverse spaces unconfined by conventional territorial or geographic markers (Drummond 2006), but also such areas as 'information flows' encompassing the internet and global conferences (Merry 2000: 131) or world media (Eide 2010) in its diaspora.

*A Perspective on Migrants*

One area where multi-sited ethnography is especially pertinent is in addressing research on migration and in following the trajectories of migrants' multi-sited lives. For the transnationalisation of law across national boundaries is not the exclusive domain of powerful inter- and trans-national actors, but also pertains to ordinary migrants, businessmen and traders who do not belong to the political and intellectual elite that feature so prominently in discussions on globalization of law. The literature on migration usually describes one aspect of these processes: migrants taking their law to the new country of domicile. This involves the customary or religious law of their place of origin, as well as (to some extent) their national law that does not lose its relevance for migrants after they have arrived in their new domicile. This law is usually seen as opposing the law of the receiving national state, creating a host of problems for politicians, lawyers and for the migrants (Foblets 2005).

In these processes migrants are important actors in the dynamic reconfigurations of law at the different localities with which they are involved. What happens in one of the localities may have important implications for the way law develops in the other localities. However, the changes may occur at different paces and have different results depending on the specifics of the various localities involved. Nuijten (2005), for example focuses on the experience of migrants who move back and forth between La Canoa, a rural village in Western Mexico, and the USA. She explores contrasting normative values that migrants are confronted with in their transnational existence and which, in the process of confrontation and reflection, transform their identities. As Rabo observes in her study of Syrian transnational families and family law, exploring intersections cannot only be understood in terms of differing legal systems or laws that collide, but requires an understanding of how "people actually practise family relations across national borders" (Rabo 2010: 31).[14] From another perspective, that of ethnographic research carried out in Germany, the USA and Haiti, Glick Schiller (2005) makes the case for a new category of citizenship for migrants, that of 'transborder citizenship" that explicitly takes account of their multi-sited lives.

*Polycentric Relations*

What has emerged from adopting these approaches to legal pluralism is a less clear cut 'top down', or 'bottom up' perspective - that is linear and mono-causal or centric in its orientation – in favour of one that is multi-dimensional and polycentric in nature and that encompasses networks or webs of relations. In exploring these dimensions, that some scholars refer to as pathways (A. Griffiths 2009b) or trails (Greenhouse 2009), there is a recognition that what constitutes knowledge or understanding of these domains is not a given but is always partial and contingent. This standpoint is consonant with an interpretive and reflexive form of anthropology that explores how knowledge is produced and represented (Clifford and Marcus 1986; Clifford 1988; Harraway 1991; Hastrup 1992; Marcus and Fisher 1989; Okely 1992; Ong 1996; Wolf 1996; Yang 1996). For knowledge "is not transcendental, but is situated, negotiated and part of an on-going process...[that] spans personal, professional and cultural domains" (Narayan 1997: 37). Such reflexivity in relation to the construction of knowledge and its application may be contrasted with law's claims, under models of legal positivism or centralism, to authenticity and exclusivity.

## The Contingency of Knowledge: Deciphering Law

An example of how such an approach challenges state centred perspectives on law is provided by Drummond (2006). In her investigation of family law in the city of Jerez in Spain, she refers to her research as a "voyage" that forms part of an "itinerary" (Drummond 2006: 4). This represents a conscious strategy on her part to provide the reader with different points of orientation to the material, bringing

[14] This is in tune with Drummond (2006) in critiquing approaches to comparative law that promote grand narratives that operate to exclude other visions of law.

different perspectives to bear on a set of interrelated themes dealing with state, culture and marriage that form the three chapters of the book. By presenting several perspectives from which law might be viewed the author aims to bring "various projections of law" more clearly into view thus allowing for "some of law's itineraries (in the sense of both agenda and trajectory)" to "emerge in a place-neutralizing world "(Drummond 2006: 6). As a result of this type of analysis Drummond challenges the grand narratives of comparative law that adopt a linear overview of legal development in Europe emphasising "the convergence and harmonisation of legal traditions" (Drummond 2006: 18). This has involved interpreting the spread of secular family law across Europe with no-fault divorce regimes as representing "the apex of a modernising homogeneity" (Drummond 2006: 86) in which the "culture and practice of family law in Spain" is seen to be "in conformity with a single, Western, globally disseminated 'modern' model" (Drummond 2006: 47). Yet, as Drummond points out, "such a rendering of the history of marriage in Western Europe is one that has been written as though there is one Western family about which a single history can be written" (Drummond 2006: 188). As a consequence, what is represented as universal in fact represents "an exclusive and extraordinarily narrow band of the European population" (Drummond 2006:188).

By focusing on space and place in the form of the city of Jerez de la Frontera Drummond explores what constitutes the 'local' or 'locale' through an analysis of perceptions of locality and community that are discursively and historically constructed, rather than treating it as a given. This perception is one that is not bounded by state notions of territoriality or jurisdiction. This approach is also in keeping with a shift in anthropological perceptions of space in physical or material terms to an interest in the spatial dimensions of culture (Gupta and Ferguson 1997) through the recognition "that all behaviour is located in and constructed of space" (Low and Zuniga 2003:1). The locale that forms the subject matter of Drummond's study is not just a place where things happen but represents "a specific site in which social relations are bounded and locally constituted, while the sense of place relates to the experiences and representational map constructed of a specific place by its occupants" (Blomley 1994: 112). Thus for her the concept of 'place' is "the central analytical problematic of the book", which encompasses the actual city as well as the "metaphorical city of the book's theoretical musings" (Drummond 2006: 4). Such musings are in keeping with Lefebvre's observations that "space is not a scientific object removed from ideology or politics, it has always been political and strategic" (Lefebvre 1991: 31). In this way Drummond's study, although located in a place that is a physical space, nonetheless represents a form of deterritorialized ethnography

## Remapping Legal Pluralism

Delineating place and space in this way has implications for the ways in which law and legal pluralism may be perceived. Through scholars' ethnographic approaches to the study of law, based on specific, concrete and lived-experiences, other narratives emerge that provide a counterpoint to the analyses of law based on abstract legal theory. While there has been a recognition of the need to rethink the traditional doctrine of the sources of law (Teubner 1997) such reappraisal does not mark a new development, as such challenges to doctrine have long been articulated by scholars who view state law as representing only one form of political organisation that exists alongside other local, territorial, tribal, political or religious organizations with their own forms of law. In many cases these challenges to 'traditional doctrine' involve a study of law from below that explores specific responses to globalization from local perspectives. They explore spatial and temporal dimensions of the globalization of law, tracing the emergence, flow and influence of transnational legal forms into small-scale social fields. These may be lower levels of state administration, or villages, or social fields and arenas interconnecting actors at different levels of political organization. Such studies contribute to a growing body of research on the globalization of law in social fields or levels of state administration that exist below the national arena.[15]

### *Reconfiguring States: Citizenship*

One area where state centred views of law have been heavily contested is that of citizenship. Over the years it has been the focus of much attention, given transnational migration discussed earlier and the displacement of persons from countries of origin due to wars or conflicts that have forced individuals to become refugees or asylum seekers. In dealing with the classification of persons, citizenship raises questions about defining who is to be included as a citizen within a state and who is to be excluded from this status. The scope of the concept of citizen is limited by policies implemented in formal laws, leading to a set of criteria applied in making this decision,[16] along with bureaucratic regulatory

[15] See Stewart (2011) on plural governance chains molding constructions of gender in ways that lead to the unequal distribution of the benefits of globalization.

[16] For the complexities involved in determining formal choice of law questions and

institutions that implement them (Morgan 2003). Those that fail to meet the criteria and who remain in the state acquire an "illegal" status in law rendering them liable to deportation and expulsion (De Genova 2002). The formal criteria for citizenship tend to be somewhat narrow, based on country of birth, marriage, official residence and so on, and have been subject to critique (Coutin 2000).

Attempts have been made to displace the status quo by framing a category of "social citizenship" as a step towards challenging and broadening formal, legal definitions of citizenship when it comes to dealing with undocumented persons within a nation state. Such new criteria include, period of de facto residence, contributions to and engagement with the local community, birth of children within the country, among other factors (Coutin 2000). It comes as no surprise that many of those constructing categories of social citizenship tend to be anthropologists, sociologists and socio-legal scholars who have a more social-scientific perspective on law and its relationship with society and who seek to apply this perspective to create more inclusive definitions of law.

Other examples include regulatory frameworks that are not formally recognised by state law but that have legitimacy and authority in the eyes of those communities that apply them. This, for example, includes the favellas in Brazil or the barrios of Columbia, which were viewed until recently as illegal, squatter settlements by state law. In recent years attempts have been made in Columbia to recognise and regularise some of these settlements under certain conditions. Another example is that of People's Courts in South Africa that sprang up under the old apartheid regime with no formal legal status but used by local groups to control and regulate life in the townships.

*Indigenous Peoples: Strategies for Recognition*

Another arena of contestation in recent years has been the recognition of indigenous peoples and their laws and rights to self-governance. It has provided an ongoing focus for legal pluralism research and has had ramifications through inquiries into how the concept of indigeneity is constructed within local, national and transnational domains. Merry has long observed that "indigenous groups often define themselves in terms being developed by the global movement of indigenous peoples human rights and the provision of state law" (Merry 2000: 127). This is

dual citizenship see Foblets (2005).

important because "the legal provision of the nation in which an indigenous community lives as well as those of the international order affect how a particular indigenous community presents itself and the kinds of identities it assumes" (Merry 2000: 127). These represent in part "accommodations to the shifting global and national frameworks of power and meaning in which the community lives" (Merry 2000: 127).

Early strategies for recognition adopted different means. The strategy behind the Mabo case[17] in Australia, for example, was to make the national legal system recognize native title, demonstrating that indigenous laws, customs and traditions, could be accommodated within the Common Law paradigm. While native title could be extinguished in a number of ways, the decision opened up the way for indigenous groups to claim interest in large segments of their traditional lands if they could demonstrate the required continuing connection with those lands. In contrast, the WAI 262 proceedings in New Zealand[18] dealing with the issue of folklore protection alleged, amongst other things, that the Crown, by entering into a number of key intellectual property law instruments without proper consultation with the Maori, breached its obligations under the treaty of Waitangi. The claimants starting point in these proceedings was not the traditional taxonomy of intellectual property rights and a demonstration of how the concerns of the Maori Iwi could be accommodated within the traditional heuristic structure of intellectual property law, but rather the treaty of Waitangi and its guarantee of the right to sovereignty which they claimed the Crown had breached.

*Tribal Constitutionalism: Towards a New Form of Pluralism*

In responding to claims and rights asserted by indigenous peoples, states such as Australia, New Zealand, Canada and the United States have required such peoples to adopt a written constitution on membership rules. Such rules operate as a condition of official recognition. This requirement has given rise to 'tribal constitutionalism' that generates a new legal and political distinction between indigeneity and tribal membership (Gover 2010). This creates "a jurisdictional split between the category of indigenous persons identified by the state, and the

[17] *Mabo v Queensland [No 2]* (1992) 175 CLR 1. For discussion see Sackville (2003).

[18] For discussion see Austin (2003).

category of tribal members identified by officially recognized tribes" (Gover 2010: 1). This is problematic because these classifications create a situation where some "legally indigenous persons are not tribal members" while "some tribal members would not qualify as indigenous under public law definitions" (Gover 2010: 1). In the settler states she deals with, Gover observes that one of two models are applied to recognition based on race or the nation (Gover 2010:10). The first model, based on race, prioritises indigenous ancestry, while the second, based on the nation, prioritises tribal membership. They operate in opposition to one another with the effect that "either tribal self-governance is undermined by the State's dealing with non-tribal indigenous people, or a large and growing number of indigenous people are shut out of the State-indigenous relationship by the mediating institutions of tribes" (Gover 2010: 10).

Yet, Gover argues, the concept of indigeneity extends beyond that of a narrowly construed emphasis on tribal membership, for many non-tribal persons are recognized by tribes and by other indigenous communities. This is something of which neither model of recognition takes account because "neither acknowledges the role played by indigenous communities in the construction of indigeneity" (Gover 2010: 10). In accommodating this excluded perspective, Gover advocates adopting a concept of 'inter-indigenous' recognition. This would extend the legal category of 'public indigeneity' beyond members of officially recognized tribes to include "the cultural concept [of indigneity] as it emerges from indigenous practices of recognition" (Gover 2010: 10).

## Moving Beyond the State: Appeals to Transnational Regulation

Defining concepts of indigeneity, involving recognition of membership within social groups and of rights ascribed to their status, entails configuring relations between indigenous peoples and states. This not only involves internal processes of negotiation located within the geographic territories of states but may also involve appeals to transnational forms of governance that may be used to reshape negotiations within these arenas. For example, UN Declaration on the Rights of Indigenous Peoples (UNDRIP)[19] provides an international instrument that may be utilized by indigenous peoples in the quest for recognition and implementation of

[19] This was passed by a resolution of the General Assembly, GA Res 61/295, adopted on 13th September 2007.

international human rights standards to legitimate their claims on states. Framed in terms of international law, UNDRIP refers to international law norms, human rights law, treaties between states and indigenous peoples, state law, and without distinction, to indigenous 'laws, traditions [and] customs'. As such, it marks a significant advance in the recognition of indigenous peoples as subjects of international law, with recognition of their collective rights that may be viewed as separate and distinct from the body of international human rights law (geared to individual rights) and the related rights of minorities. As a resolution, UNDRIP is not a treaty establishing international obligations for those states that consented to its adoption. Nonetheless, it has provided an important mechanism for developing a system of global governance and international human rights law. As Wheatley observes "applications from indigenous groups have been important in developing the 'case law' of the Human Rights Committee on Article 27, International Covenant on Civil and Political Rights (the minority right to a distinctive 'way of life')" (Wheatley 2009: 383).

What UNDRIP creates is space for "political participation in legal regimes outside of the state" that "allows the possibility of regime capture (or at least influence) with the authority of the international law system then seen to conflict with the state law system" (Wheatley 2009: 383). In appealing to norms developed outside state legal systems, indigenous peoples may challenge legal norms within their own domestic legal systems. This gives rise to a legal pluralism that requires a "shift in the thinking of public international lawyers." They must make sense of the "new complexities" and take account of "global governance, and the relevance of democracy and democratic legitimacy in the exercise of political authority", including a recognition of the social, economic and political life of indigenous peoples (Wheatley 2009: 384).

Outside of states, bodies that may be used to push the implementation of human rights within states include the Inter-American Commission on Human Rights (IACHR) and the Inter-American Court of Human Rights that regulate the Inter-American Human Rights System. A recent case, *La Oraya Community v Peru*, pursues the relationship between environmental health and human rights. It seeks to extend the responsibility of a state for the violation of human rights of a non-indigenous community through contamination of the environment. As Spieler observes the case is significant because it "has the potential to expand the concept that environmental protection is closely related to human rights promotion and effectiveness" (Spieler 2010: 27). If the IACHR issues a report in favour of the petitioners, the people of La Oroya, and the state of Peru fails to address the concerns of the IACHR it could remit the case to the Inter-American Court. While the Court has issued judgments dealing with environmental degradation, these have, to date, been confined to dealing with indigenous communities and the protection of their rights and territories. In opening up the scope for recognition of the interrelationship between environmental health and human rights in general, the case has the potential for holding a state accountable for human rights violations in a broader arena. This could include violations of the right to health, life or personal integrity of a community, caused by environmental contamination in a whole range of circumstances, such as pesticide contamination, or air pollution in cities (Spieler 2010: 23).

*Mobilizing Legal Change: Social Movements and Constitutional Reform*

Mobilizing for change within states is not confined to the struggles of indigenous peoples. It can involve widespread political mobilization for radical legal reform as in the case of several Latin American countries (Houtzager 2005; Restrepo Amariles 2010). In his study, Houtzager examines the impact of social movements in challenging systemic and durable forms of exclusion. In his case, in the context of the struggle for land engaged in by the Movement of the Landless (MST) in Brazil. He analyses the success of the MST, that has made access to land more equitable in parts of Brazil by redefining property rights in practice, in terms of juridical mobilization through the juridical field. This field is constituted through a wide range of actors and institutions including judges and judicial institutions, private lawyers and law firms, public prosecutors, law school professors, NGOs and professional legal associations. Such mobilization takes places across multiple fields that "integrate juridical action into broader political mobilization, politicizing struggles before they become juridified, and mobilizing sophisticated legal skills from diverse actors" (Houtzager 2005: 219). In addition, support was also garnered from other sources that were "religious (through the progressive wing of the Catholic Church and pastoral organizations), political (through the Workers' Party in particular), labor (through the labor organization *Central Unica dos Trabalhadores),* academic, and within international advocacy groups and NGOs" (Houtzager 2005: 225). Such support was set in motion because of the transition to democracy.

What Houtzager demonstrates is how substantial legal change may be generated "when dynamics in the movement field and the political arena converged to alter that of the juridical field" (Houtzager 2005: 220). Even where this does not occur he shows how change on a smaller and more incremental scale can be brought about through mobilization across multiple fields. In these processes the modalities of legal change may vary. Drawing on the case of land occupation Pontal do Paranapanema, he demonstrates how the movement's land occupation strategy and juridical mobilization can combine to set in motion different types of modalities of legal change. In Pontal do Paranapanema three modalities were visible, these were "[1] state enforcement of a *de jure* legality that was ignored in practice, [2] a significant procedural innovation that speeded up the judicial clock, and [3] a shift in the sources of law and reinterpretation of substantive legal norms" (Houtzager 2005: 225).

Underpinning these developments is recognition that ever since the 1990's the efforts to constitutionalise law have played a critical role in facilitating judicial modalities of legal change. Such efforts have been strengthened through networks of progressive lawyers, especially the National Network of Popular Lawyers, formally constituted in 1996. Their commitment to the constitutionalisation process within the juridical field "played an important role in synchronizing the juridical and movement fields" (Houtzager 2005: 237). It has "played a substantial role in altering a highly exclusionary legality by compelling public authorities to implement existing agrarian reform legislation, by helping to create and institutionalize novel interpretations of the social function of property and an expanded notion of civil disobedience" (Houtzager 2005: 238). What is key in this process is an understanding of the dialectical relationship existing between the movement and juridical fields that illuminates how "relations between fields can alter their respective internal logics" to mobilize new perspectives on law (Houtzager 2005: 223).

Turning to other parts of Latin America, Restrepo Amariles draws attention to constitutional change in Columbia (1991), Venezuela (1999) and Bolivia (2009), focused on popular sovereignty as a means of refounding the state (Restrepo Amariles 2010). Promoted by the Latin American neo-constitutional movement and its radical wing, constitutional reforms in these countries aim at institutionalising popular sovereignty - based on legitimacy - over legal sovereignty - founded on legality, in the foundation, structure and functioning of the state. What this entails is establishing "original constituent powers" derived from the people, the promotion of active political participation and a focus on the justiciability of constitutional rights. To this end, and in order to include minorities and historically excluded groups in the process of constitutional reform, Columbia established a constitutional assembly. This was derived out of a national consensus "that claimed for itself the original constituent power" and thus "the legitimate constitutional power of the Columbian State" (Restrepo Amariles 2010: 89). According to Restrepo Amariles the constitutional assembly was characterised by its legitimacy rather than by its legality because it was "a constituent power and not a constituted power". It was "a source of law because it was built upon popular sovereignty" (Restrepo Amariles 2010: 89).

Venezuela went further than Columbia in its mechanisms for participation by holding a referendum on whether or not to establish a constitutional assembly, and by presenting the final draft of the constitution prepared by it to the people for approbation in another referendum. The Venezuelan Constitution "established by the sovereign people - in exercise of their constituent power" (Restrepo Amariles 2010: 95) constructed an institutional arrangement of that state that allows for permanent popular participation through creating a new public electoral power. This independent electoral power was established to enable citizens to control state abuses. It does so by guaranteeing the expression of the people's sovereignty "through vote, referendum, consultation of public opinion, mandate revocation" and other mechanisms as well as "open forums and meetings of citizens whose decisions are binding' (Restrepo Amariles 2010: 98). What is key here is the potential for strengthening civil society organisations and social networks of co-operation without the intermediation of political parties. The electoral power promotes a direct link among citizens and between citizens and the state.

To strengthen this type of participation the Columbian Constitution provides another mechanism for assuring popular legitimacy in the functioning of the state. This is through provision for the justiciability of constitutional fundamental rights that allow for "actualizing rather than merely protecting these constitutional rights" (Restrepo Amariles 2010: 104).[20] In this process the Constitutional Court "has used judicial review not only to decide particular cases, but to advance the social agenda of the constitution and promote structural changes that eliminate permanent threats to fundamental rights" (Restrepo Amariles 2010: 110). Restrepo Amariles argues further that with the introduction of constitutional actions for the actualisation of fundamental rights "constitutional review becomes more than an instrument of legality; it becomes a means of achieving popular legitimacy for the state" (Restrepo Amariles 2010: 113). This is especially the case given that it is

[20] This is done through four different types of constitutional actions, the fulfillment action (Art 87); the popular action (Art 88); the group action (Art 88) and the Tutela action (Art 86). For details see Restrepo Amariles (2010: 104-112).

not only negative liberty rights that are protected by the constitutional judges but also positive rights, such as housing, work and social security that increase "the legitimizing potential of constitutional review" (Restrepo Amariles 2010: 113).

These processes underpin broader notions of legitimacy with regard to state policies and actions, as well as providing for greater popular participation in the affairs of state through the development of a concept of popular sovereignty.[21] As such these developments represent radical changes in the interpretive legal process as well as in the accountability of the state that is expanded through constitutional reform. To be successful they require concerted political action and convergence of interests, as well as the mobilisation of forces that cut across multiple social fields.

## Virtual Worlds and Ephemeral Domains: New Horizons on Law

Rethinking questions of authority and legitimacy with regard to law also arise in spaces that elude conventional approaches to doctrinal analysis. One such arena concerns the internet. Given its global reach there has been much discussion over the years as to whom should regulate it, what form this regulation should take and for what purposes. Such deliberations give rise to competing approaches to perceptions of what the 'global commons' entails in a virtual world (Bernstorff 2004; Dizon 2010; Paliwala 2010). Much of the discussion centres on the potential for democratic governance and the ways in which this may be ordered. For Dizon the flaws in popular theories of democracy and Information and Communications Technology (ICT), be they utopian, dystopian or reinforcement, derive from the fact that "they have a very limited and singular view of what democracy is, where to look for it, and who are involved in its constitution" (Dizon 2010: 7). For this reason he advocates the need to "deconstruct and re-imagine the conception of democracy itself beyond the traditionalist state-centred and legal centralist

[21] Restrepo Amariles however challenges the view put forward by the radical wing of the neo constitutionalist movement, that popular sovereignty has replaced legal sovereignty underlying the modern political project by producing an alternative refoundation project. He argues that the latter is in fact "essentially a way of recovering the faith in modern ideals...[by creating] a new ideological artifact of modern thought aiming to recover faith in itself" (Restrepo Amariles 2010: 124-125).

assumptions" (Dizon 2010: 7). He proposes to do this by expanding the concept "beyond governmental regulation and political activity" which allows for "a broader yet more socially-intimate and fine grained experience of democracy" to be comprehended (Dizon 2010: 9).

Another approach is adopted by Paliwala who explores the way cyberspace's construction of new internet cultures also transforms economic and regulatory cultures that compete with one another (Paliwala 2010). On the one hand, he draw attention to cyberspace's potential for creating a new space for collaborative, non-capitalist, democratic engagement that is emancipatory for its constituents or the 'multitude'. However, he also highlights a competing approach that seeks to defend state and property interests by harnessing the power of capital to develop and control new modes of regulation and production with their inclusionary and exclusionary powers. What emerges are contradictory interpretations of what virtual space embodies. Thus Baxi and others such as Klein and Rajan stress that far from being emancipatory the internet represents new techno-scientific modes of production that stand for new modes of domination (Baxi 2006; Klein 2005: Rajan 2006).

From yet another perspective, Ali examines the discourse of internet *fatwa* and how this affects women and gender relations in a transnational sphere (Ali 2010). In exploring selected *fatwas* from three internet sites she asks the question "whether this burgeoning field of communication reflects emerging discursive sites for Muslim women within a counter-hegemonic transnational and global 'virtual' space" (Ali 2011: 118). In addressing this issue her study reveals how these new cyber space regulation mechanisms serve global Muslim space. As such, they generate an international discourse encompassing a wide spectrum of interacting norms that highlight "the 'irrepressible' plurality of the Islamic tradition" (Ali 2011: 118). She demonstrates how these sites have enabled Muslim women to raise questions about their lives that "they would not have been able to frame in a 'face to face' encounter due to the sensitive, private and at time challenging nature of the enquiry" (Ali 2011: 118). Thus she highlights the transformative potential of internet *fatwas* and the implications that this has for transnational and international family law norms within plural Islamic legal traditions. Her approach challenges existing hegemonies within an Islamic tradition that is predicated upon ethnicity, schools of juristic thought and territorial locations.

Moving in and out of engagements with multi-sited, transnational arenas poses problems about how to study a world in which all "is in flux, order is transient, nothing is independent, everything relates to everything else, and no one subsystem is necessarily continuously in charge" (Martin 1994: 250). It is a problem at the other end of the scale from deriving law and order from the territorial and sovereign claims of nation-states. While anthropological and/or social-scientific approaches to law have provided alternative visions of legal pluralism from those based on state centred frameworks, this has generally been accomplished through ethnographic and empirical studies derived from a focus on the "field" as a locus of study. What this entails has been subject to change over time, from earlier studies of village life to multi-sited or deterritorialised ethnography discussed earlier. It is constantly undergoing reconceptualisation and adapting to new challenges, as for example, how to conduct research where there is no easily discernible 'social field'. This is most evident in, but not confined to, moments of political reconstruction and instability (Greenhouse, Mertz and Warren 2002).

An example of the challenges this poses is provided by Zabusky's study of space-science mission development in Europe (Zabusky 2002). In examining the worlds of big science and European integration Zabusky elected to study the Space Science Department (SSD), within the European Space Research and Technology Centre located in the Netherlands, where most of the technical and scientific work is carried out. Zabusky identified what she considered to be a manageable social field for study, one where staff scientists are responsible for co-ordinating the efforts of other scientists, engineers and technicians from across Europe in designing, developing and manufacturing European Space Agency space-science missions. However, it soon became clear that the SSD "was not a relevant ...even genuine, social field for European scientists" (Zabusky 2002: 125), so she reoriented her focus away from the SSD itself to space-science missions. But this also presented difficulties because there was no central locus of decision-making that could be grasped, or tangible space that presented itself for study.

Instead, she encountered ephemeral virtual networks, such as international review boards that "did not exist anywhere but appeared only at the moment when called into being by a set of rules and regulations and by ongoing practices of participants" (Zabusky 2002: 129). For staff participating in mission development this gave rise to a sense of vulnerability and uncertainty in a world where "networks of people in different locations" working "toward a common goal" were continually being made and unmade "in decision-making processes that were constantly taking on different forms, subject to shifting centres of power that in turn dissolved and became reconstituted elsewhere" (Zabusky 2002:125). The problem for Zabuksy was that these processes "seemed more defined by constant change than by definitive structures; at every moment, political, economic, and organizational realities shifted"; this challenged Zabusky's ability "to hone in on a place I could call the field" (Zabusky 2002: 115). These experiences raised questions about where was "Europe (as opposed to its constituent nation-states)?", along with the problems of identifying "the international scientific community" since it was, by definition, everywhere?" (Zabusky 2002: 121). Nonetheless, she continued to grapple with these processes that she viewed as "widening gyres" where no-one is in control of this ongoing "gyration" that involves "the making and unmaking of centres" (Zabusky 2002: 113).

In exposing and exploring these dimensions Zabusky reveals how productivity in space-science mission development, far from being the product of political stability, in fact results from "participants experiences of instability and uncertainty as they improvise moments of clarity in which work can get done" (Zabusky 2002: 114). For participants working at the intersection of two powerful transnational processes, European integration and big science, this is an uphill struggle, as they are faced with constructing missions in the light of forces that are often at odds with one another. They must "meet their professional or intellectual needs" that are required for their projects "in the face of constant shifts in political priorities, organisational policies, and economic real-locations over which they have little or no control" (Zabusky 2002: 114). Under such circumstances what becomes apparent is the contingent and highly mobile nature of the world in which space-science missions come into being.[22]

## Shifting Paradigms: Legal Pluralism and the Mobilization of Power

This paper has explored forms of legal pluralism that highlight the multi-spatial contextualization of law. It provides a perspective on legal pluralism that highlights the mobile and contingent nature of law that reflects an ongoing process. Thus it challenges conventional analyses of law that are centred on and derive from a state centred perspective. It demonstrates the multiple ways in which international, transnational, national and local domains intersect with one another in a whole variety of ways that undermine any grand narrative of globalization and

[22] See Brumann (2012) on the importance of engaging in a discursive ethnography of interaction in studying the World Heritage arena.

concomitant vision of law. It displaces the latter, that underpins discussions of a uniform tendency towards homogenization, or alternatively, to fragmentation in the globalization literature, by highlighting the ways in which the effects of globalization reveal themselves to be highly different in specific contexts. This is accomplished through an analysis that sets out the complex relationships derived from intersections between transnational forms of law, such as human rights and religious law, and local legal orders, such as customary or traditional law, emanating from a plurality of sources within and beyond the state.

The importance of this perspective on law is that it reconstitutes spaces for action and the redrawing of boundaries within an environment in which state sources of law represent only one of a number of elements that may be at work. It also reveals the multi-stranded composition of state legal pluralism that discloses more shifting alliances and transitory bases for action.[23] In addition, it makes visible the transformative potential for law that derives from the new kinds of political and legal spaces that are in the making, that elude the boundaries of the territorial state and traditional legal scholarship. Such an approach reframes the discussion of institutions and specific practices - both public and private- "away from historically shaped national logics" (Sassen 2008: 2). Such visibility is critical for acquiring a proper understanding of processes of gloablization that, among other things, are "taking place inside the national to a far larger extent than is usually recognized" (Sassen 2008: 1).

In pursuing this form of analysis an understanding of the ways in which law is spatialized becomes apparent. It demonstrates how legal representation of space must be seen "as constituted by - and in turn, constituted of - complex, normatively charged and often competing vision of social and political life under law" (Blomley 1994: xi). In struggling to make sense of the complexity and ambiguity of social life "legal agents - whether judges, legal theorists, administrative officers or ordinary people - represent and evaluate space in different ways" (Blomley 1994: xi). What is foregrounded under plural legal conditions are the diverse and often contradictory notions of spaces and boundaries

[23] Merry and Woodman have long called for the need for a more serious investigation into what state legal pluralism involves, to examine the nation-state's ideological claims to legal uniformity and coherence that are used to construct a meta narrative that challenges "other" forms of ordering (Merry 1988; Woodman 1998). Studies on governance and governmentality have contributed to dismantling this image (Griffiths 2009a; Zips and Weilenmann 2011).

or borderlands that come to exist. In acknowledging these diverse legal constructions that come into being, what becomes visible the "multiple arenas for the exercise of political authority, the localization of rights and obligations, as well as the creation of social relationships and institutions that are characterized by different degrees of abstractions, different temporalities and moral connotations" (F. von Benda-Beckmann et al. 2009b: 4).

What emerges from these more broadly construed perspectives on law are the different actors who are engaged in contestations over who has the power and authority to generate law and construct its meaning. This is especially pertinent in plural legal constellations where there may be contestation over what is the 'correct' law in particular contexts. The power struggles that emerge under these circumstances often reflect asymmetrical power relations among parties and among legal orders. This affects the ways in which law's legitimacy is constituted and reconstructed. For law plays an important part in creating, producing and enforcing meanings of concepts such as 'justice', 'authority' and 'rights', and in instantiating notions of 'legality' that may be invoked by different social actors in their construction of hegemonic and counter-hegemonic discourses. Such discourses not only operate on a rhetorical or ideological level but may also serve to underpin the actual use of force or violence to achieve their ends.[24]

The recognition and prioritizing of legal orders today continues to create dilemmas and opportunities for contestation. These are ongoing because of a lack of consensus on how relationships between competing legal orders are to be determined. This involves questions about the extent to which such orders can co-exist, or the conditions under which one law takes precedence over another. In these negotiations legal pluralism provides a repertoire on which social actors can draw in constructing discourses of legitimacy that may be used to promote and justify multiple forms of intervention, action and policy-making in many different arenas. This is so, whether it is utilized to provide a form of higher legitimacy derived from rhetorical claims or whether it is mobilized for more concrete and instrumental purposes. Comprehending what these dimensions entail engages with the multifaceted nature of law that constitutes legal pluralism. It also underlines the extent to which legal spaces are embedded in broader social and political claims that involve complex negotiations over power[25] that cannot be ignored.

---

[24] See Baxi (2009), Greenhouse (2009) and Nader (2009) on the power of legal discourse in the 'war on terror'.

[25] For discussion of the multiple dimensions that power embodies see F. von

## References

ALI, Shaheen S.
2010 'Behind the Cyberspace Veil: Online Fatwas on Women's Family Rights.' Pp 117-137 in Hellum et al 2010.
ALLOTT, Antony and Gordon WOODMAN (eds.)
1985 *People's Law and State Law: The Bellagio Papers.* Dordrecht (Netherlands) and Cinnaminson (USA): Foris Publications.
APPANDURI, Arjun
1996 *Modernity at Large: Cultural Dimensions of Globalization.* (Public Worlds Series). Minneapolis: University of Minnesota Press.
2003 'Sovereignty without Territoriality: Notes of a Post-national Geography.' Pp. 337-349 in Low and Lawrence-Zuniga 2003.
AUSTIN, Graeme W.
2003 'Re-treating Intellectual Property? The WAI 262 Proceeding and the Heuristics of Intellectual Property law.' *Cardozo Journal of International and Comparative Law* 11: 333-363.
BAXI, Upendra
2006 *The Future of Human Rights. New* Delhi: Oxford University Press.
2009 'The Globalization of Fatwas Amidst the Terror Wars Against Pluralism.' Pp. 96-114 in F. von Benda-Beckmann et al. 2009a.
BENDA-BECKMANN, Franz von
1998 'Comment on Merry.' *Law and Society Review* 22(5): 897-901
BENDA-BECKMANN, Franz von, Keebet von BENDA-BECKMANN and Anne GRIFFITHS (eds.)
2005 *Mobile People, Mobile Law: Expanding Legal Relations in a Contracting World.* Aldershot (UK) and Burlington (USA): Ashgate.
2009a *The Power of Law in a Transnational World; Anthropological Enquiries.* Oxford (UK) and New York (USA): Berghahn Books.
2009b *Spatializing Law: An Anthropological Geography of Law in Society.* Aldershot (UK) and Burlington (USA): Ashgate.
BENDA-BECKMANN, Keebet von
2001 'Legal Pluralism.' *Tai Culture* VI(1/2):18-40.
BERMAN, Paul S.
2007 'Global Legal Pluralism'. *Southern California Law Review* 80(6): 1155-

Benda-Beckmann et al. (2009a: 2-6).

1237.

BERNSTORFF, Jochen von

2004 'The Structural Limitation of Network Governance: ICANN as a Case in Point.' Pp. 257-282 in Christian Joerges, Inger-Johanne Sand and Günther Teubner (eds.), *Transnational Governance and Constitutionalism.* Oxford and Portland: Hart Publishing.

BLOMLEY, Nicholas K.

1994 *Law, Space and the Geographies of Power.* New York: The Guilford Press.

BRUMANN, Christoph

2012 *Multilateral Ethnography: Entering the World Heritage Arena.* Working Paper No. 136, Max Planck Institute for Social Anthropology Working Papers, Halle/Saale.

CLIFFORD, James

1988 *The Predicament of Culture: Twentieth Century Ethnography, Literature, and the Arts.* Cambridge: Harvard University Press.

CLIFFORD, James and George E. MARCUS (eds.)

1986 *Writing Culture.* Berkeley: University of California Press.

COUTIN, Susan

2000 *Legalizing Moves: Salvadoran Immigrants' Struggle for U.S. Residency.* Ann Arbor: University of Michigan Press.

COWAN Jane A, Marie-Benedicte DEMBOUR and Richard A. WILSON (eds.)

2001 *Culture and Rights: Anthropological Perspectives.* Cambridge and New York: Cambridge University Press.

DE GENOVA, Nicholas P.

2002 'Migrant "Illegality" and Deportability in Everyday Life.' *Annual Review of Anthropology* 31: 419-447.

DEZALAY, Yves and Bryant G. GARTH

1996 *Dealing in Virtue: Commercial Arbitration and the Constructions of a Transnational Legal Order.* Chicago and London: University of Chicago Press.

2012 *Lawyers and the Construction of Transnational Justice (Law, Development and Globalization).* Oxon and New York: Routledge.

DIZON, Michael

2010 'Participatory democracy and information and communications technology: legal pluralist perspective.' *European Journal of Law and Technology* 1(3):1-36.

DRUMMOND, Susan G.

2006 *Mapping Marriage Law in Spanish Gitano Communities.* Vancouver:

UBC Press.

EIDE, Elisabeth

2010 'Differing Standards of Free Expression: Clashing of Laws during the Cartoon Controversy.' Pp. 227-298 in Hellum et al. 2010.

FOBLETS, Marie-Claire

2005 'Mobility *versus* Law, Mobility *in* the Law? Judges in Europe are Confronted with the Thorny Question "Which Law Applies to Litigants of Migrant Origin"?' Pp. 297-315 in F. von Benda-Beckmann et al. 2005.

GLICK SCHILLER, Nina

2005 'Transborder Citizenship: An Outcome of Legal Pluralism within Transnational Social Fields.' Pp. 27-49 in F. von Benda-Beckmann et al. 2010.

GOODALE, Mark

2007 'Introduction Locating rights, envisioning law between the local and the global.' Pp. 1-38 in Mark Goodale and Sally E. Merry (eds.), *The Practice of Human Rights: Tracking Law Between the Global and the Local*. Cambridge UK and New York: Cambridge University Press.

GOVER, Kirsty

2010 *Tribal Consitutionalism: States, Tribes and the Governance of Membership*. Oxford and New York: Oxford University Press.

GREENHOUSE, Carol

1998 'Legal Pluralism and Cultural Difference: What is the Difference? A Response to Professor Woodman.' *Journal of Legal Pluralism* 42: 61-72.

2009 'The Military Order of 13 November 2001: An Ethnographic Reading.' Pp 33-53 in F. von Benda-Beckmann et al. 2009a.

GREENHOUSE, Carol, Elizabeth MERTZ and Kay B. WARREN (eds.)

2002 *Ethnography in Unstable Places: Everyday Lives in Contexts of Dramatic Political Change*. Durham and London: Duke University Press.

GRIFFITHS, Anne

1997 *In the Shadow of Marriage: Gender and Justice in an African Community*. London and Chicago: University of Chicago Press.

2002 'Legal Pluralism.' Pp. 289-310 in R. Banakar and M. Travers (eds.), *An Introduction to Law and Social Theory*. Oxford and Portland Oregon: Hart Publishing.

2009a 'Anthropological Perspectives on Legal Pluralism and Governance in a Transnational World.' Pp. 164-186 in M. Freeman and D. Napier (eds.), *Law and Anthropology*, *Current Legal Issues*. Vol. 12. Oxford: Oxford University Press.

2009b 'Law, Space and Place: Reframing Comparative Law and Legal

Anthropology.' *Law and Social Inquiry* 34(2): 495-507.

GRIFFITHS, John
1986 'What is Legal Pluralism?' *Journal of Legal Pluralism and Unofficial Law* 24: 1-56.

GUPTA, Akhil and James FERGUSON
1992 'Beyond "Culture": Space, Identity and the Politics of Difference.' *Cultural Anthropology* 17: 6-23.

GUPTA, Akhil and James FERGUSON (eds.)
1997 *Culture, Power Place: Explorations in Critical Anthropology*. Durham and London: Duke University Press.

HAAS, Peter M.
1992 'Introduction: Epistemic communities and international policy coordination.' *International Organization* 46(1): 1-35.

HARRAWAY, Donna
1991 *Simians, Cyborgs and Women: The Reinvention of Nature*. New York: Routledge.

HASTRUP, Kirsten
1992 'Writing ethnography; state of the art.' Pp. 116-133 in Judith Okely and Helen Calloway (eds.), *Anthropology and Autobiography*. London and New York: Routledge.

HELLUM, Anne, Shaheen S. ALI and Anne GRIFFITHS (eds.)
2010 *From Transnational Relations to Transnational Laws: Northern European Laws at the Crossroads*. Aldershot (UK) and Burlington (USA): Ashgate.

HOUTZAGER, Peter P.
2005 'Movement of the Landless (MST) and Juridical Modalities of Legal Change in Brazil.' Pp. 218-240 in Boaventura de Souza Santos and Cesar A. Rodriguez-Garavito (eds.), *Law and Globalization from Below: Towards a Cosmopolitan Legality*. Cambridge: Cambridge University Press.

ICHRP (INTERNATIONAL COUNCIL FOR HUMAN RIGHTS POLICY)
2009 *When Legal Worlds Overlap: Human rights, State and Non-State Law*. Geneva: ICHRP.

KLEIN, Urusla
2005 'Introduction: Techno-scientifc productivity.' *Perspectives on Sciences* 13(2): 39-141.

KOH, Harold H.
2002 'Opening Remarks: Transnational Legal Process Illuminated.' Pp. 327-332 in Michael Likosky (ed.), *Transnational Legal Processes: Globalization and Power Disparities*. London: Butterworths.

LEFEBVRE, Henri
1991 *The Production of Space*, translated by Donald Nicholson Smith. Oxford: Blackwell [1979].
LOW, Setha M. and Denise LAWRENCE-ZUNIGA (eds.)
2003 *The Anthropology of Space and Place: Locating Culture*. Oxford and Berlin: Blackwell Publishing and Carlton.
MAHER, Imelda
2002 'Competition Law in the international domain: Networks as a new form of governance.' *Journal of Law and Society* 29(1): 111-136.
MARCUS, George E.
1995 'Ethnography in/of the World System: The Emergence of Multi-Sited Ethnography.' *Annual Review of Anthropology* 24: 95-117.
MARCUS, George E. and Michael FISHER (eds.)
1989 *Anthropology as Cultural Critique*. Chicago: University of Chicago Press.
MARTIN, Emily
1994 *Flexible Bodies: Tracking Immunity in American Culture from the Days of Polio to the Age of AIDS*. Boston: Beacon.
McBARNET, Doreen
2002 'Transnational Transactions: Legal Work, Cross Border Commerce and Global Regulation.' Pp. 98-113 in Michael Likosky (ed.), *Transnational Legal Processes: Globalization and Power Disparities*. London: Butterworths.
McBARNET, Doreen, Aurora VOICULESCU and Tom CAMPBELL (eds.)
2007 *The New Corporate Accountability: Corporate Social Responsibility and the Law*. Cambridge and New York: Cambridge University Press.
MERRY, Sally E.
1988 'Legal Pluralism'. *Law and Society Review* 22(5): 869-896.
2000 'Crossing Boundaries: Ethnographies in the Twenty-First Century.' *PoLAR* 23(2): 127-133.
2006 *Human Rights and Gender Violence: Translating International Law into Local Justice*. Chicago: University of Chicago Press.
MICHAELS, Ralf
2005 'The Re-State-Ment of Non-State Law: The State, Choice of Law, and the Challenge from Global Legal Pluralism.' *Wayne L. Review* 51: 1210-1254.
MORGAN, Bronwen
2003 *Social Citizenship and the Shadow of Competition: The Bureaucratic Politics of Regulatory Justification*. Aldershot UK) and Burlington (USA): Ashgate.

NADER, Laura
2009 'Law and the Frontiers of Illegality.' Pp. 54-73 in F. von Benda-Beckmann et al. 2009a.

NARAYAN, Kirin
1997 'How Native is the "Native" Anthropologist?' Pp. 23-41 in Louise Lamphere, Helena Ragone and Patricia Zavella (eds.), *Situated Lives: Gender and Culture in Everyday Life*. New York and London: Routledge.

NUIJTEN, Monique
2005 'Transnational Migration and Re-Framing of Normative Values.' Pp. 51-68 in F. von Benda-Beckmann et al. 2005.

OKELY, Judith
1992 'Anthropology and autobiography: Participatory experience and embodied knowledge.' Pp. 1-28 in Judith Okely and Helen Calloway (eds.), *Anthropology and Autobiography*. London and New York: Routledge.

ONG, Aihwa
1996 'Anthropology, China and modernities: the geopolitics of cultural knowledge.' Pp. 60-92 in Henrietta L. Moore (ed.), *The Future of Anthropological Knowledge*. London and New York: Routledge.

PALIWALA, Abdul
2010 'Regulating Cyberspace: Modes of Production, Modes of Regulation and Modes of Resistance.' Pp. 229-250 in Hellum et al.

RABO, Annika
2010 'Syrian Transnational Families and Family Law.' Pp. 29-49 in Hellum et al. 2010.

RAJAN, Kaushik S.
2006 *Biocaptial: The Constitution of Postgenomic Life*. Durham: Duke University Press.

RANDERIA, Shalini
2003 'Glocalization of law; Environmental justice, World Bank, NGOs and the cunning state in India.' *Current Sociology* 51: 307-330.

RESTREPO AMARILES, David
2010 *Legality and Legitimacy: The Legal and Political Philosophy of Popular Sovereignty in the New Latin American Constitutions*. Saarbrucken, Germany: Lambert Academic Publishing.

ROBERTS, Simon A.
2005 'After Government? On Representing Law Without the State.' *Modern Law Review* 68(1): 1-24.

ROULAND, Norbert
1994 *Legal Anthropology* (trans. Philippe G. Planel). London: Athlone Press.

SACKVILLE, Justice Ronald
2003 'The Legal Protection of Indigenous Culture in Australia.' *Cardozo Journal of International and Comparative Law* 11: 711-745.
SASSEN, Saskia
2008 *Territory, Authority, Rights: From Medieval to Global Assemblages.* Princeton and Oxford: Princeton University Press.
SPEILER, Paula
2010 'The Le Oroya Case: The Relationship Between Environmental Degradation and Human Rights Violations.' *Human Rights Brief* 18(1): 19-23.
STEWART, Ann
2011 *Gender, Law and Justice in a Global Market.* Cambridge and New York: Cambridge University Press.
TAMANAHA, Brian Z.
1993 'The Folly of the "Social Scientific" Theory of Legal Pluralism.' *Journal of Law and Society* 192-217.
2008 'Understanding Legal Pluralism: Past to Present, Local to Global.' *Sydney Law Review* 30: 375-411.
TEUBNER, Günther (ed.)
1997 *Global Law without a State.* Aldershot: Dartmouth.
TIE, Warwick
1999 *Legal Pluralism: Toward a multicultural perception of law.* Aldershot and Brookfield: Ashgate.
TWINING, William
2009-2010 'Normative and Legal Pluralism: A Global Perspective.' *Duke Journal of Comparative and International Law* 20: 473-517.
VANDERLINDEN, Jacques
1970 'Le pluralisme juridique: Essai de Synthese'. Pp. 19-56 in J. Gilissen (ed.), *Le pluralisme juridique'*. Brussels: l'Université Bruxelles.
1989 'Return to Legal Pluralism: Twenty Years Later.' *Journal of Legal Pluralism* 28: 149-158.
WEILENMANN, Markus
2009 'Project Law – a Power Instrument of Development Agencies: a Case Study from Burundi.' Pp 156-175 in F. von Benda-Beckmann et al. 2009a.
WHEATLEY, Steven
2009 'Indigenous Peoples and the Right of Political Autonomy in an Age of Global Legal Pluralism.' Pp. 351-384 in Michael Freeman and David Napier (eds.), *Law and Anthropology, Current Legal Issues Vol. 12.*

Oxford: Oxford University Press.

WIBER, Melanie

2005 'Mobile Law and Globalization: Epistemic Communities versus Community-Based Innovation in the Fisheries Sector.' Pp. 131-151 in F. von Benda-Beckmann et al. 2005.

WOLF, Diane L.

1996 'Situating Feminist Dilemmas in Fieldwork.' in Diane L. Wolf (ed.), *Feminist Dilemmas in Fieldwork.*" Westview Press.

WOODMAN, Gordon R.

1998 'Ideological Combat and Social Observation: Recent Debate about Legal Pluralism.' *Journal of Legal Pluralism* 42: 21-59.

YANG, Mayfair

1996 'Tradition, travelling theory, anthropology and the discourse of modernity in China.' Pp. 93-114 in Henrietta L. Moore (ed.), *The Future of Anthropological Knowledge.* London and New York: Routledge.

ZABUSKY, Stacia

2002 'Ethnography in/of Transnational Processes: following Gyres in the Worlds of Big Science and European Integration.' Pp. 113-145 in Carol J. Greenhouse, Elizabeth Mertz and Kay B. Warren (eds.), *Ethnography in Unstable Places: Everyday Life in Contexts of Dramatic Political Change.* Durham and London: Duke University Press.

ZIPS, Werner and Markus WEILENMANN (eds.)

2011 *The Governance of legal Pluralism: Empirical Studies from Africa and Beyond.* Vienna and Berlin: Lit Verlag.

# BOOK REVIEW

Deborah Isser (ed.), *Customary Justice and the Rule of Law in War-Torn Societies*. Washington DC: United States Institute of Peace Press, 2011. xiv + 386 pp.

Irene I. Hadiprayitno

The book is an edited volume of inter-disciplinary case studies that analyze the plural legal systems in seven countries. Authors of this well-written edited volume examine in depth the dynamic of the justice sector in Mozambique (Stephen C. Lubkemann, Helene Maria Kyed and Jennifer Garvey), Guatemala (Jan Hessbruegge and Carlos Fredy Ochoa Garcia), East Timor (Tanja Copra, Christian Ranheim and Rod Nixon), Afghanistan (Thomas Barfield, Neamat Nojumi and Alexander Thier), Liberia (Stephen C. Lubkemann, Deborah Isser, and Philip A.Z. Banks), Iraq (Patricio Asfura-Heim) and Sudan (Francis M. Deng).

The case studies go beyond traditional legal analysis to include a broad historical perspective on the legal structure of each country. The inquiry mostly goes back to the colonial period, a view that is sometimes neglected in legal positivist academic reporting. Considering the nature of the cases, it proves beneficial to move beyond a myopic focus on common juridical analysis in war-torn societies. In such circumstances, the nation building effort is at risk if plural legal systems are perceived as a given rather than as a result of social construction. In addition, each case study scrutinizes customary law and its connection with formal law in the context of various legal and practical modes, giving the book a central cohesiveness. Analyzing customary justice this way allows the authors, who consist of reputable scholars and experienced practitioners, to investigate the ways that customary justice systems further the goals of the rule of law and stability in post-conflict societies.

In the case studies, formal and non-formal legal systems are (differently) connected for many diverse reasons. In Mozambique, the developing interaction between state-centered and customary justice systems relies on the historical post-colonial legacy that gave legitimacy to customary law; this shapes modern daily politics as well. The connection was made possible in Guatemala by a remarkable acknowledgment of indigenous people of Mayan descent in the peace accords that ended the country's internal conflict of thirty-four years. Such an attempt brings a promise of legal pluralism in formal political practices, as is demonstrated by the codification of Mayan law in the constitutional amendment. In post-Taliban Afghanistan the formal justice system has limited reach and legitimacy, which creates a need for an accessible customary justice system. Similarly, alongside the globally celebrated flow of democratization in Liberia, customary institutions continue to function in small communities, where formal courts often do not even exist.

As these case studies observe, formal and customary justice systems coexist, and in their different ways not only provide the victims of post-conflict periods with access to justice, but also enable communities to adjust and adapt to the transitional situations. Both community-based authorities and local state officials in Guatemala are offered a *de facto* framework for action through practices that recognize the social legitimacy of customary justice systems. This *de facto* framework is marked by forms of collaboration that coexist side by side with forms of competition in different forms of collaboration. In Mozambique practicing customary law could fill the gap in the formal legal framework by setting *de facto* rules for articulation and jurisdiction. *Jirgas* and *shuras*, forms of non-formal dispute settlement mechanisms in Afghanistan, have also played a critical role in resolving certain kinds of crime. While in Iraq, tribal customary law could expand its task from resolving conflict to limiting the scale of conflicts.

Naturally, the existence of customary systems is not without contestation. Many different groups in society ultimately challenge the existence of customary systems. Such is the case with Mayan law, which is persistently contested by right wing or religious groups. In East Timor, the United Nations Transitional Administration sought to build a Western-style formal justice system with little regard for the socio-economic and capacity realities in the country. Yet local justice systems continue to adapt to native values that give meaning to sensitive crimes such as rape, or property issues such as land tenure. In the Sudan, the colonial legacy formally acknowledged religious and indigenous judicial systems that adjudicated personal matters, but this has been contested by demands to modernize the customary legal system, including the codification of customary law.

This edited book appeals for two reasons. First, the authors have carefully considered the caveats arising from the reach of customary law. Apart from the advantage of social adaptability and accessibility, the informal system still in many cases poses challenges with regard to gender discrimination. In the case of Afghanistan, customary justice may give individuals the power to seek their own justice, but also inhibits the community from punishing perpetrators who assert their right to revenge or defense of honor. Furthermore, customary systems are generally powerless in disputes or offences involving outsiders, government actors, or other powerful people, including those protected by militia commanders or criminal networks, as observed in the case of Liberia. Second, the authors offer a list of practical recommendations at the end of each chapter. While this pragmatic stance is tailored with respect to each case study, the recommendations offer rule of law practitioners evidence for informed policy and programming. A lesson learned from the case of East Timor is relevant in this regard, where a top down effort to initiate transnational justice failed to deal with conflicts arising at the inter-communal level, which in effect seriously threatened the stability of the country.

In the context where formal legal systems are in transition, the case studies in this book provide us with insights regarding the realities of actors and actions in practicing customary justice. Obviously, there is no such thing as 'one size fits all' to deal with the complexity of legal systems, especially in post-conflict societies. The victims and survivors in such societies have experienced conditions that demand sensitive and long-term solutions. As the concluding chapter of the book highlights, attempts to address the unique problem of post conflict situations, as well as navigating the changes in transitional societies, should be undertaken in coherence with a comprehensive understanding of current social and political contexts. This means observing the complexity that follows on the co-existence of formal and customary legal systems as well as the possibilities for creating a dialectical space, which in turn implies analyzing the long-term impact of the implementation of both legal systems to the changing perceptions of justice and to creating access to justice in society. Drawing on decades of experience, the authors in this book have delivered a sound examination of social practices of customary justice that can contribute to a better practice for the global effort to promote legal empowerment in an increasingly plural world.

## BOOKS AVAILABLE FOR REVIEW IN THE JLP

The *Journal of Legal Pluralism* is sometimes notified by publishers of the availability of review copies of recent publications likely to be of interest to the readership of the *Journal*. The following list consists of the most recent titles. Readers who are interested in submitting book reviews to the JLP for may obtain these from the addresses given.

1. *Legitimacy, Legal Development and Change - Law and Modernization Reconsidered*, edited by David K. Linnan, University of South Carolina School of Law. ISBN: 978-0-7546-7728-4. Published June 2012. Full details and page extracts are available at www.ashgate.com/isbn/9780754677284. For a review copy, contact:

Eleazer D. Durfee (Mr.)
Ashgate/Lund Humphries Publishing Company
101 Cherry Street, Suite #420
Burlington, VT 05401
802-865-7641 x314
802-865-7847 fax
www.ashgate.com
www.lundhumphries.com

2. *Adjudication in Action - An Ethnomethodology of Law, Morality and Justice*, by Baudouin Dupret. Series: Directions in Ethnomethodology and Conversation Analysis. ISBN: 978-1-4094-3150-3. Published November 2011. Full details are available at www.ashgate.com/isbn/9781409431503. Contacts for a review copy are as for **1** above.

3. *The Tobacco Challenge: Legal Policy and Consumer Protection,* by Geraint Howells, University of Manchester, UK. Further details are available at: http://www.ashgate.com/isbn/9780754645702. For a review copy, contact:

Debbie Fattore
Marketing Assistant, Social Sciences
Ashgate Publishing, Social Sciences Marketing Dept.
Wey Court East, Union Road
Farnham, Surrey, GU9 7PT
tel: 01252 736600 - fax: 01252 736736

www.ashgate.com/reviews

**4.** *At the Edge of Law: Emergent and Divergent Models of Legal Professionalism*, by Andrew Francis, Keele University, UK. Further details are available at: http://www.ashgate.com/isbn/9780754677444. Contacts for a review copy are as for **3** above.

**5.** *Regulating Marriage Migration into the UK: A Stranger in the Home*, by Helena Wray, Middlesex University, London, UK. Further details are available at: http://www.ashgate.com/isbn/9781409403388. Contacts for a review copy are as for **3** above.

**6.** *Interdisciplinary Research in Jurisprudence and Constitutionalism*, edited by Stephan Kirste, Anne van Aaken, Michael Anderheiden, and Pasquale Policastro. ISBN: 978-3-515-09941-7. Published by Franz Steiner Verlag, 2012. For a review copy, contact:

Regina Maaß
Rezensionsabteilung, Franz Steiner Verlag GmbH
Birkenwaldstr. 44
D-70191 Stuttgart
Germany
Tel.: 0711 2582-301
Fax: 0711 2582-390
rmaass@steiner-verlag.de
www.steiner-verlag.de

**7.** *Introduction to South Pacific Law,* 3rd Edition, by Jennifer Corrin and Don Paterson. ISBN: 978-1-4202-5657-4. Published by Palgrave Macmillan, 2011 (1st ed. 1999). For a review copy, contact:

Melanie G. Wiber
Editor-in-Chief
Journal of Legal Pluralism
wiber@unb.ca

**The Journal of Legal Pluralism and Unofficial Law**
published by the Foundation for the Journal of Legal Pluralism
Editor in Chief: Prof. Dr. Melanie G. Wiber (University of New Brunswick)

Melanie Wiber; Gordon R. Woodman (Eds.)
**The Journal of Legal Pluralism and Unofficial Law 62/2010**
Bräuchler examines the Indonesian decentralisation process and the revival of tradition and cultural self-determination in the Moluccas. Tuori studies restatements and codifications of customary laws in Africa. Harboe Knudsen considers European Union regulation of the marketing of dairy products in Lithuania. Douglas and Hersi examine the attitudes of Muslims to the smoking of khat. Simarmata studies the contrast between Indonesian state law and local officials' practice regarding natural resources use in East Kalimantan.
Bd. 62, 2011, 168 S., 29,90 €, br., ISBN 978-3-643-99895-8

LIT Verlag Berlin – Münster – Wien – Zürich – London
Auslieferung Deutschland / Österreich / Schweiz: siehe Impressumsseite

Yüksel Sezgin (Guest Editor)
**Human Rights and Legal Pluralism**
This issue opens with an article on how to integrate Human Rights into customary and religious legal systems generally (Y. Sezgin), and then presents special studies of the issues in a "tribal" women's forum in South Rajastan, India (M.Hong Tschalaer), in customary justice in post-conflict Sierra Leone (K. Inksater), in indigenous justice systems in Latin America (G. Corradi) and in deep legal pluralism in South Africa (C. Rautenbach)
Bd. 60, 2011, 208 S., 29,90 €, br., ISBN 978-3-643-99905-4

LIT Verlag Berlin – Münster – Wien – Zürich – London
Auslieferung Deutschland / Österreich / Schweiz: siehe Impressumsseite